PS   71-1191
221   French
F66   The fifties: fiction,
       poetry, drama.

Date Due   JUL 2000

Manufactured in the United States of America by
E. O. Painter Printing Co., DeLand, Florida

To celebrate
the long and distinguished services to
American literature
of
HARRY R. WARFEL.

Contents

The Fifties:
Fiction,
Poetry,
Drama

Introduction

This survey of the American literature of the 50s has required a different organization from the companion volumes of the 30s and 40s. The 30s book was organized around the traditional division of literature into fiction, poetry, and drama, befitting the study of a sorry era that witnessed the collapse of outworn traditions. In the 40s World War II dominated American life and the most appropriate plan for the study of the literature of the period called for its division into two bodies — those works directly connected with the war and those flashing "highlights" that suggested directions for an as yet uncertain future.

During the 50s — as American life settled into a depressing new routine and literary activity became more channeled than in the chaotic 40s — "movements" mattered more than genres—the "Beat" outburst, the "Black" rising, the growth of a Jewish-American movement in fiction, a new academicism in poetry, an "off-Broadway" movement in drama. The record of the decade was not impressive, but the way was paved for solider achievements in the 60s.

Accordingly it seemed most fitting to organize this book around three major essays interlinked by a group of shorter ones focusing on significant individual writers and works. The book begins with a study of the appeal of the stories of the writer who gave "The Age of Salinger" its name, set against the background of a general summary of the literary achievements of the decade.

A consideration of other fiction writers leads to a long essay on the Beat Generation, which greatly influenced both fiction and poetry. From the Beats we move to other poets whose works received attention — often long overdue. Among the outstanding poets of the decade was Gwendolyn Brooks, whose work leads to a consideration of other Black writers of the decade, including dramatist Lorraine Hansberry; and from Miss Hansberry, we proceed to consider some of the major theatrical writers of the decade. Our survey concludes on a perhaps appropriately downbeat note with an appraisal of the ill-starred efforts to produce a significant, original television drama.

Within the section on fiction a further grouping may be

observed. The first three essays deal with important late works of the older writers who have since World War II won the Nobel Prize for literature. Then five essays treat two male and three female writers distinctively identified with the immediate post-war age. A final group of three essays considers three of the outstanding fiction writers to emerge during the 50s.

Like *The Thirties* and *The Forties,* this book consists entirely of original essays commissioned for this project. It is largely the work of a group of widely scattered friends. Inevitably some contributors have not been able to participate in the whole series and newcomers — especially able young critics — have taken their places. The aim of this changing group remains, however, constant — to produce an account of the literature of a decade that is not so much a formal history as a conversation between friends. Regrettably the need for making each essay part of a balanced whole made essential substantial editorial cuts in some essays — especially Mark Leaf's on Faulkner and William Freedman's on Malamud — after their authors had left this country. I hope that in eliminating some of the detailed development of their positions, I have remained faithful to the spirit of these positions.

Since the 50s are still close to us, this volume is more speculative than its predecessors. The reputations of some of the writers discussed will continue to rise, others will fall. Many readers will be disappointed to find a favorite writer — especially a novelist — neglected. Much has already been written , however, about the fiction of the 50s, and some frequently discussed writers have had to be omitted in order to focus attention on others who may not previously have received the consideration that they deserve.

This group of co-workers will not produce a book on the Sixties. One is being planned, but it will embody a novel approach suited to the evaluation of a fresh, new literature. Both the editor and the contributors will belong to what we hope will prove the rising generation of critics. One of the most promising of this group, Donald Pease, has already not only contributed to this book an essay on James Purdy that may be a harbinger of the *new* criticism of the 70s, but has also assisted greatly with the preliminary editing of this volume. While the "60s project" is underway, those of us who started out in the 30s to survey three decades of American literature will turn our attention back to the first three decades of this century.

—WARREN FRENCH

The Age of Salinger

by WARREN FRENCH

I

"Tacky," which Webster's controversial Third International Dictionary defines as meaning "marked by a lack of style or good taste," is *the* word for the 50s.

Looking backward with little nostalgia, we can see that the seemingly shapeless decade was actually as clearly demarcated as the twittering 20s, the threadbare 30s, or the flaming 40s, even though there were no such vivid watersheds as a Versailles Conference, a Stock Market crash, an outbreak of a World War to drop a cataclysmic final curtain on an era of political egomania, financial fantasy, or psychological barbarism. The febrile 50s as a distinctive era in the history of human folly might be said to have begun late and confusingly on June 24 (our time) or June 25 (their time) when either the artificial, Communist-propped Republic of North Korea invaded the artificial, American-propped Republic of South Korea, or vice versa. (The facts in this lingering squabble between Tweedledum and Tweedledee will probably never get sorted out.) The 50s ended—although few groggy witnesses would have ventured to say so—almost exactly ten years later when on July 14, 1960, John Fitzgerald Kennedy defeated for the Democratic Presidential nomination the self-effacing standard-bearer of the exhausted liberal hopes of the 50s, Adlai Stevenson.

We contemplate now the magazines, the movies, the music, the TV shows, the dress, the hairdos of the ten years that dragged between those two long, hot summers with astonishment. How could

1

we ever have put up with such dowdiness? The emblem that leaps to mind for these years is the Statue of Liberty transformed into the figure of Mamie Eisenhower, sculpted in one of her inaugural gowns, holding an extinguished torch that may be only an empty bottle. Why didn't we die laughing at the ridiculous spectacle we made of ourselves?

Because those weren't laughing years! Hovering vulture-like over the desiccated decade are the twin spectres of Senator Joseph McCarthy and the Sputnik.

For the dates suggested above as terminal posts for the 50s, we might substitute those of two events in the down-at-the-heels state of West Virginia, which has served usually only as a historical afterthought. On February 9, 1950 Senator Joseph McCarthy of Wisconsin made a speech in the state's bustling city of Wheeling, in which he charged that the State Department was loaded with Communists whose names were known even to the Secretary of State. Reports of this epochal event—like those of many others during the 50s—were confused. It was disputed how many Reds the Senator said infested Foggy Bottom, but there were surely a lot! And what matters was that they were still working and making policies after their identities had been ferreted out. On May 10, 1960 John F. Kennedy, a Senator from Massachusetts, won a smashing upset victory over his principal opponent, Minnesota Senator Hubert Humphrey in the West Virginia Democratic presidential preferential primary. Humphrey's subsequent withdrawal from the race was a major step in wrapping up the nomination for Kennedy. These events catapulted Senator McCarthy and later Senator Kennedy into national and international celebrity. McCarthy's repressionist and Kennedy's expansionist personalities provide the keys to understanding the successive decades that these men and their memories dominated.

McCarthy's reign of terror terminated on December 2, 1954, when his Senate colleagues voted 67-22 to censure him for his contempt of the Subcommittee on Privileges and Elections and for acting contrary to Senatorial ethics. The Senator had been able to dominate events for four years in part because of American disillusionment with the aftermath of World War II, especially the fall to the Communists of Czechoslovakia in 1948 and China in 1949. The world we had fought to win seemed to be being wrested from us; and newspaper headlines that bristled with the names of suspected spies fed our fears of domestic subversion. Despite the failure to substantiate his charges, McCarthy seemed to be in such an impregnable position that even a greatly respected President from the Senator's own party quailed at the thought of confronting him. Finally, however, in the fashion of most fanatics, McCarthy overreached himself by recklessly and ruthlessly pursuing innocents. He died three years after his censure, of some kind of internal complications apparently associated with heavy drinking. The suspicions bred by his irresponsible charges had, however, cast a spell over the nation; and gray-flannel men, indistinguishable in appearance and opinion, moved like zombies through a blasted landscape and spent much of their time reading bulletins from the President's hospital rooms as he—like the nation he emblematized—endured a variety of complaints that almost undid him.

So demoralized was this country by the McCarthy years that—despite loud talk about freeing "captive nations"—it stood silently by while Russia stamped out the Hungarian revolt of October, 1956, and adopted a holier-than-thou attitude when Israel, France, and England attempted to defend their interests against Egyptian aggression. The nation was still recovering from its humiliation when on October 4, 1957—a few months after McCarthy passed away—it was further humbled by Russia's successfully orbiting around the earth Sputnik I, the first man-made satellite.

Reaction to Sputnik unleashed one of this nation's unloveliest drives—an aggressive hysteria that is the opposite side of the coin from the McCarthy-inspired defensive hysteria. The 50s demonstrated the contrasting facets of our national propensity to panic. The response to the Soviet achievement took the form of a crash program to make up for years of shameful undernourishment of our educational system. Something, it was resolved, must be done quickly to improve training in the sciences, not so that Americans might lead better-informed, more satisfying lives, but so that we might catch up with those Russian destroyers of Eisenhower tranquillity.

We more than caught up, of course, before another decade ended. Less than a dozen years after the launching of the first Sputnik, the United States placed the first man on the moon. Americans have always shown a phenomenal capacity for rising speedily to a direct challenge and mounting a massive effort to achieve some formidable goal, whether it be the industrialization of an agrarian society, the conquest of the frontier, or the defeat of Germany and Japan. The dramatic decade of the 60s was energized by the space race, in which America left all competitors behind.

As Sinclair Lewis, for one, pointed out, however, American energy expends itself quickly in convulsive movements to attain a frantically coveted goal. Once this goal is attained, the frontiersman-turned-businessman is content to settle back and revel in his prejudices at revival services, lodge meetings, communions-at-home with TV's ritual Western and domestic fantasies. Americans have never craved an intellectual life that results in more than the creation of fantastic technological gimmicks like electric scissors or moon-landing craft. There is in this country no concept of a "continuing city," no vision that outlasts the most transient forms of self-gratification. Lewis described the process nearly half a century ago in *Main Street*:

> The citizen of the prairie drifts always westward. It may be because he is the heir of ancient migrations—and it may be because he finds within his own spirit so little adventure that he is driven to seek it by changing his horizon. The towns remain unvaried, yet the individual faces alter like classes in college. The Gopher Prairie jeweler sells out, for no discernible reason, and moves on to Alberta or the state of Washington, to open a shop precisely like his former one, in a town precisely like the one he has left. There is, except among professional men and the wealthy, small permanence either of residence or occupation. A man becomes farmer, grocer, town policeman, garageman, restaurant-owner, postmaster, insurance-agent, and farmer all over again, and the community more or less patiently suffers from his lack of knowledge in each of his experiments.

An itemizing of the "philosophy complete" of the Champ Perrys—pioneer settlers of the Midwest in this same novel—concludes, "There would be no more trouble or discontent in the world if everybody worked as hard as Pa did when he cleared our first farm." But even Pa no longer works that hard. Having lost his money in unsound investment "experiments," he weighs "wagons of wheat" and naps betweentimes "in the dusty peace of his office."

The American tradition—rooted in a distrust of intellectualism—has not been steady movement toward consistent accomplishment but "boom or bust," hysterical over-exertion followed by a long nap (possibly induced by tranquilizers). Sputnik triggered a renewal of this process as have few other events except the opening of the Cimarron strip and the sneaky attack on Pearl Harbor. The 60s were an exhilarating, eventful decade. (Not all the events were pleasant. They included riots and an unjustifiable war. But there was action! The outlook for the 70s if the nation settles back into a new complacency under the phantom President Nixon is discomforting.) During the doldrums that were the 50s, however, only some widely castigated Supreme Court decisions indicated that the spirit of progress was not carrion for the vultures. In December, 1950, the Court ruled that under the Fifth Amendment to the Constitution no one could be forced to testify against himself; and in May, 1954, racial segregation in public schools was ruled unconstitutional. The Court, however, was moving too fast for a suspicious nation and throughout the country signs sprung up demanding the impeachment of the generous-minded and dignified Chief Justice Earl Warren. In some places the posting of the "Bill of Rights" was banned because these first ten amendments to the Constitution were controversial.

Over the 50s presided the benign cipher Eisenhower. If not the worst American President (there are too many contenders to award that honor lightly), he was surely the least effectual since President William Henry Harrison, who was seized with a fatal illness at his inauguration. In the aimless confusion of his thinking, "Ike" is an ideal symbol for the period. He had made his way through the backbiting ranks of the military hierarchy by serving as smiling flunky to strong men like MacArthur. He had headed one of the largest armies in history—as Ernest Hemingway cattily pointed out in *Across the River and into the Trees*—from farther back than any one else had ever commanded. Unlike Arthur Miller's archetypal salesman, Eisenhower had made his fortune out of being "well-liked." He had thought that he might be a Democrat until he had made enough money to impress his new-found Republican cronies with the idea that he might salvage the fading fortunes of a party that had been ideologically bankrupt since 1912. His regime—with Congress three-fourths of the time in control of the opposition party—produced nothing of lasting significance but a magnificent Interstate Highway system and even that had to be justified on the grounds of military security rather than as a contribution to the safety and attractiveness of pleasure travel. Even the triumphs of the American way of life are often the fruits of paranoia.

Small wonder that those growing up during the 50s were lampooned as "the silent generation." Talk was dangerous, and it was more fun to listen to the endless inanities of television. Until the Sputnik scare, the aim of education in the United States was to turn out regiments of interchangeable, crew-cut conformists to assume silently and respectfully the functions of those being pensioned off to Golden Age communities in the Arizona deserts and Florida swamps.

The decade fostered a literature that mirrored its own lack of luster. The best American play of the period had been written years earlier by a man who allowed it to be produced only after his death. One of the most impressive poetic achievements was making a best-seller out of a translation of Dante's fourteenth-century *Inferno*. The most widely read and most influential serious novel of the decade was the account of a touchy young man's being badgered into resignation and conformity. Few established writers found much to say worth hearing; few new writers could—before 1959—break through the smog of apathy and suspicion that hid the landscape.

The disparity between American accomplishment in fiction (for which a large audience still existed), on one hand, and poetry (for which little audience existed) and drama (for which there was a dwindling, undiscriminating audience), on the other, grew even more embarrassingly conspicuous than during the two previous decades. Yet, though the novel continued to dominate the American literary landscape, little was heard from representatives of the five groups of writers who had been prominent during the 30s.

Of those who had begun to publish in that hazy, golden day before World War I only Upton Sinclair—now in his seventies—remained active; but few people even noticed, except as antiquarian curiosities, such productions as *Another Pamela* (1950), a harking back to Richardson's prototypical novel in an effort to rejuvenate the genre, or *The Return of Lanny Budd* (1953), a postscript to a long series of novels about an American diplomatic superman. Sinclair remained quixotically undaunted after all his former colleagues had laid down their arms, but the windmills were disappearing. Little note was given either to several novels (including *Mrs. Reynolds,* 1952) that were exhumed from the papers that Gertrude Stein had willed to Yale at her death in 1946.

The voices of the regional iconoclasts who had given new impetus to American fiction immediately after World War I were being stilled. The last important representatives of the group, Sinclair Lewis and James Branch Cabell, died in the early 50s.

The oldest group to make a substantial contribution to the fiction of the 50s were the surviving members of the "lost generation" of once expatriated writers. John Dos Passos increased, if anything, his phenomenal output, but *Chosen Country* (1951), *Most Likely to Succeed* (1954), *The Great Days* (1958) and other products of the decade failed to attract the attention that the *U.S.A.* trilogy had in the 30s to this writer who had shifted politically from extreme left to extreme right. The most venerable writer to produce a significant work in the 50s was the only one of the old expatriate crowd to carry off a Nobel Prize for literature, Ernest Hemingway. After failing to impress readers with his broodings over the post-World-War-II world in *Across the River and into the Trees* (1950), "Papa" Hemingway made a remarkable comeback to win new honors for his powerful, touching fable *The Old Man and the Sea* (1952, Pulitzer Prize 1953).

Maybe one wins the Nobel Prize for pertinacity as much as anything else. Certainly the only two American novelists besides Hemingway to win the award since World War II have demonstrated this quality. In *The Thirties,* I observed that "What seems unquestionably the major body of American fiction produced during the 30s is the work of three men who published their first major novels in the year the depression began—Thomas Wolfe, John Steinbeck, and William Faulkner." Wolfe had died young, but Steinbeck and Faulkner had not only endured, but prevailed well enough to continue to write voluminously. After 1945, however, critics noted a decline in the quality of their labors. Steinbeck's high hopes for his vast chronicle novel about California's Salinas Valley and the problem of free will, *East of Eden* (1952) were not realized; and *Burning Bright* (1950) and *Sweet Thursday* (1954) parodied rather than recaptured the qualities of earlier related works like *Of Mice and Men* and *Cannery Row*. Only in an engaging satire of French politics, *The Short Reign of Pippin IV,* and an ironic short story of the loss of American values, "How Mr. Hogan Robbed a Bank," (both 1957) did Steinbeck begin to open up a new and promising vein that he subsequently failed to exploit.

Faulkner also faltered early in the 50s. Both *Requiem for a Nun* (1951), a tricky combination of nostalgic short stories and Gothic drama, and *A Fable* (1954, Pulitzer Prize in 1955) proved pretentious bores. When late in the decade, however, Faulkner returned to the "Snopes trilogy" that he had abandoned after publishing *The Hamlet* in 1940, he proved in *The Town* (1957) and *The Mansion* (1959) that he had an almost unique capacity not only to recapture the style and subject matter of his most brilliant period but also to reformulate a vast history of the destructive consequences of greed in the twentieth century to accommodate developments since World War II. Few writers have staged such a comeback to demonstrate conclusively their right to be included among the world's great artists.

Those writers who started out in the 30s made little showing in the 50s; they had seemingly run out of steam during World War II. Perhaps they, too, had discovered as John Steinbeck complained, "Thirty years ago you could tell an underdog. Today it is rather harder to recognize one." Of the "proletarian-tough guy" chroniclers of the underdog celebrated by editor David Madden in two anthologies on the writers of the 30s, Erskine Caldwell and James T. Farrell kept busy, but watched their once enthusiastic audiences evaporate. John O'Hara continued to win admiration for his masterful, ironic short stories rather than for bulky novels like *Ten North Frederick* (1955) and *From the Terrace* (1958), in which he sought to extract from the stubborn soil of the Pennsylvania Dutch country an equivalent of Faulkner's epic of the red clay hills of Mississippi. The best "tough guy" novel of the 50s was Nelson Algren's raffish legend of prostitutes and drifters, *A Walk on the Wild Side* (1956).

James Gould Cozzens is difficult to place in relation to any of these groups. He had begun to publish fiction away back in the 20s, but he failed to attract substantial attention until the appearance in the 30s of *The Last Adam* and *The Just and the Unjust*. He won still greater acclaim in the 40s for *Guard of Honor,* one of the few memorable reports on life in a stateside military training camp during World War II. When nearly a decade passed, however, without Cozzens' being heard from again, readers assumed that like most of his contemporaries he had sunk into a silence inspired by a distaste for the times. In 1957 he shook the somnolent literary world and seemingly proved that he was one writer who grew better as the years rolled by with *By Love Possessed,* a huge, ruminative work in the seemingly exhausted vein of "the genteel tradition" of the respectable, decorous, small-town, Protestant, upper middle class. Polite circles in mourning since the deaths of Willa Cather and Ellen Glasgow cast off their weeds and hysterically acclaimed

Cozzens' behemoth as "the great American novel." No better example of the tackiness of the times can be found than in the excited response to this ponderous, pedestrian account of the inflated tribulations of a tribe of pompous small-town Pennsylvanians and the widespread confusion of Cozzens' sluggish, obscure style with elegant writing. Not only were adulatory reviews published—a whole issue of a critical journal was devoted to the brief resuscitation of Cozzens' reputation.

Probably the reason for this flurry of enthusiasm was that the long beleaguered partisans of gentility were encouraged by the vacuous proprieties of the Eisenhower administration to believe that "normalcy" might at last be restored to a land blighted since the levying of a graduated income tax. *By Love Possessed* was to art what the conservative policies of Senator Robert Taft were to political theory. Cozzens' novel arrived, however, too late with too little about the same time as the Sputnik whizzed overhead, and the adultation for its passive exaltation of the consolations of a fat bank account died out as the hysterical drive for technological supremacy was launched.

Another surviving exponent of the genteel tradition, its mildly ironic New England cataloguer, J. P. Marquand, continued his exploration of affluent bourgeois types with tales of the Army, *Melville Goodwin, USA* (1951), and big business, *Sincerely, Willis Wayde* (1955), but neither generated the pleasure that *The Late George Apley* and *Wickford Point* did before World War II undermined the market for discerning nostalgia. The remaining adherents of the New England-New York tradition of mercantile gentility rallied to the support of a new spokesman, stock-broker-turned-novelist Louis Auchincloss, who foreshadowed with works like *The Great World and Timothy Colt* (1956), the enormous success that he would enjoy in the 60s with *The Rector of Justin.*

The Southern brand of seignorial gentility fared less well during the 50s. Andrew Lytle published *The Velvet Horn* (1957), a cryptic, poetic tale of youth's reluctant coming-of-age in a pastoral society; and Caroline Gordon lambasted such modern abominations as the artificial insemination of cattle in *The Malefactors* (1956). Despite the bulkiness of *World Enough and Time* (1950—the rehashing of a nineteenth-century Kentucky scandal) and *Band of Angels* (1955), Robert Penn Warren failed to enlarge the reputation that he had won with *All the King's Men.*

The more sardonic Southern writers who had established their reputations during the 40s also generally failed to develop them. Carson McCullers' *The Ballad of the Sad Cafe* (1950), Truman Capote's *The Grass Harp* (1951), and Eudora Welty's *The Ponder Heart* (1954) proved ingratiating, but thin follow-ups to earlier works. Only Elizabeth Spencer strengthened her reputation with *This Crooked Way* (1952), a candid tale of Mississippi's planter class, and *The Voice at the Back Door* (1956), one of the best fictional analyses that has been made of the conflict between ambition and conscience among Southern whites.

Disappointing, too, were the writings of those who had made strong impressions in the late 40s with tales of World War II. Norman Mailer's preachy *Barbary Shore* (1951) and chaotic *Deer Park* (1955) discouraged those who had admired *The Naked and the Dead. Advertisements for Myself* (1959) suggested that Mailer's future reputation would rest upon a form of self-exploiting journalism rather than on his entirely fictional efforts. John Hersey's *The Wall* (1950) and *The War Lover* (1955) were well received and provoked considerable discussion of touchy issues, but have failed to live because of the author's inability to produce more than effective journalism. Gore Vidal failed to score a success with *Messiah* (1954) and turned to other media, after having dashed off seven novels and three mystery stories in eight years. John Hawkes produced no impressive sequel to *The Cannibal* (1949), nor did Paul Bowles match in *Let It Come Down* (1952) and *The Spider's House* (1955), the frightening fantasy of *The Sheltering Sky*.

Only four of the writers to make their reputations in the 40s continued to develop. Wright Morris produced five capable novels during the 50s; and if indeed Americans were a tougher breed than they are, Morris might have become—what a few critics have fancied him—the literary spokesman for the 50s. In *Love Among the Cannibals* (1957) especially, Morris dramatizes a process of shucking off the past that characterized American life during the decade. As the novelist said in an interview, this work is the first "in which the past does not exist. We begin with the present, we live in the present, and it is an effort to come to terms with the present, in terms of only the present." This vision—as bleakly existential as Morris' native Midwestern prairies—was too disenchanting for most Americans. Morris seemingly envisions man stripped down to a kind of D. H. Lawrentian paganism—with, as Marcus Klein suggests in *After Alienation*—sex as the only "Real" alternative to living by the clichés of the past. Americans were not quite ready, however, like the song-writer-protagonist of *Love Among the Cannibals*, to strip themselves of all the baggage of the past. They preferred, like Salinger's Eloise in "Uncle Wiggily in Connecticut" to ask plaintively—in expectation of an affirmative answer—"I was a nice girl, wasn't I?," not granting that the American concept of "nice" is a cliché of the deodorant commercial. Morris tried to rub our noses in our tackiness. While most Americans, however, were willing to live lives without style as penance for fancied offenses, they would not belligerently defend those lives. They fled the austerities of Lone Tree, Nebraska, for the spurious glamour of Miami Beach. After all, even Eisenhower refused to return to the drab homeliness of Abilene, Kansas. The Age of L.B.J. was not yet.

Mary McCarthy came closer to the American heart of the 50s with *The Groves of Academe* (1952), a vitriolic satire of college life that inspired Randall Jarrell to write the equally malicious and witty *Pictures from an Institution* (1954). The academy, however, still seemed in the 50s to most Americans too exotic to serve as more than a stopping-off place on the way to suburbia, and those who made caution the cardinal rule of their lives found Miss McCarthy's acerbity too bold to serve even as an ideal.

The man who came closer to balancing a harsh critique of American life with a vision acceptable to a tasteless age was Saul Bellow in his picaresque tale of a young Chicagoan on the make, *The Adventures of Augie March* (1953) and his cryptic fable of the effort to master an obsessive ego, *Henderson, the Rain King* (1959); but although many critics consider Bellow a much better writer than J. D. Salinger, Bellow's works were never quite as enthusiastically received perhaps because his self-contained intellectual style made too many demands on readers addicted to the banalities of the 50s.

The man to come even closer than Bellow to serving as a literary emblem for the period is not an American at all, but a Russian emigré who had to develop an entirely new style in a new language. Vladimir Nabokov had been publishing works in English since the early 40s, but his reputation was consolidated with his scandalous, panoramic view of American tackiness, *Lolita* (1955). Curiously this work, perhaps now most famous for its portrayal of the motels and other landmarks of this nation at which lecherous Humbert Humbert and his "nymphet" enjoy their orgies during a cross-country junket, was at first considered too strong for American tastes and had to be published in Paris by the notorious Olympia Press.

It was cautiously introduced to the American public by Columbia University's F. W. Dupee in the second (and last) issue of the *Anchor Review,* a pretentious effort—characteristic of the 50s—to give snob value (Marguerite Yourcenar, W. H. Auden, etc.) to paperback books by wrapping them in dowdy covers. Since then, however, *Lolita* has been enormously successful—and only occasionally attacked—in an American edition and film version. If Nabokov has never won hearts as Salinger has, it may be because he has not chosen to. Discussing his work in a piece called "On a Book Entitled *Lolita,*" he remarks, "I am neither a reader nor a writer of didactic fiction . . . and *Lolita* has no moral in tow. . . . An American critic suggested that *Lolita* was the record of my love affair with the romantic novel. The substitution 'English language' for 'romantic novel' would make this elegant formula more correct." Americans are not happy in such a rarefied aesthetic atmosphere; they are also bruised by the withering contempt of Nabokov's description of early reactions to *Lolita*: "One reader suggested that his firm might consider publication if I turned my Lolita into a twelve-year-old lad and had him seduced by Humbert, a farmer, in a barn, amidst gaunt and arid surroundings, all this set forth in short, strong, 'realistic' sentences." The sensational success of *Lolita* has unfortunately served to obscure the merits of another of Nabokov's fictional reactions to the American scene, *Pnin* (1957), the tale of a refugee teacher in an American college that belies its author's avowed disinterest in romanticism and didacticism and displays a witty compassion missing in the brittle exposés of Mary McCarthy and Randall Jarrell.

Unquestionably the novelist who dominated the 50s was J. D. Salinger, whose generally available writings are contained in four rather slender volumes—*The Catcher in the Rye* (1951), *Nine Stories* (1953), *Franny and Zooey* (1961), and *"Raise High the Roof Beam, Carpenters"* and *"Seymour: An Introduction"* (1963), all composed of material originally published between 1948 and 1959. Despite his limited production Salinger with his complementary creations of Holden Caulfield and Seymour Glass (both surrounded by siblings) so captivated the fancies of the Americans of this intellectually and emotionally arid era that the decade of the 50s can justly be called from more than a literary point of view

"The Age of Salinger." The relationship between the world of Salinger's fiction and the world outside is complex, but it is perhaps best suggested in Holden Caulfield's despairing cry after he searches for a "place that's nice and peaceful," "There isn't any."

One can place into four groups all but one of the dozen other novelists who began to publish during the 50s and who appeared after the end of another decade to have succeeded in establishing lasting reputations.

The seemingly indefatigable South followed up the Agrarian school of the 30s and the "precious" school of the 40s with what may be called the "religious school" of the 50s, composed of intense young writers moved by spiritual distress to a bizarre mixture of sentimentalism and cynicism. James Agee had been writing for a number of years, but his novel *The Morning Watch* did not appear until 1951 and *A Death in the Family* (Pulitzer Prize, 1958) was not published until after his death in 1955. Also in 1951 William Styron published his only major work of the decade, *Lie Down in Darkness*. The next year, Flannery O'Connor, who was to remain best known for her short stories, published her first novel, *Wise Blood*.

Despite its strong regional character, Miss O'Connor's novel could also be appropriately categorized as a predecessor to the writings of a group of powerful fabulists who were to become known collectively as "black humorists." "Black Humor" has not yet been satisfactorily defined, but it is apparent that all the works to which the term has been applied have much in common with the traditional American tall tale as exemplified by Mark Twain's "Celebrated Jumping Frog of Calaveras County." They are all grotesque stories of lofty ambition and ignominious defeat.

Although John Barth's *The Floating Opera* appeared in an altered version in 1956 (the original text was not published until 1967), it was not until 1958 that this country felt the full impact of "black humor" in Barth's *End of the Road* and an expurgated American edition of J. P. Donleavy's *The Ginger Man* (originally published in Paris in 1955, the unexpurgated text did not appear in this country until 1965). About the same time the work of the darkest and sharpest of these critics of American life, James Purdy, began to circulate, although *63: Dream Palace* and the stories collected under the title *Color of Darkness* had been privately printed earlier. Purdy's *Malcolm* (1959) brought the literary decade to a distinguished close and foreshadowed some of the outstanding productions of the 60s. John Updike, another distinguished fabulist-critic, also began to publish in 1959 with the surrealistic *The Poorhouse Fair,* but his major work is distinctly a part of the culture of the 60s.

These "black humorists" are, ironically, all white, but the 50s also saw the rise in importance of the Negro novel, and also the Jewish novel. Curiously, few distinguished Black or Jewish novelists began to publish during the decade. Of the former only James Baldwin with *Go Tell It on the Mountain* (1953) and *Giovanni's Room* (1956) and Ralph Ellison (*Invisible Man,* 1952) evidence strong survival value, though Ellison's elaborate *bildungsroman* is clearly one of the most important works produced during the period. Richard Wright, whose *Native Son* had been acclaimed in 1940, returned after years of writing non-fiction to the novel and produced *The Outsider* (1953) and *The Long Dream* (1958), but even his warmest partisans find that these works lack the concentrated power of his early stories.

The only Jewish writer to achieve a reputation anything like Saul Bellow's is Bernard Malamud, whose *The Natural* (1953) was promoted by controversial critic Leslie Fiedler and whose *The Assistant* (1957), a haunting tale of a potential hood's spiritual travail, made its author one of the most talked about writers of a decade that induced great anguish in people of sensibility. Although Philip Roth's *Goodbye, Columbus* appeared in 1959, its author—like John Updike—is stylistically and attitudinally associated with the 60s.

The writer-without-a-camp who some impressionable reviewers thought might prove the most lustrous luminary of the decade is that arch-apostle of disaffiliation, Jack Kerouac. His works have a curious publishing history. He actually greeted the decade with a conventional coming-of-age tale, *The Town and the City* (1950); but then he went underground, and his *On the Road* gained a reputation as one of the most famous unpublished works of the period. It reached print at last in 1957, and before the decade was over Kerouac had in print five more novels—many of them dashed off during his years of obscurity. Of these only *The Subterraneans* (1958)—an exposition of the Beat mystique—has fictional merit; for some of his effusions Kerouac could find publishers willing to risk only cheap paperbacked editions.

With mention of Kerouac and the "Beats," one might expect to hear also of William Burroughs and Henry Miller; but even more than Purdy, Updike, and Philip Roth, these men and their productions are a feature of the 60s. Burroughs' *Naked Lunch* appeared in Paris in 1959, but not in New York until 1962, the year after Miller's *Tropic of Cancer* (originally published in Paris in 1934) appeared at last in an American edition and became a target of widespread obscenity litigation.

As the work of Miller and Burroughs suggests, it is difficult to draw a fine line between the fiction of the 50s and 60s because many important works did appear at the very end of the earlier decade. While the dividing point is hard to find, something had surely happened to alter American literary values between 1957 when *By Love Possessed* lumbered on to the scene and 1961 when Henry Miller's most famous work was published at last in his native land. For that reason it is most fitting to say that the story of the fiction of the 50s concludes with the appearance in June, 1959, of J. D. Salinger's "Seymour: An Introduction," the story that provided a saint for a sinner-conscious era. It must also be said that although the novel was the dominant form during the decade, the 50s saw the production of fewer works of lasting interest than the three preceding or the succeeding decades. Except for *The Old Man and the Sea, The Mansion, The Adventures of Augie March, The Assistant, Invisible Man, Lolita, The Catcher in the Rye,* and *Malcolm,* it is difficult to argue that one finds much more than interesting and craftsmanlike work. One must resort to that most damning of all phrases, it was "a promising period."

One must fall back on the same cliché to describe poetic and dramatic achievement during the 50s.

As the list of Pulitzer Prize winners in poetry for the first half of the decade indicates, these were years of the consolidation of reputations. Four of the five prizes went to collections of the poetry of those who had long since done their major work— Marianne Moore, Carl Sandburg, Archibald MacLeish, Wallace Stevens. Stevens, in fact, was beginning at last to receive the honor that he had deserved for a third of a century. With the appearance of his *Collected Poems* in 1954, Stevens began to dominate the imagination of a rising generation as Frost and Eliot had earlier. The providing in *Opus Posthumous* (1957) of many of the works that Stevens had omitted from the collection of those he wished to preserve further encouraged study of this aloof genius who probably would have been relieved that he died before his following reached its zenith. The appearance in 1951 of the *Selected Poems* of Richard Eberhart also brought fresh recognition to this gentle romantic who failed to share his age's preoccupation with technical innovation.

The poets who got their start during World War II did little to advance their positions. John Ciardi became increasingly known as a shrewd editor and translator. Richard Wilbur did interesting work for the theatre. Theodore Roethke won a reputation as one of our most colorful poetic figures since Ezra Pound. Karl Shapiro became much better known as polemicist than poet. Peter Viereck disappeared from sight. None had found the poetic formula for rousing readers from the lethargy of the period as Frost had in the elegant-minded teens and Eliot, in the frivolous-minded 20s. In fact the poet who dominated the American scene in the early 50s was not an American at all. It was Welshman Dylan Thomas, whose impassioned readings made poetry once again live for his auditors. When death prematurely ended his tours in 1953, his "sullen art" itself seemed dead.

The sorry state of poetry in the middle of the 50s is illustrated by the fate of one of the few imaginative ventures to involve those emerging poets that did attract new readers. After World War II a group of artists, poets, and architects—many of them European refugees—founded in the beautiful mountains of North Carolina near Thomas Wolfe's Asheville, Black Mountain College, with poet Charles Olson as Rector. The college attracted the brilliant, restless students of the period; and its *Black Mountain Review* was one of the few distinguished avant garde publications of the decade. Black Mountain gave support to one of the few significant poetic movements of the period—projective verse—which was explained by Olson and practiced most successfully by his student—and later colleague—Robert Creeley. The college could have been a center for a new creative society, but its aims were too visionary for a tacky era. It went bankrupt, and its grounds are now a fundamentalist summer colony.

Anyone appraising the situation in the mid-50s who would have been brash enough to predict a future for poetry in the United States should have been denounced as a "cockeyed optimist," if not blacklisted—in the typical fashion of the period—as a Red agent. Yet a perceptive observer of the parched landscape might have detected some promising sprouts in the San Francisco Bay area. No matter what one may think of the "Beats"—and a dozen years after they burst upon us many guardians of culture have not grown reconciled to these latter-day Whitmaniacs—one must admit that if the United States has been saved for poetry except as a pale pursuit of cultists, those Beats saved it!

The origin of the Beat movement is obscure. Some people associated with it—Brother Antoninus under his lay name of William Everson, Philip Lamantia, William Burroughs—had been publishing before 1955; but in that year the movement gained momentum when Lawrence Ferlinghetti began publishing under the imprint of his City Lights Bookshop in San Francisco's North Beach district a series of pamphlets, including a collection of his own poems called *Pictures of the Gone World.*

The nation generally was made aware of the movement, however, only after the publication by City Lights in 1956 of Allen Ginsberg's *Howl and Other Poems.* Sometime around June 1, 1957, Captain William Hanrahan of the Juvenile Department of the San Francisco police (the prototypical "fuzz") arrested Ferlinghetti for publishing and selling Ginsberg's book. The ensuing trial brought the Beats to the attention of the nation, with Kenneth Rexroth—who had just a few months earlier begun beating the drum by contributing "Disengagement: The Art of the Beat Generation" to *New World Writing*—as their advance man. Before the year was out the venturesome new *Evergreen Review* had devoted its second issue to the "San Francisco Scene," including selections from the works of Brother Antoninus, Ferlinghetti, Gary Snyder, Ginsberg, and Jack Kerouac. Ferlinghetti's *A Coney Island of the Mind* appeared in 1958— along with Gregory Corso's *Gasoline*—and sold so unexpectedly well that it proved there was still an enthusiastic American audience for poetry. Mimeographed "little magazines" like *Beatitude* and *Underhound* began to appear. Older writers like Henry Miller and Kenneth Patchen became patron saints of the new movement, which Norman Podhoretz felt compelled to denounce as early as 1958 in an essay for *Partisan Review,* "The Know-Nothing Bohemians." By February 1960 John Ciardi believed that he was able to announce in the *Saturday Review* the death of the movement; its colorful history had already been chronicled by Lawrence Lipton in *The Holy Barbarians* (1959). Thomas Parkinson was able to employ it as the subject for a "casebook" by 1961.

The movement proved, however, to have more staying power than one would have expected in view of the premature flood of publicity it received and the early public obsequies. The Beats have abandoned North Beach, which after giving the United States the coffee house as an institution became a trap for tourists with a taste for topless dancers; but the dispersed clan has provided the incentive for subsequent movements emphasizing a disaffiliation from the dehumanizing Establishment in many places in this country and throughout the world. Many pioneering Beats moved to New York to recapture Greenwich Village from the Italian politicians. A lasting movement has developed in Los Angeles and its seedier environs (especially Venice West), centered on the outspoken, volatile Charles Bukowski. San Francisco itself has spawned in its Haight-Ashbury district the Hippie movement that many view as the logical continuation of the impulse generated by the Beats. Allen Ginsberg is still around (everywhere!) and still one of the most powerful influences upon young American thought. No subsequent school of poets has captured the American imagination as effectively and completely as the Beats.

The difference between the Beats and their contemporaries like Lowell and Ciardi, for example, can be illustrated by a conversation between Holden Caulfield and his girl friend in *The Catcher in the Rye*. Holden begins:

"I mean do you like school, and all that stuff?"

"It's a terrific *bore*."

"I mean do you hate it? I know it's a terrific bore, but do you *hate* it, is what I mean."

"Well, I don't exactly *hate* it. You always have to—."

"Well, *I* hate it. Boy, do I hate it."

The United States bores those poets that Wilbur calls "the whiskey generation," but they don't actually hate it. The Beats do. Their manifesto is no series of abstract propositions about the hope of social justice, but the opening words of Ginsberg's "Howl": "I saw the best minds of my generation destroyed by madness, starving hysterical naked." The Beats perceived that the United States—especially during the 50s—was indeed *destroying* its best minds, maddening them with vague charges of disloyalty, with the stultifying demands of technological conformity, with the insistence that they perpetuate meretricious tranquility.

The other poets—many of whom had taken refuge under the rock of the academy—were too loyal to the faded vision they had fought for or too decorous to use the only language that could smite the smog of fear and indifference that hung over the land—the howl that Ginsberg sounded from the streets. The other poets wrote not to waken the multitude, but to win the favor of their finicky peers. They took refuge with Auden in the idea that "poetry makes nothing happen," and they kept alive the hope that somehow art was compatible with suburbia. Not until Lyndon Johnson wantonly accelerated the Viet Nam War late in the 60s did most poets recognize that their compatriots had indeed been brainwashed and raise their voices in anything like angry unison. In the interim it was the Beats and those whom they turned on who remained tuned in to restless American youth.

The Beats were encouraged during the 50s not only by many "little magazines"—often painstakingly produced on hand presses—but also by two ambitious journals. Brainchild of Arabella Porter, *New World Writing,* which began to appear on newsstands in 1952, was sponsored by a major publisher of paperbacks. Fifteen issues appeared during the decade, and there was even a more expensive successor bearing the same name early in the 60s; but neither it nor several short-lived emulators of the earlier magazine, like *Discovery* and *Noonday,* shared its success in bringing new poets, short story writers, and essayists from all over the world before the American audience.

Evergreen Review, which began publication late in the decade under the aegis of the spunky Grove Press, specialized in bringing even more avant garde writing than *New World Writing* championed before a freshly alerted public. Although with its change in format and emphasis in the 60s to the slick equivalent of a "skin flick" it has ceased to be taken seriously, it did a great deal to shatter the stifling Puritanical complacency of the 50s and to make young Americans aware of exciting new currents in literature at home and abroad.

The situation on Broadway was even worse than at Manhattan's 92nd St. YM-YWHA, where promising poets are invited to display their wares on a famous program of readings. The legitimate theatre failed to produce any new playwright of significance until nearly the end of the decade when *J.B.* introduced to playgoers the work of 65-year-old poet Archibald MacLeish, who had twenty years earlier been a pioneer in the creation of a now virtually vanished radio drama. The theatre relied for serious fare principally upon two men who had captivated audiences in the 40s; but though Tennessee Williams' *Camino Real* and *Cat on a Hot Tin Roof* and Arthur Miller's *The Crucible* and *A View from the Bridge* won respect, they failed to repeat the successes of *A Streetcar*

Named Desire and *Death of a Salesman*. William Inge, the fledgling playwright whom the 50s took most seriously, ground out *Come Back, Little Sheba; Picnic; Bus Stop; The Dark at the Top of the Stairs* in rapid succession; but his popular works have never been esteemed by critics.

Unquestionably the greatest play to open on Broadway during the decade was Eugene O'Neill's *Long Day's Journey into Night,* but even O'Neill's other posthumous works like *Hughie* and *More Stately Mansions* failed to attract audiences. Only O'Neill's haunting probing into his own family's past penetrated the evasions of the era and made people take a frighteningly honest look at the failure of one glimmering facet of the American dream.

The musical theatre flourished, but generally the most successful works—*The Most Happy Fella, Guys and Dolls, Wonderful Town, My Fair Lady, The Music Man, Flower Drum Song*—were in the now established manner that Rodgers and Hammerstein had created in the 40s. Only *Candide* (1956), a collaboration between Leonard Bernstein, Lillian Hellman, and Richard Wilbur brought musical novelty and fresh verbal wit into the theatre; and *Candide* bombed at its premiere, although it is still being pushed by its supporters as a classic of the American lyric stage. The audiences of the 50s failed even to recognize outstanding works that demanded a fresh response.

If Broadway was moribund, however, great promise for a theatrical awakening was evidenced by the development during the 50s of Off-Broadway theatre. "Off-Broadway" was not a new concept in 1950. Small, inexpensive theatres—often obscurely located and supported by minority groups—had operated in New York throughout its theatrical history. O'Neill's plays had first reached the city through such groups; but in general "little theatres" specialized in revivals of works in the public domain that could be produced cheaply. The general public and the drama critics usually ignored them.

A change was evident in off-Broadway activities, however, from the onset of the 50s. On May 31, 1950 the first arena theatre in New York opened in the Hotel Edison with veteran actor Lee Tracy starring in a revival of George Kelly's *The Show-Off.* In November ANTA (American National Theatre and Academy) launched its own productions with Robinson Jeffers' demanding poetic drama, "The Tower Beyond Tragedy," starring Judith Anderson.

In August, 1951 Greenwich Village roused from its 20-year-sleep as a thralldom of Tammany Hall and began to assert itself anew as a theatrical center with the establishment of the Circle-in-the-Square (Sheridan, that was). This arena venture attracted attention particularly in March, 1952, when it successfully produced a revival starring Geraldine Page of Tennessee Williams' *Summer and Smoke,* which had failed on Broadway. Four years later it was to repeat its achievement with its successful revival of Eugene O'Neill's *The Iceman Cometh.* A major step in the development of a new off-Broadway theatre was the opening on October 28, 1952 of the Theatre de Lys. Although *Frankie and Johnny,* its initial production, was a flop, William de Lys was subsequently to see his small house become a national institution because of its revival of Bertolt Brecht's *Three-Penny Opera,* which enjoyed one of the longest runs in the history of the New York theatre.

In *The Best Plays of 1953-1954,* Garrison P. Sherwood was compelled to admit that off-Broadway had changed from "little theatre" to "big business." His concession was inspired primarily by the opening on December 1, 1953 of the Phoenix Theatre at 12th St. and 2nd Ave. The first play to rise from its ashes was Sidney Howard's *Madam, Will You Walk?,* which had originally been scheduled for production in 1939. So successful were developments off-Broadway in luring theatre-goers far from their customary haunts that by 1956 cautious uptown producers felt compelled to respond to the challenge from the Village by offering a bewildered public Bert Lahr in Samuel Beckett's *Waiting for Godot,* a work that prompted supercilious taste-maker Louis Kronenberger to observe in *The Best Plays of 1956-1957.* "Not in some years has Broadway been given anything that, in terms of meaning and merit, was more inevitably 'controversial.'" By the 1957-58 season over forty off-Broadway theatres were operating. Their new prestige and the real threat that they posed to the established theatre became manifest in January, 1958 when one of the country's most important playwrights, Tennessee Williams, chose to have produced off-Broadway his *Garden District,* a pairing of two short plays, one of which—*Suddenly, Last Summer*—critics and public agreed was his most powerful work of the decade. Two months later another off-Broadway theatre successfully revived Arthur Miller's *The Crucible,* which earlier audiences had found heavy going. During the 1958-59 season off-Broadway houses presented Samuel Beckett's *Endgame, The Quare Fellow* (the first play by Brendan Behan to reach New York) and plays by Engene Ionesco. The *New Yorker* began to feature regular reviews of off-Broadway openings.

Henry Hewes could still complain in *The Best Plays of 1958-1959,* however, that despite the importance of off-Broadway theatres in sponsoring revivals of neglected American works and introducing important foreign playwrights, they had not been "very successful in the matter of developing new native playwrights." On July 15, 1959 this claim could be set aside when the Living Theatre opened its production of Jack Gelber's *The Connection,* a haunting drama of dope addiction that marked a step forward in breaking down the barriers between action and audience. Six months later the Provincetown Playhouse gave some glimpse of the extraordinary promise of the 60s when it offered the first American production of Edward Albee's *The Zoo Story.*

The health of off-Broadway theatre was boosted by the publication beginning in September, 1955 of the *Village Voice,* a weekly newspaper sponsored by, among others, Norman Mailer. Although the uptown dailies and national magazines had been slow to take an interest in goings-on off-Broadway, the *Voice* encouraged small-scale operations from its outset. Its scarce files are a principal source of information about the varying but generally steadily growing fortunes of this effort to rejuvenate American theatre.

The *Voice* was also one of the first American periodicals to recognize the motion picture as not just transient entertainment, but an increasingly important twentieth-century art form. The growing addiction to television had driven the American film industry to seek new gimmicks with which to sustain itself. The early 50s saw an experiment beginning with *Bwana Devil* to project motion pictures in three dimensions. The need for special viewing glasses cooled, however, public enthusiasm for this medium. (The only important film to be made in it, *Kiss Me, Kate,* appeared also and survives only in conventional form.) Hollywood then turned to Cinerama, a three-screen process, and such cheaper wide-screen processes as Cinemascope. These, audiences accepted; by the end of the decade the "wide screen" had become the American standard and almost all films were being made in color.

Few Hollywood films of this desperate decade were artistic triumphs; yet the studios showed daring by filming Tennessee Williams' *A Streetcar Named Desire* and Arthur Miller's *Death of a Salesman* (which brought out American Legion pickets) and *A Place in the Sun,* based upon Theodore Dreiser's *An American*

Tragedy. In 1954 the first American to achieve a major artistic reputation primarily as a writer of television dramas and screenplays, Paddy Chayevsky, carried off the best picture honors from the Academy of Motion Picture Arts and Sciences for his *Marty,* the ingratiating tale of a timid butcher's romance. Meanwhile the impressive films of foreign directors like Ingmar Bergman and Federico Fellini were beginning to reach this country through "art theatres," whose growth parallelled the development of the off-Broadway theatres.

The 50s were, in short, an artistically as well as politically tacky decade during which the Establishment accomplished virtually nothing (Faulkner, Stevens, and O'Neill—the older writers whose works gave the decade its greatest distinction—never played the "game" of literary politics), while dissident groups made clear the necessity for a remodeling program. The 60s were to witness the disappearance from the scene of not only most writers active before World War II, but even of such recently risen favorites as Tennessee Williams and J. D. Salinger, along with the emergence of tough, critical, outspoken young writers attuned to the restlessness of a time that was to witness a vast relaxation of bigoted standards of censorship that had only begun to give way in the 50s.

II

But can such a decade be labeled with the name of one writer? During the 1950s, Jerome David Salinger published his single novel to date, *The Catcher in the Rye,* and eight rather long stories — all but one of them connected at least thematically with the saga of a family named Glass. (All but one of the stories also originally appeared in the *New Yorker.*) This small body of work enjoyed a popularity unparalleled during the decade. Especially in a paperbacked edition, *The Catcher in the Rye* sold hundreds of thousands of copies for years. *Nine Stories* outsold any similar collection during a period when the market for short story collections was evaporating. Until the four long stories about the Glass family — beginning in 1955 with "Franny" and ending in 1959 with 'Seymour: An Introduction"—appeared some years later in book form, issues of the *New Yorker* containing them sold for up to ten dollars when they could be located. So much more was written about Salinger than he wrote himself that George Steiner was able to write derogatorily about "The Salinger Industry."

Salinger's significant writing was almost entirely confined to the 50s. Since 1959, he has made only a single lengthy addition to the Glass family saga, 'Hapworth 16, 1924," a tale of Buddy and Seymour Glass as children at a boys' camp; and even Salinger's most enthusiastic admirers have found this pretentious tale almost a parody of his earlier concise and understated stories. Before 1950 he had published 26 mostly quite short stories, only five of which he chose to include in *Nine Stories*. The others remain uncollected in magazine files and out-of-print short story anthologies. Only the longest, "The Inverted Forest" (*Cosmopolitan,* December, 1947; reprinted, March, 1961) is of major importance in understanding Salinger's artistic vision and techniques. Two of these stories ("I'm Crazy" and "Slight Rebellion off Madison") are preliminary sketches, containing material subsequently incorporated in different form into *The Catcher in the Rye.* Two more ("The Last Day of the Last Furlough" and "This Sandwich Has No Mayonnaise") are World War II stories, notable for the mention of an earlier Holden Caulfield, who is killed during the war. Four are examples of the once fashionable "short, short story," a quick, slickly told anecdote; and the four contributed to *Story* magazine (edited by Whit Burnett, who reputedly "discovered" Salinger in a creative writing class at Columbia University) are apprentice efforts to explore the psychology of the same urban upper middle-class that the Caulfields and Glasses belong to. Although seven of these stories were selected for inclusion in annual surveys of the best short fiction, only three of them ("A Perfect Day for Bananafish," "Uncle Wiggily in Connecticut," "Down at the Dinghey" — all contributions to the Glass family saga) are usually mentioned among Salinger's best works, and all three of these are closely linked with his major writings of the 50s. If ever a writer has been inextricably identified with a single decade, Salinger is with the 50s.

Certainly no writer has won a remotely similar place in American affections during the 60s; nor did any single writer so largely monopolize readers during any earlier decade. Because of the singular relationship between Salinger and the years of the "silent generation," it would seem that we might learn something about the feelings of the inarticulate youth of the period by examining the assumptions underlying the fiction of the writer that most attracted them.

First, though, we must bear in mind that Salinger was not

universally acclaimed during the 50s. His works have always polarized opinion. *The Catcher in the Rye* was widely denounced and rejected. Older critics dismissed it impatiently; school boards and self-appointed professional moralists objected to its colloquial style and obscene language. Although some older readers had the perceptiveness to admire Salinger, his novel appealed principally to high school and college students; and he is important — among other things — as one of the earliest chroniclers of the now formidable "generation gap."

The first and last of Salinger's stories to attract widespread attention concerned the same event — the suicide of Seymour Glass in a Miami Beach hotel. Indeed "The Age of Salinger" can be precisely designated as extending from January, 1948, when "A Perfect Day for Bananafish" introduced readers of the *New Yorker* to the extraordinary Glass family to June, 1959, when the far longer and more garrulous "Seymour: An Introduction" appeared in the same magazine and cleared up the most important chapter in this family chronicle. These dates are important in discussing the rage for Salinger, because not since the enthusiasm during the early Romantic period for Goethe's young Werther had fictional characters so completely dominated the imaginative fancies of a decade as Seymour Glass and Holden Caulfield dominated the dim, defensive 50s. When in the 60s John F. Kennedy helped inspire a new dynamic activism among American youth, interest in Salinger and his creations began to dwindle.

With a decade's perspective on the body of Salinger's major work, we can see that Holden and Seymour are actually polar opposites and that from the contrast between them we can achieve a sharply black-and-white outline of the hopes, fears, and convictions of the sensitive young people growing up during the 50s. Both Seymour and Holden are, paradoxically, triumphant and defeated figures, depending upon the code of values of the perceiver. For those who believe in the sacredness of the life force, who feel that survival even at the expense of repression is the highest value, Holden Caulfield is a hero of his time and Seymour Glass is anomic, the personification of neurotic self-righteousness. For those who believe that the maintenance of principle is worth any sacrifice ("Better dead than red," as some shouted during the 50s), who find their highest values in personal integrity even at the sacrifice of their lives, Seymour Glass is not just a hero, but a saint — a spiritual exemplar to less noble and dedicated men, and

Holden Caulfield is a "cop-out," a man who demeans himself by compromising in the interest of self-preservation. To do justice to Salinger, it is important to observe that Holden does not — like his older brother, D. B. — actually sell out to the Establishment. He is unhappy about the concessions that he must make, but he acknowledges that there is "no nice place." He is resigned — like Eloise in "Uncle Wiggily in Connecticut" and Zooey Glass — to living with this knowledge. Seymour refuses. Salinger has little to say about those like Lane Coutell in "Franny" or Joanie in "Pretty Mouth and Green My Eyes" or Seymour's mother-in-law or Holden Caulfield's father, who not only sell out to the world, but who enjoy selling out and revel in their phoniness. These ashen spectacles are too dreadful to contemplate.

If we can correctly assume that Salinger's values are representative of those of a sizeable and influential segment of the youth of the 50s (and this argument remains hypothetical because the 50s are still close enough to remain an exasperating puzzle), it is clear that a principal conviction of this witch-hunting era was that a man could not retain his integrity and stay alive. In my book about Salinger I argue that "Uncle Wiggily in Connecticut" is a key to understanding the author's writings as a whole because in it he directly contrasts the squalor of the real world, which Holden Caulfield calls "phony," with the "nice" world of the imagination, in which man is happy. This "nice" world, however, doesn't really exist and Eloise's cry at the end of the story, "I was a nice girl, wasn't I?" is the plaint of everyone who has compromised his vision.

Holden Caulfield's dream as he drifts about New York City during his flight from the confinement of home and school is of protecting children so that they will not be contaminated by the "phony" world. In one of the most famous passages in Salinger's work, Holden shares his dream with his sister Phoebe:

> "Anyway I keep picturing all these little kids playing some game in this big field of rye and all. Thousands of little kids, and nobody's around — nobody big, I mean — except me. And I'm standing on the edge of some crazy cliff. What I have to do, I have to catch everybody if they start to go over the cliff—I mean if they're running and they don't look where they're going I have to come out from somewhere

and *catch* them. That's all I'd do all day. I'd just be the catcher in the rye and all."

But when Holden discovers obscenities scratched where small children can see them, he comes reluctantly to the conclusion that "you can't ever find a place that's nice and peaceful, because there isn't any." This realization forces him to make the choice "to be or not to be" that ultimately confronts Seymour Glass. Throughout *The Catcher in the Rye* Holden has intimations that he may "disappear," and he calls upon his dead brother Allie to help him. He enters the latrine in the Museum of Natural History and suffers a "fall" (perhaps the one foreseen by his former teacher Antolini) that could kill him. But all he does is "sort of land" on his side; and after he recovers, he feels better — not "so damn dizzy any more."

He learns that his allegiance must be not to the dead (Allie and the mummies) but to the living when his young sister Phoebe announces she is running away with him. He recognizes that in order to get her home, he must go home himself. Then watching her ride the carrousel in Central Park that is playing "Smoke Gets in Your Eyes," "very jazzy and funny," he admits,

> All the kids kept trying to grab for the gold ring, and so was old Phoebe, and I was sort of afraid she'd fall off the goddam horse, but I didn't say anything or do anything. The thing with kids is, if they want to grab for the gold ring, you have to let them do it, and not say anything. If they fall off, they fall off, but it's bad if you say anything to them.

The dream of the catcher has evaporated. If you start telling anybody anything, Holden observes at the end of the book, "you start missing everybody." If you start thinking about the living instead of the dead, the changing rather than the immutable, you become involved in all life and you recognize that you must forego your private vision and at least make an effort to conform to the world. "If you want to stay alive," Holden observes, "you have to say that stuff," like "Glad to've met you" to people you're not at all glad to meet.

Holden surely spoke for many of his contemporaries even if they didn't always recognize his message. The 50s were a period of supreme disillusionment. Men had fought for years and millions had died in the hope of defeating the forces of evil and madness and creating a better world; but by 1949 it was painfully apparent that the Western Allies had enjoyed a material triumph, but a spiritual defeat. Sheer physical power and technical know-how had brought the fanatical Germans and Japanese to their knees; but with the slicing up of Germany and Korea, the collapse of China, the erection of an iron curtain, suspicion drove out love. People, it was demonstrated, could band together to die, but could not learn to live together. The naive idealism of American and British wartime leaders was directly or indirectly discredited, while obsessively vindictive men like Stalin and smiling hollow men like Eisenhower flourished.

Most people of the 50s resembled Holden Caulfield. When he says, "If you want to stay alive, you have to say that stuff," he speaks for his readers. Extraordinarily for a book that has been so frequently and intensively read, *The Catcher in the Rye* has often been completely misinterpreted. Both youthful partisans and older fault-finders have viewed the novel as an account of a callow rebellion against pompous propriety. On the contrary, the book preaches not rebellion, but resignation. More than that, it is not even romantic in its approach. Jacques Barzun in *Classic, Romantic, and Modern* explains the difference between the first two of these views of life as they are exemplified by works of Descartes and Goethe:

> In the romantic view, the lesson of Faust has to be relearned individually through experience. The lesson of Descartes can presumably be learned from reading the remainder of the *Discourse on Method*. Descartes has alone done the perilous work; he has taken the risks and wrested the true answers from his experiences. The lesson that Faust learns can only be found in the undergoing of experience itself.

The clearest indication of the intention of *The Catcher in the Rye* is found in Holden's remark after spending a night in the waiting room at Grand Central Station, "It wasn't too nice. Don't ever try it. I mean it. It'll depress you." Even at the climax of the novel, though Holden realizes that kids can't be protected from falling over "some crazy cliff," he continues to tell *the reader* what to do, "The thing with kids is, if they want to grab for the gold ring,

you have to let them do it, and not say anything." Holden is not
a Romantic urging his readers — like the later Beatniks — to go
"on the road" and discover life for themselves. Barzun's remark
about Descartes applies exactly to Holden as Salinger presents
him, he "has alone done the perilous work; he has taken the
risks and wrested the true answers from his experiences." The
reader can learn his lesson by reading the book. Far from encouraging rebellion and flight, Salinger atempts to make *The Catcher
in the Rye* a surrogate for them, so that the reader by vicariously
sharing Holden's depressing experiences need not himself undergo
a parallel ordeal.

Although few young readers could probably have articulated
their response to the book and although few of them probably
even tried to analyze this response (as Holden said of Jesus,
"He didn't have time to go around analyzing everybody"), many of
them probably were provided by the novel with the vicarious
experience that enabled them to compromise with their own
private, impractical dreams — the aesthetic resolution of their
frustrations. In the many battles that has raged over *The Catcher
in the Rye,* few have noted that the novel is a virtually flawless
fictional embodiment of the traumatic experience of accepting
the destruction of one's illusions as the price for moving from
childhood to manhood. One of my students, Greg Naganuma,
expresses the concept behind the book memorably when he writes
that the "responsibility" of education is to help one "to learn to
compromise with his surroundings." The book depicts the moral
growth that is the necessary complement to Holden's rapid physical growth if he is not to remain — like so many Americans — a
child in an adult's body. The picture that the novel offers of
this painful process of maturation is likely to be the quality that
will insure its survival when its fascinating portrayal of a particular
era becomes of only historical interest.

Something else that the horde glossing *The Catcher in the Rye*
has failed to notice is that Holden Caulfield is a masochist. He
discloses an irrational aspect of his personality when he comments after looking out the window of a hotel of the "perverts" in
the other rooms, "The trouble was, that kind of junk is sort of
fascinating to watch, even if you don't want it to be." On other
occasions, he observes, "I hate the movies like poison, but I get
a bang imitating them" and, after a fight with a pimp who is
attempting to cheat him, "I had blood all over my mouth and chin

and even on my pajamas and bathrobe. It partly scared me and it partly fascinated me." Most significantly, at the end of the book he climaxes his recital of his new feelings of communality with the statement, "I think I even miss that goddam Maurice." Maurice, the pimp, is the man who has hurt Holden most both physically and ethically (by taking deliberate advantage of his naivete). Holden recognizes that an acceptance of the world involves an acceptance of suffering. Reflecting on the "perverty bum" who he imagines wrote the obscene phrase on the wall of Phoebe's school, Holden writes,

> I kept wanting to kill whoever'd written it. . . . I kept
> picturing myself catching him at it, and how I'd smash his
> head on the stone steps till he was good and goddam dead
> and bloody. But I knew, too, I wouldn't have the guts to
> do it. I knew that. That made me even more depressed.
> I hardly even had the guts to rub it off the wall with my
> *hand,* if you want to know the truth. I was afraid some
> teacher would catch me rubbing it off and would think *I'd*
> written it.

Again Holden serves as a perfect reflector of his time. He not only knows that he is incapable of initiating any risky positive action to benefit others because he feels his motives may be misconstrued by the authorities. He is in precisely the position of the conscientious but timid people of the 50s who were intimidated by the irresponsible persecution of the Joseph McCarthys. Everyone could envision himself as the kind of victim of "guilt-by-association" that Dr. J. Robert Oppenheimer became. As a result a significant portion of our society was morally immobilized at a time when constructive action was desperately needed to avert a racial crisis at home and to support dynamic rather than decadent regimes abroad (like those in China and Viet Nam). *The Catcher in the Rye* gratified its audience not only by providing it with an aesthetic resolution of its frustrations in a colloquial language that it could understand, but also by providing it with the consolation of an understanding portrayal of its irresolute and irrational behavior. Salinger imposed upon a tacky age the style that it lacked.

Seymour Glass is the necessary complement to Holden Caulfield. We can, in fact, only fully grasp the significance of Holden by contemplating his polar alternative. Holden's old teacher Antolini urges upon Holden a quotation from Wilhelm Stekel, " 'The mark of the immature man is that he wants to die nobly for a cause, while the mark of the mature man is that he wants to live humbly for one.' " Whether Antolini is good angel or devil's advocate (and I doubt that Salinger accepts the idea that to die nobly for a cause is a mark of immaturity), the statement that he treasures does express what Salinger conceives to be the only alternatives open to people. Either one lives humbly (as Holden will if he continues to accept suffering) for a cause or one dies nobly for it. Salinger seems to reject the Socratic posibility of leading the truly "examined life" (like Jesus, one doesn't have time to go around "analyzing everybody"), but so probably did most of his contemporaries, too caught up in the "rat race" to have the leisure or even the inclination to scrutinize their own and other's behavior.

Seymour Glass embodies the possibility of dying nobly (and the danger of viewing the talkative Antolini as Salinger's spokesman is shown by the tenderness with which the author presents a character for whom Holden's teacher would have to feel great distaste). The motive behind Seymour's suicide remains enigmatic in "A Perfect Day for Bananafish," The only clue to his behavior is found in his earlier explanation of the bananafish to a little girl Sybil (who calls him "Seemore Glass"):

> "Well, they swim into a hole where there's a lot of bananas. They're very ordinary-looking fish when they swim *in*. But once they get in, they behave like pigs. . . . Naturally, after that they're so fat they can't get out of the hole again. Can't fit through the door. . . . They die. . . . They get banana fever. It's a terrible disease."

A possible interpretation of this fable is that Seymour sees himself as a bananafish, doomed by his addiction to material things; but this explanation scarcely holds water because Seymour kills himself quite deliberately, whereas the bananafish enter blithely upon their doomed course without understanding the consequences. They behave just like the little kids in *The Catcher in the Rye* grabbing for the gold ring. It is more likely that the other characters are the bananafish. Seymour's wife Muriel and her mother, for example, are clearly obsessed with material things, so that their doom is certain. Seymour finds the only escape from their vulgar obsession with "things" (Salinger could scarcely have set the story in a more appropriate place than Miami Beach, which must be the most garishly vulgar place in the world) in the childlike innocence of Sybil; but when Sybil says that she sees the bananafish, Seymour recognizes that she is going to go the way that Muriel has gone — that he can't prevent her falling any more than Holden can prevent the kids in the field of rye from doing so and that, therefore, there is literally nothing that he can do to save this world while he remains alive. (In her yellow bathing suit, Sybil must even look like a bananafish. When Seymour says that her bathing suit is blue — a color associated with innocence — Sybil insists, "This is a *yellow*.") Sybil's seeing the fish with six bananas in his mouth can be interpreted in the same way that Holden interprets the kids' behavior on the carrousel, "If they want to grab for the gold ring, you have to let them do it." But you don't have to stand around resignedly and watch them. Holden does accept Phoebe's behavior and goes home with her to try to help her live as happy a life as possible in a squalid world. Seymour, however, refuses to capitulate. Having already been rejected by Muriel (who hasn't gotten around to reading the work of "the *only great poet of the century*"), Seymour sees in Sybil's response to his parable the blighting of his last hope for a materialistic world. Though she has not had enough, he refuses to dally with her any more and returns to end his life.

Salinger returned to the problem of Seymour's suicide at the end of his great decade (whether or not he continued to brood on this event throughout the decade is a question that I shall attack finally). In "Seymour: An Introduction," Buddy Glass is quite explicit about Seymour's reasons for taking his life: "I say that the true artist-seer, the heavenly fool who can and does produce beauty, is mainly dazzled to death by his own scruples, the blinding shapes and colors of his own sacred human conscience."

I don't think that it matters whether or not Salinger actually had this clearly articulated concept in mind when he wrote the first story about Seymour. The important thing is that although there are differences between the early and the late Seymour Glass, both manifestations of the character are incapable of "adjusting" to the "phony" world. That Seymour is not intimidated as Holden is by the knowledge that "If you want to stay alive, you have to say that stuff" is evident from his conversations about an imaginary tattoo and his remark to a woman whom he accuses of looking at his feet. In both stories, he will not compromise with squalor; and this refusal makes it impossible for him to continue to live in a squalid world.

Salinger's other major stories are principally reinforcements or elaborations of the principles laid down in his portraits of Holden and Seymour. In some lines from the work of the poet who is the principal character in the regrettably neglected "The Inverted Forest," Salinger suggests that one can find joy only within one's self. Slapping indirectly at T. S. Eliot, the poet writes that the world is "Not wasteland, but a great inverted forest/with all foliage underground." Also in this story, Salinger voices one of his most powerful complaints against phoniness when he has his hero observe, "A poet doesn't invent his poetry — he finds it." "Uncle Wiggily in Connecticut," as I have already pointed out, contrasts the "phony" and the "nice" worlds and shows through the portrait of Eloise what happens to the person who compromises. "Down at the Dinghey" and "For Esmé — with Love and Squalor" are rare examples in Salinger's work of his attempting to show how a generous gesture may help to maintain the illusion of love in a squalid world. Some critics have tried, quite plausibly, to associate Sergeant X in this story with Seymour Glass. If the two can be equated, it becomes clear that even the kind of loving gesture that Esmé is capable of is but a stopgap measure that may preserve one temporarily from madness but that cannot reconcile one permanently to squalor.

After publishing *The Catcher in the Rye,* Salinger turned away from his preoccupation with the Glass family, of whose history he had given us only some colorful glimpses. Without access to his manuscripts, we cannot tell whether he continued to write about these characters; but from the public record, there is reason to suspect that he put them aside, only to return again in "Franny" — with "DeDaumier-Smith's Blue Period" and "Teddy" as transitional steps — to an extended reconsideration of them.

The support for this hypothesis is a story unique among Salinger's works that has never received adequate attention, "Pretty Mouth and Green My Eyes," his only picture of adult life in the "phony" world. The principal character is one of the slick successes that Salinger usually avoided dealing with. He is in bed with the wife of one of his associates when he receives two phone calls from the man that he is cuckolding. The first is a request for help in locating the other man's wife who has disappeared after a party; the second reports that the wife — who is still in her paramour's bed — has returned home. The story reveals in a few pages not only the amoral squalor of the adult world, but the fear of those trapped in the "rat-race" of exposing their fears. Ironically, the man trying to keep up a brave front has nowhere to turn except to one of his destroyers.

If Salinger had pursued the vein that he opened in this story, he might have given us a frightening picture of the adult world of the 50s to match the one that he had already presented in *The Catcher in the Rye* and most of his stories of the experience of growing up in such a world. In his next stories, however, he returned to the mystical investigation of childhood innocence. Perhaps he found squalor too frightening to contemplate; more likely the importunities that he had to endure as a result of the success of *The Catcher in the Rye*, which appeared at almost the same time as "Pretty Mouth and Green My Eyes," drove Salinger out of the adult world altogether, back to the privacy of his own visions in the "inverted forest."

"De Daumier-Smith's Blue Period" is an arch and rambling effort to present the impact of the revelations that Holden Caulfield experiences in *The Catcher in the Rye* upon an older, more self-consciously introspective artist, who tries to play "catcher in the rye" to his pupils. In the end, gazing into a window full of bedpans and surgical appliances, he learns to accept the world and frees his students to fulfill their own destinies.

"Teddy," which Buddy Glass in *Seymour: An Introduction* includes in the Glass family canon, is perhaps Salinger's most chilling portrayal of the impossibility of innocence in this squalid world. At the end of the story the clairvoyant ten-year-old boy named by the title either destroys himself or allows his little sister — another aggressor like Sybil and Phoebe Caulfield — to destroy him, while a sympathetic educator sits hopelessly by. In this story Salinger heightens his attack on the illusion that man is rational by shifting from the metaphorical presentation of human irrationality in *The Catcher in the Rye* to a frontal assault on logic, which Teddy says is what was in the apple that Adam ate in the Garden of Eden. "You have to vomit it up," he explains, "to see things as they really are." At ten Teddy is already a strong advocate of the idea that Holden Caulfield learns only years later that "it's bad if you say anything" to kids to try to make them change. Teddy says that his parents don't seem able to love him and his sister "just the way we are. . . . They don't seem able to love us unless they can keep changing us a little bit."

In the major stories about the Glass family, Salinger investigates the possibility of leaving people alone and thus keeping alive without completely selling out in such a dog-eat-dog profession as acting. When Zooey Glass encourages his distraught sister Franny to act for "the Fat Lady out there," who is "Christ Himself, Buddy," he preaches exactly the same kind of resigned acceptance at which Holden Caulfield finally arrives:

> ". . . you raved and bitched when you came home about the stupidity of audiences. The goddam 'unskilled laughter' coming from the fifth row. And that's right, that's right — God knows it's depressing. I'm not saying it isn't. But that's none of your business, really. That's none of your business, Franny. An artist's only concern is to shoot for some kind of perfection, and *on his own terms,* not anybody else's. You have no right to think about those things. Not in any real sense, anyway."

Like Holden, Franny calls upon the dead (Jesus — through the pilgrim's prayer — and Seymour), but receives assistance actually from the living Zooey masquerading as his brother Buddy. The great voices from the past become meaningful only when they find living spokesmen.

The final two major stories of the Glass saga illustrate this process of re-embodiment that makes living truths of dead words by characterizing Seymour's devoted brother Buddy as a kind of selfless medium.

"Raise High the Roof Beam, Carpenters" shows us Buddy's concept of Seymour as a man who would not yield to pressure from his in-laws-to-be to make a public spectacle of his private feelings at a conventional society wedding. An excerpt from a journal of Seymour's that Buddy reads recalls the days when the Glass children performed on a radio quiz show called "It's a Wise Child" and suggests Seymour's concept of the impossibility of verbal communication between the "phony" and "nice" worlds. He reports a conversation with a phychoanalyst:

> "He'd actually heard the Lincoln broadcast, but he had the

impression that I'd said over the air that the Gettysburg Address was 'bad for children.' Not true. I told him I'd said I thought it was a bad speech for children to have to memorize in school. He also had the impression I'd said it was a dishonest speech. I told him I'd said that 51,112 men were casualties at Gettysburg, and that if someone *had* to speak at the anniversary of the event, he should simply have come forward and shaken his fist at his audience and then walked out — that is, if the speaker was an absolutely honest man."

The trouble, it would seem, is in trying to bring about any change in people — reasoning with those who are the unreasoning slaves of their greedy impulses. In "Seymour: An Introduction," Buddy recalls some remarks that Seymour made as he watched Buddy playing marbles with a friend. Buddy has been using a technique of Seymour's and has been losing steadily, when Seymour addresses him:

"Could you try not aiming so much?" he asked me, still standing there. "If you hit him when you aim, it'll just be luck." . . . "How can it be *luck* if I *aim?*" I said back to him, not loud (despite the italics) but with rather more irritation in my voice than I was actually feeling. He didn't say anything for a moment but simply stood balanced on the curb, looking at me, I knew imperfectly, with love. Because it will be," he said. "You'll be *glad* if you hit his marble — Ira's marble — won't you? Won't you be *glad?* And if you're *glad* when you hit somebody's marble, then you sort of secretly didn't expect too much to do it. So there'd have to be some luck in it, there'd have to be slightly quite a lot of *accident* in it."

What Salinger sems to have Buddy saying is something that might explain the difficult line in T. S. Eliot's "Ash Wednesday," "Teach us to care and not to care." Teach us, that is, to want to do something perfectly for its own sake, but not to want to do it so badly that our satisfaction depends upon impressing another — to care for the action, not the audience response, as Zooey advises Franny in his remarks about the Fat Lady. Standards must be exclusively one's own; they cannot be imposed upon the world. One must either be content to be equally responsive to all others in the world—making no invidious distinctions no matter how much they may please or offend — or else one must leave this world behind.

The range of ideas in Salinger's work is extremely narrow. He is like a searchlight exploring a small area intensely rather than like a sun illuminating a landscape. (The simile is doubly appropriate because his vision is nocturnal. Most of the action in his stories takes place at night, and the characters tend to spend their days largely in dim apartments or darkened theatres.) He sees the material world as absolutely corrupt (once more he recalls Eliot, whose "Gerontion" observes ". . . what is kept must be adulterated"). One can save one's self only by limiting one's criticism to one's self and resisting the temptation for public acclaim. The man whose vision is too clear to enable him to close his eyes to this world cannot hope to communicate with it. He can hope to make a spectacular exit that may keep alive some glimmering memory of the "niceness" we can know only momentarily.

It is easy to see that these ideas had enormous appeal to young people of the 50s. The continued cold War, the venal leadership of the "industrial-military" complex, the "crew-cut" mentality that denounced any deviation as heresy made the world seem squalid indeed. One could enjoy his vision only — like the poet in "The Inverted Forest" — by throwing away his glasses so that he could not see the "phony" world and keeping quiet about the world inside his head. Survival demanded either a debasing acceptance of the acclaim of an "unskilled" public or else an undiscriminating acceptance of all men and things. (Significantly, Eisenhower, the most appropriate figurehead the age could have found, had a reputation based on his being undiscrimiatingly "liked" by everyone on the basis of a vacuous smile that served to hide any ideas or visions he might have had.) The man who would not compromise his vision was either literally driven to his death (like French film director Max Ophuls or Czech leader Jan Masaryk) or into long seclusion (like Charles DeGaulle or Boris Pasternak). The direction of society was left in the grasping hands of insensitive egotists like Lane Coutell.

Since the end of the 50s Salinger's works — though still widely read and admired — have declined in popularity. Sensitive youth has turned activist in the 60s, and Salinger does not speak as clearly to a dynamic generation as he did to a passive one. The shortcoming of the quite justified attitude of withdrawal from the world held by sensitive people of the 50s is that it is self-indulgent. By assuming that any effort to improve conditions is going to be defeated and will probably simply get one into trouble, one can rationalize a failure even to make any effort. Celebrity is undoubtedly accompanied by formidable problems; but Salinger's characters — and Salinger himself — never tried to surmount these problems. Instead he withdrew into his own "inverted forest" in New Hampshire. While it is undeniable that too many public demands may be destructive of one's career, so also may too much isolation from the world. Brooding in his retreat over the history of the Glass family, Salinger lost touch with a changing world.

His behavior is, of course, his own business; but our concern is not with Salinger the man so much as with Salinger the spokesman for the 50s. His resigned refusal to try to make the world come around to his terms is characteristic of his audience's. The result is that an entire generation of Americans lacked either any constructive ideas or the will to implement them. It is ironic that when John F. Kennedy came along at last, he could not stimulate a sufficiently lasting program of action among mature people to keep the country from falling, upon his inopportune death, into the hands of people like Lyndon Johnson, whose thinking was geared to the crises of the 30s and 40s, and even Barry Goldwater, whose thinking was geared to the irresponsible individualism of the 1880s and 90s. The young people who had rallied to Kennedy's support were too young to take over control; the old people were stuck with visions inspired by Hoover or Roosevelt, and the mature people of Salinger's generation were either devoid of ideals or too touchy to risk fighting for their vision.

"The Age of Salinger" provides compelling reasons for describing as sentimental and decadent an "either/or" vision which perceives defeat or death as the only alternatives in the struggle between the affectionate individual and squalid society. None of Salinger's characters ever expresses the attitude championed by Marlow in Conrad's *Heart of Darkness* that "for good or evil mine is the speech that cannot be silenced."

What a writer has his characters say is, of course, as much his own business as his attitude toward the world. What matters is not that a defeatist attitude underlies Salinger's work, but that works embodying such an attitude were extremely popular during the 50s. Salinger's writings have sometimes been called "decadent" for the wrong reasons by unthinking people reacting automatically to words or incidents in the stories. Perhaps in the long run the most important contribution made by *The Catcher in the Rye* to the development of American literature was the novel's providing the perennially necessary refurbishing of the colloquial idiom; and Salinger needed to "invent" very few of the things that happen to Holden. As the poet in "The Inverted Forest" insisted one should, the novelist "found" his material by observing the world around him.

The Catcher in the Rye is, however, like most of Salinger's work, decadent from one point of view because it expresses a hopeless acquiescence in squalor. "It didn't seem at all like Christmas was coming soon. It didn't seem like *anything* was coming," Holden Caulfield says at one point as he surveys Central Park. Christmas had become a commercial orgy, not the mystical celebration of a promised rejuvenation of the world. It did look to the people of the 50s indeed as if "nothing was coming." It was a black-and-white decade — the white of horrified faces slashed with the black of willful violence. It was not one of those eras whose features we necessarily crave to see fixed in art; but the era found in J. D. Salinger the artist who fixed those features. Through his work those of us who endured the 50s can re-experience them (from an aesthetic distance, happily) and those who did not can grasp the feeling of living in that age of decadent apathy as they cannot such periods as the campy 60s, which seem not to have found their artistic match, or the fearful 40s, which were too much for any one man to contain.

Hemingway's Craft in The Old Man and the Sea

by Sheldon Norman Grebstein

The Old Man and the Sea, published in 1952, was the last major work of fiction by Hemingway to appear in his lifetime. Although several years of creative effort remained to him before his death in 1961, the writing of those years is not likely to either enhance or materially alter his reputation — at least in the opinions of Carlos Baker and Philip Young, who have examined the writer's unpublished papers. If this is indeed the case, *The Old Man and the Sea* will probably solidify its position as the final boundary of Hemingway's career, just as *In Our Time* marks its beginning. The judgment of the Nobel Committee, which singled out *The Old Man and the Sea* for special praise in its award of the 1954 Literature prize to Hemingway, has proved to be unusually percipient.

Nor have critics neglected the work. Soon after its publication it became the subject for serious and generally sympathetic commentary, continuing to this moment. Some have hailed *The Old Man and the Sea* as Hemingway's affirmation and reconciliation of man and nature; others have interpreted it as Hemingway's reiteration of man's tragic or ironic defeat by insuperable forces. The story's allegorical dimensions have also been examined, especially its use of Christian symbolism and the parallels between Santiago's ordeal and Christ's, or that of a mythic quest-hero. An early and persistent reading holds that the novella poses a parable of Hemingway's own literary fate, with himself as the gallant fisherman and his career as the splendid marlin devoured by bloodthirsty shark-critics. In sum, *The Old Man and the Sea* would not seem to be a neglected work.

Nevertheless, while the story's themes, characters, and dominant symbols have been carefully examined, as in the recent study by Bickford Sylvester which also reviews the various critical interpretations (PMLA, 71:130-38, 1966), many of the work's vital elements of structure and some of its most effective techniques remain unnoticed. This despite the common agreement that Hemingway's narrative art has never been better than in *The Old Man and the Sea*. I am convinced that much of the hostility to Hemingway, seemingly more virulent and frequent with each passing year, and the oft-heard and influential view of him as a minor writer of narrow range and scanty achievement, derive from too much emphasis on his ideas, his world view, the "meaning" of his work. However important the Hemingway "Code" and the Hemingway "Hero" have been to our literary imagination, we are a little tired of hearing about them. Literature will owe more to his technique than to his vision of life; after him the writing of prose narrative was not the same. It is the craft, then, of *The Old Man and the Sea* that this essay proposes to treat.

One of the characteristic effects of Hemingway's good work is that of wholeness, completeness, symmetry. What has usually been attributed to the Hemingway Code, the sense of rigid control over painful or turbulent feelings, is as much an attribute of form — of a violent pattern of action contained within a strong but unobtrusive structure. This structure must never be ignored in the reading of a Hemingway narrative, yet, surprisingly, one finds relatively little attention to it.

First, the essential design of *The Old Man and the Sea* can be compared to that of the drama, for the narrative moves through three distinct phases of action which are symmetrically proportioned in relation both to one another and to the whole. In the first part, or act, Hemingway establishes the old man's relationship with the boy, Santiago's uniqueness and potentiality for tragic stature, the ethical values to be tested, and the voyage out to sea. This part occupies almost exactly one-fourth of the entire work. The second section, act two in the drama, is introduced by Santiago's twice-repeated "yes" and begins at the moment when the great marlin takes the fisherman's bait. It proceeds to describe the harrowing combat between man and fish, and concludes with

Santiago's killing of the marlin. This section is virtually twice the length of the opening phase and occupies the middle half of the work. The concluding section, the dénouement, completes the symmetry for it is the same length as part one. It narrates the voyage back, the destruction of the marlin by sharks, and the old man's reconciliation with the boy. Thus the story comes full circle. This sequence of action, then, in its proportional arrangement, comprises the work's basic architecture. However, this is hardly its only structural principle. The large frame is reinforced by other, more intricate designs.

Among the essential symbolic patterns which support the structure of *The Old Man and the Sea,* as of other Hemingway narratives, is the movement from inside to outside, or, conversely, from outside to inside. This movement sometimes applies literally as the progression from in-doors to out-of-doors (or the reverse), from nature to dwelling or dwelling to nature, as in "Indian Camp," "Three-Day Blow," "An Alpine Idyll," and many others. In some instances the pattern has only two phases, in others three, with the action returning to the place or sphere of origin. The inside-outside pattern has many ramifications, of course, which break through the literal naming and which inherently convey deep emotional associations and values: in here — out there, home — abroad, familiar — strange, tame — wild, predictable — unpredictable, and so on.

Furthermore, the values which gather around each of these polarities are themselves ironically ambivalent, alternately desirable or repugnant, good or evil. For example, in "Indian Camp" the out-of-doors — especially the lake which Nick Adams crosses to and from the Indian settlement — represents the seeming peace, serenity, and infinity of untrammeled nature, which the naive boy contrasts with the dark hut where a woman has screamed in the agony of childbirth and a man has cut his throat. The symbolic possibilities of the contrast are manifold: Eden before and after the Fall, marriage and single life. Yet the placid lake which assures Nick of his immortality is but a mirror of his innocence. It may be immortal; he, of flesh, is not.

In *The Old Man and the Sea* the same pattern applies but in a slightly different form. Here the movement is from shore to sea to shore, and we have at once a credible imitation of life (is this not the way of fishermen?) and the archetypal associations which sea and shore inspire. Carlos Baker has rightly insisted that the simultaneous creation of a vivid surface reality and strong symbolic undercurrents is fundamental to Hemingway's method and among his greatest achievements. This is in part what Hemingway meant when he spoke of the "iceberg principle," a famous but not wholly understood phrase.

But these associations, as I have noted, are more complex than they may seem at first. Irony and symbolism, E. M. Halliday reminds us, are often inseparable in Hemingway. Shore means home, safety, comradeship; it is the locale for the story's portrayal of the love between Santiago and Manolin. It represents peace, rest, even perhaps an ultimate destiny, in two senses: first in the untranslatable but portentous image of lions playing on African beaches, second in the possibility that (as Bickford Sylvester argues) Santiago returns to die. The shore's negative or hostile function is emphasized when we recall that here Santiago lives in total poverty and is mocked by other fishermen, and that here, at the end, obtuse tourists mistake the marlin's skeleton for a shark's — the very monster which destroyed it. If the shore is thus the affirmative symbol of the closest human relationship Santiago has ever known, it also represents corrupt and confused standards of judgment.

Just as Hemingway establishes paradoxical values for the land, he bestows even more ironically ambiguous meanings upon the sea. As the vast arena for Santiago's struggle with the great marlin, it is that sphere in which man becomes most intensely alive, most severely tested, most heroic. The sea is beneficent, the source of peace and nourishment, and of inexpressible grandeur. But it is a trap, too, the element populated by deceptively beautiful yet poisonous creatures such as the Portuguese Man-of-War, and by the vicious sharks. The sea succors and exalts man even as it overwhelms and ruins him. This is what Santiago means when he says repeatedly in the book's concluding section that he has gone out "too far." The sea becomes, finally, the obective correlative for the abstractions we name Nature, Fate.

Thus the work's narrative pattern and frame, the land-sea-land movement, embodies also the polarities of its meanings: the known against the unknown, the human against the infinite. Furthermore, Hemingway strengthens the principal narrative pattern by interweaving two other sub-patterns, which serve to reduplicate the three-part structure: together-alone-together, darkness-light-darkness.

In the together-alone-together design the narrative opens with its depiction of Santiago's intimate comradeship with the boy, takes him out to sea alone, then closes with the renewed and intensified love of the boy, who resolves henceforth to defy his natural father and always accompany his spiritual father. Whatever one's interpretation of the significance of Santiago's solitary trial against marlin and shark, affirmative, negative, or ironic, the final phase of this design seems to allow little ambiguity; from his aloneness on the sea Santiago is restored to human love on shore. We surmise, too, that other fishermen will no longer mock him for his bad luck. The secular prayer the old man utters recurrently during his exhausting contest, "I wish I had the boy," is fulfilled at the story's end. He will have the boy for as long as he lives, and the boy — as he did at the beginning — is keeping him alive, with food, admiration, and hope. Structure becomes parable; our children extend us.

The second related pattern, darkness-light-darkness, is clear enough in its literal or realistic appearance but contains subtle implications. That is, as fishermen do, Santiago sets out before dawn, captures his fish in daylight (though not of the same day), and returns to port at night. Because the quest itself begins and ends in darkness, the response elicited would seem to be tragic, with darkness functioning first as foreshadowing and then confirmation of failure, loss, defeat, or, at the extreme, the fisherman's death. In darkness also the sharks complete their savage work, as we associate darkness with bestiality and sin. Yet here is the paradox. That the marlin is first hooked and then killed in daylight, that the first shark attacks when the sun is still high, as in daylight Santiago begins to question the ethics of his actions, all suggest that slaughter and moral awareness occur simultaneously and that both are forms of illumination. Indeed, Santiago's reflections upon the joy, the pride, and the evil of killing, ideas stated in full consciousness (in broad daylight, as it were) rehearse a life-long preoccupation of Hemingway's and perhaps his most profound and disturbing literary idea. The killing of the fish, another of Hemingway's deaths in the afternoon, and the old man's thoughts about it remind us of Hemingway's overt statement of that idea in the opening pages of the earlier book: that for him the most intense, the truest art, occurs in the presence and with the inspiration of violent death.

The narrative and symbolic pattern of light-darkness can be studied in further detail, for it serves in the story both as simple external frame and as internal imagery. As frame, the story begins and ends in daylight, from the late afternoon of the eighty-fourth day Santiago has gone unlucky to the afternoon three days later, when the tourists comment ignorantly while Santiago sleeps exhausted. More important, Hemingway uses a recurrent imagery of light and darkness. The sun on the sea hurts Santiago's eyes but it also warms him and helps unclench his crippled left hand. He dreams of white and gold beaches where the lions play. He is fed by white turtle eggs and gold and silver-sided fish. The moon and stars are his friends, and he associates the great fish with the celestial bodies. He knows he cannot be lost at sea because he will be guided by the glow of lights from shore — related, too, to the land-sea symbolism. But silver is also the color of extinction, as the marlin changes from its regal and vibrant blue-purple of life to the pale hue of death: "the color of the silver backing of a mirror." The sea, in contrast, is always and only dark. In fact, the word assumes almost the significance of leitmotif. I count "dark" (or darkness) used thirty times in the story, usually in connection with sea or water, yet never obtrusively. It works as a subtle form of incremental repetition, underscoring the sea's inscrutability, its archetypal mystery, for example in Santiago's thought: "The dark water of the true gulf is the greatest healer that there is."

We must consider, finally, the techniques by which Hemingway portrays his hero, and here again there appears a kind of ambivalence. That is, Hemingway commends Santiago to our affection and admiration; at the same time, he carefully foreshadows the story's tragic or ironic outcome and demonstrates the protagonist's frailties as a man. Hemingway's method is dual: first, he establishes the old man's attributes through a series of contrasts and associations which convey both strength and weakness, innocence and guilt; second, the writer makes his hero intimately familiar to us by his skillful use of a particular narrative perspective.

It was noted earlier in this essay that one of the important functions of the story's opening section is to elevate the fisherman to heroic stature. The most obvious means is direct statement, and three such assertions occur in the work's early pages. Hemingway tells us that Santiago's eyes remain "cheerful and undefeated;" the hero says of himself, "I am a strange old man;" the boy utters the highest tribute: "There are many good fishermen and some great ones. But there is only you." These statements convince us, despite their honorific content, because they are balanced against Santiago's

age, scarred hands, tattered shirt, and simple humility of speech.
Even more persuasive and revealing, however, are the characteristics
suggested by the difference or contrast between the old man (and
his relationship with the boy) and other men.

Santiago is unlucky; others, such as the boy's present master,
are lucky. The boy's father "hasn't much faith;" the boy and the
old man do. The boy's present master has poor vision, does not
allow the boy to help him carry the boat's equipment, and fishes
close to shore. The old man has keen eyes, welcomes the boy's
help, and goes far out. Other men speak of the sea as neutral or
enemy; Santiago feels the same kinship with it one has with a
woman. The old man drinks shark liver oil for its healthful
properties; other men hate it. The old man talks to himself
for company; others have radios. Santiago fishes correctly and
precisely; other men tend their lines carelessly. He thus becomes a
kind of natural aristocrat of fishing, as his idol DiMaggio is a true
prince of baseball. Even the old man's white lies to the boy
contribute to his nobility, for he wishes no pity or charity; and
the very poverty of his shack enhances the nobility of his character and the magnificence of his dreams.

Yet it must be shown that Santiago is a flawed mortal, one of the
race of Cain, born to kill his brothers and to suffer. Hemingway
reminds us of the hero's human imperfection by emphasizing the
theme of treachery, betrayal, deception, from the start. It begins
innocently enough with the old man's mention of his "tricks" as
a compensation for his waning physical strength. Although this
means simply his craft, his skill and intelligence as a fisherman
and man's principal claim to superiority over other animals, the
word itself has a sinister and negative connotation which Hemingway deliberately plays against its surface sense. The same word is
repeated a few pages later, and here Hemingway establishes as the
corollary for man's tricks the cruelty and unpredictability of the
sea, nature, and the unknown agency ("they") which makes some
creatures "too delicately" for survival. From this point on in the
story recurrent emphasis is given to deception, betrayal, and treachery, especially man's treachery. It was "treachery" to pursue the
great marlin in the deep water beyond the usual range of fishermen, as it is "unjust" to kill him. Santiago's left hand behaves
traitorously throughout much of the combat with the fish. Though
men hunt fish for food, Santiago concludes that they are unworthy
of their prey. And once the old man has conquered the fish, the

mode of conquest becomes a cause for shame. "I am only better than him through trickery and he meant me no harm," Santiago thinks as he begins the voyage home with his dead fish-brother. The connection between trick and treachery, between intelligence and sin, is now unmistakable.

In consequence, the return to shore can be compared to Santiago's penance for his crime, though full expiation is not possible because the fish is dead. The sharks, evil in themselves, assume the ironic function of moral agents: they inflict the necessary punishment. Their appearance comes sufficiently as a surprise to intensify the story's action, yet it has been foreshadowed. Subconsciously we have been waiting for them. In the novella's opening pages sharks are associated with vile smells; they are mentioned again, twice, on the voyage out, and once more after Santiago has hooked the marlin. Both their participation in the action and their moral function are specifically given when, late in the second day of the combat, Santiago says, "If sharks come, God pity him and me." And, finally, their appearance produces in him the same response as one suffering the tortures of crucifixion: in answer to the boy's question at the story's close, "How much did you suffer?" Santiago answers, "Plenty."

At last, regardless of profound symbolism and fascinating ambiguities, we must *know* the old man; we must share in his experience. The chief method by which Hemingway joins us to him — even more, by which we enter into him — is the masterly use of that narrative mode called "selective omniscience." In this mode, properly employed, the artist retains the objectivity and freedom of the omniscient, third-person, outside narrator, but takes advantage of the immediate and intimate responses — the "I am there" sense — of the first-person, inside narrator. The writer achieves this through careful selectivity and consistent focus upon one (or a few) of his characters, subtly integrating his voice and vision with theirs. Although Hemingway did not invent this mode, he refined it early in his career and used it with peculiar skill. Furthermore, he is able to avoid detection in his shifts from third-person to first-person narration, or, to say it another way, avoid discordance in his various narrative voices, by using essentially the same linguistic structures, the same level of language and diction, that his characters would naturally employ. Interior monologue thus becomes almost indistinguishable from outside narration. It is a technique that Scott Fitzgerald, for all his superb talent, never wholly mastered. Although a complete study of Hemingway's use of this technique would require more space than available here, a brief explanation is essential.

With a single exception (when we dip quickly into the mind of the boy), the third-person mode is scrupulously maintained during the book's first twenty pages which treat events on shore. We know the *contents* of Santiago's thoughts by Hemingway's statement of them but we do not share in them directly. However, once Santiago is alone and rows out to sea we enter into his mind with increasing frequency, sometimes moving from outside to inside with the traditional Hemingway cues, "he thought," "he said," sometimes gliding over directly from third person to first person. In other words, we get to know Santiago better when we have him alone. The initial instance of Santiago's voiced thought is indicated by quotation marks; after that the author uses no typographical markers except for what is actually spoken aloud. Thus to the reader third-person and first-person narration seem visually the same, as they do aurally. Likewise, the seams of the narrative, the transitions in voice, are kept from intruding upon the reader's attention. For example, here is a typical passage:

> The fish moved steadily and they travelled slowly on the calm water. The other baits were still in the water but there was nothing to be done.
>
> "I wish I had the boy," the old man said aloud. "I'm being towed by a fish and I'm the towing bitt. I could make the line fast. But then he could break it. I must hold him all I can and give him line when he must have it. Thank God he is travelling and not going down."
>
> What I will do if he decides to go down, I don't know. What I'll do if he sounds and dies I don't know. But I'll do something. There are plenty of things I can do.
>
> He held the line against his back and watched it slant in the water and the skiff moving steadily to the northwest.
>
> This will kill him, the old man thought. He can't do this forever. But four hours later the fish was still swimming steadily out to sea, towing the skiff, and the old man was still braced solidly with the line across his back.

Surely the passage appears simple enough and wholly characteristic of Hemingway, yet this seemingly transparent and artless prose employs, in sequence, four distinct narrative modes. It begins with third-person narration, but with the writer occupying the same point in time, space, and outlook as his character. It then shifts to direct utterance, set off by conventional punctuation and introduced by a conventional phrase. Next, however, there is a passage of interior monologue without any cues, followed immediately by another brief passage of outside narrative, followed in turn by a passage which integrates cued interior monologue and third-person narration.

Even in this kind of purely rational analysis of narrative technique, which allows nothing for the momentum of previous action, for the reader's already initiated identification with the protagonist, or for the rhythms of the language (note the repetitions in the passage, and the use of parallelism and balance in the sentence constructions), Hemingway's craft impresses us as remarkably *right*, totally congruent to its subject. It has been said before but it cannot be said too often: no one has written better about such things than Hemingway.

What is true of *The Old Man and the Sea* is true at large. Who does not know Hemingway's writing? Yet who can profess to understand exactly how it is made, or unriddle the secrets of its special magic? We want to know more, for at its best, as in *The Old Man and the Sea,* it partakes of the miracle of enduring art: that it can never be exhausted by critic or reader, but that it renews itself and its audience perpetually.

William Faulkner's Snopes Trilogy: The South Evolves

by MARK LEAF

Faulkner's major effort of the 50s was the reworking and the creative extension of materials, some published as early as 1931, to update his Yoknapatawpha chronicle to 1946. The Snopes trilogy was completed by the publication of *The Town* (1957) and *The Mansion* (1959). Although *The Hamlet* had been published as early as 1940, only with the publication of the two subsequent volumes was its latent promise fully realized and its theme brought into perspective.

Critical opinions of the trilogy have been markedly ambivalent. There has been widespread admiration for *The Hamlet,* but as a collection of short sketches, rather than a novel, and some misgivings — in spite of the depth of response the trilogy as a whole has stimulated in readers lay and professional — about a lack of consistency in form and tone through the later books. Generally applauded has been the character study of Flem Snopes, one of Faulkner's most complex and sensitive portraits of a type he perhaps unduly disliked. Such judgments seem to depend on a reading of the three books as an attack, primarily, on a new class in 20th century Southern society, who rise from obscurity to prominence and power, through ruthless opportunism and unethical practices. This interpretation focuses rather simply on the career

51

of Flem Snopes, who leads his family in an invasion, or rather infestation, of the hamlet of Frenchman's Bend and the town of Jefferson. On this reading, Flem is seen as exhibiting innately vicious determination, against which the longer established inhabitants of Yoknapatawpha country are powerless. It can only be checked when it meets an even more determined viciousness in the person of another Snopes, the wronged, mean and vengeful Mink. Before this happens the incisors of the infesting rodents have destroyed the roots of Yoknapatawpha life.

On this view, which assumes that the novels purport to express a well-defined moral polarity, they appear flawed because the defenders of Yoknapatawpha, free themselves from neither opportunism nor ruthlessness, are defending a way of life which is clearly not presented as admirable, while, as Malcolm Cowley says in *The Faulkner-Cowley File*, "Flem, the type of everything Faulkner detested, acquires a redeeming dignity at the end."

Formally, too, the work seems loosely controlled, the story conveyed variously by an anonymous narrator, a 'choric' commentary, and an omniscient author. Some incidents seem only marginally relevant, and the range from comedy to near-tragedy seems to cut across the simpler satiric response which, it is implied, the novels seek to arouse.

Such misgivings may stem from a misreading of the trilogy. They seem to reflect a too unreserved acceptance of the Yoknapatawpha chronicle as a kind of saga or typology devoted to the depiction of the Southern experience as elegiac epic through the life stories of exemplary characters. Since this interpretation has given rise to considerable critical uneasiness, it is worth considering whether the trilogy may not repay a different reading. We should perhaps see these three novels as an exercise in realism illustrating concretely what Allen Tate has called "a Southern mode of the imagination" and as an attempt to answer the latent queries of one confronting in puzzlement the social attitudes of the South, without undue prejudice or commitment. This will lead us to seek our theme not so much in the events to which the various narrators provide equivocal access as in the attitudes revealed in the subtly portrayed consciousness of the narrators themselves. As realistic rather than romantic fiction, the work brings into focus some of the themes and attitudes already explored, sometimes peripherally, in the earlier novels and tales of Yoknapatawpha county. Once we take this view, the form of the trilogy can be seen to exhibit a free but sure control, amounting at times to an almost cavalier confidence of manner on the part of its mature author.

If we read the trilogy as realism we may abandon speculation about the significance of the treatment of Eula Varner as part *femme fatale*, part fertility goddess, and see this treatment as an element which 'places' the narrators who subscribe to it. Light is thrown on the juxtaposition of the account of the loves of Eula in Book Two of *The Hamlet* with the comic-pathetic episode of Ike's affair with Houston's cow in Book Three if we consider how the linguistic excesses and overpowering lyricism with which they are in large part presented reveal the attitude of the narrator. The two incidents form a montage, in the second of which style becomes so intrusive as to inhibit credence in events which, baldly described, would be incredible enough. Their juxtaposition would seem at best a tasteless joke if we did not see it as another example of an irony which is directed at narrative discretion throughout the trilogy and which invites us always to treat our narrators with caution.

The use of multiple narrators permits the ingenious manipulation of this irony. The variously qualified viewpoints of V. K. Ratliff, Gavin Stevens and Charles Mallison interact with each other and with those of the anonymous narrator to produce an effect of comprehensiveness, compromised by indications of unreliability. All these are contrasted with the more normalized tone of the author's objective voice (objective because omniscient and because we have no stylistic indication of its unreliability) to draw attention to the bias that distorts the opinions and surmises which are our main source for many of the events of the main plot.

This is not to deny the partial validity of an interpretation of these events as a nostalgic account of a social order under pressure, often incorporating non-realistic matter to provide structure and reinforcement. It is rather to propose a reading of the novels in which a wider, more diffused thematic emphasis is obtained. On this reading the extension of the history of Faulkner's fictitious county is seen as a more comprehensive answer to Shreve McCannon's demand to Quentin Compson in *Absalom, Absalom!* to *"Tell about the South. What's it like there."* than the necessarily more schematic, morally simpler, interpretation of the works as saga provides. It may cast some light too on Quentin's passionate and suspect denial, *"I don't. I don't. I don't hate it! I don't hate it!"*

If we are to discover this answer, we must learn to look from the events, as we come to perceive them more clearly, to the bias with which they are presented in the distorted, and sometimes discrepant and incomplete, accounts of them which the narrators offer. Ratliff, for example, as he succeeds by unsupported innuendo and a sneering tone in presenting as unattractive Flem's meticulousness in keeping the books of Varner's store, exhibits a dislike of Flem wholly unwarranted in the face of what he reveals of Varner's own slovenly and dishonest practices. The hypothesis that the involved narrative pattern of the novels is aimed at the characterization of the narrators can be confirmed if we examine a striking emphasis in the versions of one incident, the love-making of Eula Varner and McCarron, reported once in *The Hamlet* by the anonymous narrator, whose 'actually' betrays his probable informant, and twice by Ratliff himself in *The Town* and *The Mansion*.

The details of these three versions vary so as to leave the reader without any very clear picture of the encounter. The discrepancies might at first sight seem mere authorial carelessness, through this would be an unduly crass example of a fault from which Faulkner is not entirely free. The construction of the trilogy as a whole, which requires that many of the events of one book are picked up accurately for recasting in another, suggests that Faulkner knew what he was doing here. It is more enlightening to see these discrepancies as enhancing the realism. Ratliff is plausibly uncertain, since he is surmising about an incident of which he could have had no direct knowledge, because of its essentially private nature, and about which he is expressly unfitted to speculate adequately, from the poverty (if not complete lack) of his own experience of sex.

As characterising Ratliff, these three passages are particularly telling for they contain one consistent element, which he reiterates with a persistence which comes to seem morbid. The image Ratliff never abandons is of Eula having to "actually support with her own braced arm from underneath" the injured youth as he makes love to her. Ratliff's inconsistencies are realistic since he lacks information, and this one consistent detail he obsessively reiterates can only be a pointer to the incident's chief sigificance for him. The choice of this detail is psychologically acute, not simply as a reference to the commonplace pain-and-pleasure association, but more particularly as it emphasizes Ratliff's obvious fascination with a woman strong enough and forthcoming enough to support her handicapped partner in the act of love. Taken together with what we come to discover about Ratliff's uxoriousness and sexual timidity and his significant verbal confusion of "actually" and "actively," it hints strongly at a psychological frustration on the part of one who chafes at his own inability to achieve actuality by active participation in events.

With this indication of a possible source for his unreliability, we must be wary of sharing without reserve Ratliff's bitter fascination with Manfred De Spain and his hostility tinged with reluctant admiration for Flem Snopes, since he is clearly not exempt from a distorting envy either of the one who possesses Eula in law or of the other who possesses her physically. This envy is not the only aspect of Ratliff's character which casts doubt on his reliability as an observer. His falling for Flem's trick of 'salting' the Old Frenchman Place should lead us to doubt even his shrewdness. He is clearly a match for Flem over the relatively small matter of the ten-dollar notes and can carry off successfully a vulgar trick against Clarence. But he proves a sucker in an affair more important because in it Flem's successful ploy gains him an important advantage in the half-ownership of the Jefferson back-alley restaurant. This incident shows that Ratliff is as vulnerable himself as he sees others to be, when the bait is a seeming opportunity to demonstrate his own sharpness. He is really no shrewder than Jody Varner or Jason Compson.

As narrators, the excessively talkative and romantic Gavin Stevens, and the immature, and occasionally prurient Charles Mallison, exhibit similar weaknesses. The latter's reliability is doubly suspect since he is often relying on Gavin or Ratliff or both for his information. The anonymous narrator, too, is suspect both because he too often seems to share Ratliff's viewpoint, and because his tone, early established in *The Hamlet,* betrays in him a too great preoccupation with decline and paradox as the themes of a Southern devolution.

Since these four voices carry the main burden of its narration, the reported events of the main plot and the comments with which they are explained are to be accepted as true only after much discounting. This in itself should make us wary of analysing the themes of the trilogy simply from these often confusing accounts of the advent, ascent and immolation of Flem Snopes. To do so would be to undervalue the effect of Faulkner's narrative technique. The theme rather is to be sought — as any attempt to "tell about the South" must be — in an interplay between events and the reactions they arouse in the minds of Southerners, here in the minds of the Yoknapatawpha narrators as representing the South.

The blending of viewpoints of only qualified reliability produces, as has been noticed, an effect of ironized comprehensiveness. In case we fail to identify this comprehensive view, Faulkner is at some pains to identify it for us: it is the view of Jefferson, identified explicitly with that of Charles Mallison, and through him with the other narrators, since he commonly reports Ratliff and Gavin. (It could, I think, be demonstrated that the anonymous narrator often reports them too.) In making the history of Eula and her daughter, Linda, as related by these three unreliable bachelors, representatives of town and hamlet, so central to his story, Faulkner encourages us to infer in the general attitudes of the wider Southern community, the presence of the same unsureness, conceit, immaturity, romantic obsession, and incapacity for effective action that these three exhibit in their attitudes towards the two women. We are made aware of economic and social changes in a society which cannot look coolly or objectively at the manifestation of change, which is hostile really to all change, yet incapable of resistance or conciliation because of attitudes fixed in romantic immature modes. But these attitudes are presented with a superficially compelling force, as the reader must at first accept what his narrators suggest (for all that he comes later to suspect their integrity), so that he cannot entirely resist sharing their horror at an intrusion they cannot prevent. At the same time as we become aware of their view of the unattractive pattern of the Snopeses' penetration of the society of Yoknapatawpha, however, we come to recognize in the responses of the narrators a bias and an overreaction, which forfeits to a large degree our credence.

The pattern that emerges clearly from the prejudiced accounts of the narrators is of an evolving society, in which new modes, commercial, economic, social and even political are emerging, modes which are feebly if fiercely resented by an establishment portrayed through a wide range of types. This sense of time passing and of the advent of modernity is to be seen in the changing emphasis from horse-trading to automobile-flaunting and in the contrast between Wallstreet Panic Snopes's chain groceries and Varner's store. The trilogy covers a period in which the old guard, which had managed to hang on grimly through Reconstruction, is being obliged, painfully and unwillingly, to acknowledge that old standards of economic exploitation and long outdated aristocratic social attitudes have to be modified to adapt to the realities of the twentieth century. Gavin Stevens and Manfred De Spain, the descendants of the old families of Jefferson, are no longer fitted to maintain the ascendancy of their class, any more than is Jason Compson, that corrupt survivor of the declining Compsons. The assurance of the aristocracy they so inadequately represent has disintegrated into shabby flamboyance or romantic gesture and loquacity. The rednecks who have earlier gained a secure niche in the hamlets of Mississippi by a combination of shrewdness, trickery and humble perseverance have had their day, too. The stranglehold of the Varners, practising their small-scale acquisitiveness alongside the prouder, more genteel manipulations of the Sartorises and De Spains, has relaxed. The Bookwrights, Armsteads, Tulls and, for the matter, Ratliff have never been more than marginally successful in an economic and social order which permitted their petty contrivances because they never threatened to become successful enough to disturb it.

Into this structurally weak society, the Snopeses descend. We come to see clearly (something our narrators could not conceal if they would, because it is a source of fascinated contemplation to them all, especially Ratliff) that the Snopeses succeed in establishing themselves in face of the dishonesty and hypocrisy of the established groups, by the employment of a judo-like technique, by turning against them those devices of strategem and fraud, through which the latter seek to maintain their entrenched financial and social position against newcomers. This provides a measure of sympathy for Flem, heightened by our sense he is not being given a fair deal by the commentators.

With the passing of time, the intruders become established. Flem learns the economic advantages of legality and respectability. His career follows the common *arriviste* pattern. His economic power and his new respectability even make him fairly acceptable to many Jeffersonians, since, however much they may resent his triumph, they are in no position financially or legally, to challenge it. His final destruction comes as an act of retribution, provoked by over-reaching, inexcusable malice. His death is at once satisfying and regrettable. We are left with a sense that justice has been done, but that it is a futile, because only partial justice, and, so far as we come to have some sympathy with the man so unfairly treated by the narrators, pathetic. Further, with Flem's death Jefferson seems to have lost an energy and a sense of direction, since what direction it has is nothing more positive than anti-Snopesism.

There is in fact a ray of hope to be seen in the activities of the newcomers. In Wallstreet Panic's commercial enterprise a new pattern of honest industrious activity is revealed, Snopesian in origin but anti-Snopesian too. A thematic point seems to be emerging: that only after being thoroughly shaken out of its old ways can the South be revitalised when a new class of honest, effective businessmen, themselves Snopeses, arise from the turmoil Flem's activities have produced.

But to see the themes of the novels in these terms would still be to mistake their emphasis. The trilogy resists such a relatively simple analysis. For if one attempts to extract a moral polarity from the work the difficulty (a difficulty more common in realistic than in saga-like works) becomes apparent. The theme is less neat and schematic, since Faulkner is adopting a stance less certain, a technique more inclusive and realistic. He is telling the whole truth about the Snopeses with wide implications for our understanding of the South, and qualified by ironies.

The complex moral pattern Faulkner weaves is reinforced by many comic and grotesque episodes in *The Hamlet* and *The Town*, episodes which become increasingly satiric. Ingeniously, these are made often to revolve round a characteristic American interest in transportation. Trading in horses and mules gives way to the flaunting of automobiles as a subject for comedy. The incident of Gavin and Manfred's motor-car exploits for comedy an obvious sexual display motif. The horse-and-mule-trading episodes poke tolerant fun at a common occasion for commercial opportunism.

The comic ebullience does not disguise an insight into the commercial ethic of the society and the source of the increasing mastery Flem acquires in his profit taking. Ab Snopes was no match for Pat Stamper. His attempt to work a trick fails because he ignores what Flem seems from the start to have grasped, that it is not enough to be smart or dishonest, one has to be just a little smarter than the next man. Flem, as in all his strategems, displays, in the affair of the spotted horses, a profound understanding of the avarice of the amateurs of horseflesh who compose almost the entire male population of Frenchman's Bend. In this affair in *The Hamlet*, his proceedings are questionably legitimate. In *The Town* his intervention in the quarrel between I. O. Snopes and Mrs. Hait shows us a more experienced Flem, well aware that the respectability of a bank vice-president and the legal techniques characteristic of Jefferson, so far from being a barrier against sharp practice, actually increase the possibilities of easy profits, as they render them unassailable. The contrast between Flem's growth of sophistication, and the childishness of Gavin and Manfred in comic episodes, emphasizes a contrast between the manners of the newly arrived bourgeoisie and the descendants of Southern aristocracy.

The Hamlet and *The Town* establish the moral ambivalence of Faulkner's theme, with an irony predominantly comic, so that Eula's suicide provides a reminder that there is a darker side. The tone of *The Mansion* is more sombre. If Faulkner has largely indicated in the earlier books that there is a case to be made for Flem, as even Gavin comes reluctantly and partially to recognise (*The Town*, chapter 17), in the final volume he emphasizes that however effective singleminded unscrupulousness may be in a poor man's struggle for security and economic power in a society itself unscrupulous and less singleminded, there is a limit beyond which shrewd selfishness and bitterness become unmitigated and inexcusable malevolence, and evil which invites retribution. This novel opens up a wider perspective, as Linda goes East, marries a Jewish Communist, double anathema in the South, and returns home, after experiences of love, loyalty, devotion and sacrifice, strengthened, but somehow isolated in her greater maturity, her compassion and her grief. Her deafness places her apart from the rhetoric and animosity, the sound and the fury, that continues to characterize much of Jefferson life.

As the vengeance that must overtake Flem closes in, she becomes ironically an agent in his doom. The degree of her conscious involvement is obscure. She is very marginally responsible for Flem's murder by the tormented, obsessed vengeful Mink, but her intention is not made clear in the conflicting opinions of Gavin or Ratliff, the former's chivalry, the latter's shrewdness leading them to offer appropriate and opposed interpretations. If Gavin has learned anything as he has grown older, he may have learned to mistrust Ratliff's surmises.

By the time Mink had come to trial for a murder committed out of a keen if obsessive sense of justice — another Snopesian trait, here in an extreme form, since it overrides self-interest — Flem had learned from Varner the value of respectability. He does not intervene in Mink's sordid predicament, knowing anyway, one supposes, that to do so would be vain. Mink is beyond saving, and to make a gesture of family solidarity would simply involve Flem in an incident likely to damage his plans for self-improvement. Later, however, Flem's fear of Mink's known fanatical resentment involves him in an act of cold vicious calculating self-interest and malevolence (this time not qualified for us by being reported by an unreliable narrator; the omniscient author's voice takes over this part of the story). His single act of unqualified evil, as he ensures the extension of Mink's sentence to avoid the latter's largely unjustifiable resentment, invites and receives its nemesis. This act of Flem's moreover is the only one, among many in which he preserves his self-interest without compassion, in which there is no redeeming sense of his having taken advantage of opportunities afforded him by the self-seeking strategems of others. There is no moral ambivalence here. Faulkner points clearly, through this presentation of immitigable malevolence, to a limit beyond which Snopesian contrivance cannot go unscathed.

Faulkner reinforces this point by an emphasis on the providential element in Mink's revenge. Mink sees himself as the victim of a hostile fate, but one which works through justice and so must eventually give him his chance, too. The part which Linda plays may suggest that in her new role purified by her experiences from the taint of Jeffersonian prejudice and animosity, neutral in her silent world, she is a providential accessory to Flem's punishment through an act itself inspired by compassion and justice. Faulkner introduces an irony here to underline for us the way in which the meaning of a reported action is never clear, but reveals qualities in the consciousness which observes it. If we accept Gavin's view of Linda's action as compassionate, then her good act turns her ironically into an accessory. If we accept Ratliff's, that she foresaw the consequences of her act, the act becomes vengeful, but her motive can then only be vengeance against Flem for his responsibility for the wretchedness of her mother's life and her suicide. Here the irony is parallel with one we have constantly been offered throughout the trilogy. Linda's view of Flem's responsibility is inadequate. In reality, it is clear, Eula suffers and dies at least as much, possibly more, as a consequence of Varner's original deal with Flem, her lover's pride, maternal love and her own frailty, as from any act of Flem's. Flem's final strategem, in which he unpins his $20 gold piece is not directed at his wife, but is a final twisting of the tail of Will Varner. The responsibility of Linda for the acceleration of Flem's death (intentionally or not does not matter since both alternatives are ironic) gives to his death, itself just, an overtone of irony and lends it a doubleness, like that which has marked Faulkner's treatment of events throughout the trilogy.

Flem's death is marked by inaction on his part as though, when he recognized that he had made a bad stroke, not worsted by another's smartness but through an act of his own that could carry no justification, he was prepared to abide by it. His death is really a coda to the major theme of the trilogy. Not a lame one, however. There is a neatness in the way the accounts are ruled off to close out the life of a man whose career had been marked by no other principle than the clearing of accounts, and it is the meaning of that accounting that we must understand if we are to understand the life more completely than our narrators are able to know it.

As Gavin comes to understand dimly the motivation of Flem, in a moment when his vision is less obviously untrustworthy than usual (*The Town*, Chapter 17), he confirms a view abundantly projected through the novels, that Flem is applying a lesson he has learned from Will Varner and others that "he would never have more than nothing, unless he wrested it himself from his environment and time, and the only weapon he would have to do it would be just money." Education too would be a weapon, education in the devices by which money acquires respectability — banks, furniture, property — would be necessary to protect that money, and to secure from it the advantages it gave to others. Education is seen, after that first enemy money has been assailed and taken captive, as the second more formidable enemy to be conquered, against which Flem is armed with "nothing save the will and the need the ruthlessness and the industry." It is interesting to see how Gavin comes to countenance Flem's view of banks and the credit system as a form of looting, thus providing, unconsciously it seems, in his partial understanding of Flem's motives and actions, an almost Marxist critique of the inequalities that Southern capitalism creates and enshrines.

What is really a political insight thus underlines the central theme of the trilogy. The society of the South is held together by an outdated caste and money system, reinforced by an imagination wrapped in deluding conservatism and prejudice, resisting all innovation. Faulkner demonstrates, in the career of a predator on a social order rooted in predatoriness crystallized into respectability, the power as well as the limitations of energetic farsighted unscrupulousness in a society itself unscrupulous but lacking energy and vision. Flem's death is not a sign of defeat for him so much as an indication, perhaps too optimistic even when qualified by Faulkner's more comprehensive answer to the question "What's it like there?," that the era of piracy in which Flem flourished is coming to an end, now that accounts have been ruled off.

From Commitment to Choice: Double Vision and the Problem of Vitality for John Steinbeck

by Pascal Covici, Jr.

Transcendental optimism underlies the vitality of John Steinbeck's creations through and beyond the 1930's. The awareness toward which his important characters move is of their participation in the "one big soul" that Preacher Casy and Tom Joad speak of in *The Grapes of Wrath,* an *"Oversoul"* that encompasses all mankind. They find their place in, and draw strength from, this universal oneness by heeding the promptings of their deepest feelings, even when these run counter to the conventional wisdoms of society. The lives of Danny and the other Paisanos in *Tortilla Flat* (1935), of Mac, Doc, and the Boys in *Cannery Row* (1945), of Casy and the Joads (1939), and of others, would seem to follow from Emerson's "Self-Reliance." "What have I to do with the sacredness of traditions, if I live wholly from within?" asks Emerson. And in response to "a friend's" suggestion that "these impulses may be from below, not from above," Emerson's answer speaks for Steinbeck's people, too: "[My impulses] do not seem to

63

me to be such; but if I am the Devil's child, I will live then from the Devil." With Steinbeck's people in mind, one feels a shiver of *déja vu* upon remembering that it was by no means clear to many of his contemporaries that Emerson was not "living from the Devil," Andrews Norton having called Emerson's ideas "the latest form of infidelity in Cambridge." Further, Doc's and Casy's impatience with trapped hypocrites is no greater than Emerson's with those who could not perceive the Oversoul's connection with the individual: "I would write on the lintels of the door-post, *Whim*. I hope it is somewhat better than whim at last, but we cannot spend the day in explanation."

The optimism behind both Emerson and, for example, Preacher Casy rings out a generous challenge, but such generosity is hard to accept. "To thine own self be true," smirks Polonius; "thou canst not then be false to any man." But Shakespeare's darker wisdom goes beyond Polonius; it is not so glibly easy to know who, in truth, one is; and if beneath visible reality be not the Oversoul of Emerson's monistic vision but, instead, the ambivalence of at once a Christian and a Freudian cosmology, then being true to the deepest levels of one's identity may well be living from the Devil, or at least from a basis that impels one to be false to any number of men. Steinbeck's vision of a transcendent spiritual unity, within which each man can respond to the promptings of ultimate reality as they reach him, encountered and survived the Oklahoma dustbowl and even California greed, but by the time World War II had ended — its concentration camps and atom bombs etched upon the conscience of every sensitive man — evil must have seemed to John Steinbeck to be something more than merely the absence of positive good. Juan Chicoy, whose initials and energies remind one of the power-source evoked by Jim Casy, in 1947 considers driving his Wayward Bus forever away from a more wayward society, but just as Juan decides against evasion, so the author turns in *East of Eden* (1952), his most ambitious novel, and in all of his subsequent work, to a direct confrontation of evil, and to a new kind of character, the man whose awareness is less a matter of discovering himself to be in harmony with a universal world spirit, a big soul of all mankind, than of finding within himself the power to free himself from the conditioning of his unthinking experience in order to choose deliberately actions which he knows to be right. Individual choice, rather than universal commitment, becomes the issue around which Steinbeck's fiction of the '50s revolves.

Even in the trivia of *Sweet Thursday* (1954), the curiously entertaining but finally unpersuasive presentation of Cannery Row's Doc as he struggles to learn who he is so that he can choose a new life style, this underlying concern appears. "The Great Roque War," sheer zaniness if taken out of context, belongs in the book because it recounts the deliberate choice of one man to counter the vehemence of his community's involvement in a mere game by destroying the roque-court, and thus eliminating the Guelph-and-Ghibelline quality of Pacific Grove's existence. *The Short Reign of Pippin IV* (1957) comes down to Pippin's sense of himself, of how hard it is to know the self, and to Pippin's choices concerning power. Like the gentle old man he meets, Pippin, too, is one who picks up what others have knocked over; he chooses to tell France the truth, and thus loses his kingdom. *The Winter of Our Discontent* (1961), Steinbeck's last novel but not legitimately to be discussed in a volume concerning the '50s, delineates the fragility of human morality and focuses upon the torments of choosing and of having chosen. But *East of Eden,* because it explicitly celebrates man as the creature who can choose between good and evil and because John Steinbeck saw it as the work toward which he had been moving through all of his earlier creative life, will serve to bring clearly before us the impact of a dualistic vision on, and the problem of choice in, the work of an author whose previous major novel *(The Grapes of Wrath)* had embodied a monistic reality toward which more and less fragmented characters moved.

As Lee points out to Sam Hamilton, only if man can choose evil does the capacity to choose the good "count" toward man's glory. The bee has to make honey; all man has to make is decisions. But his decisions are real ones; they represent choices between alternatives of different moral weight. Preacher Casy insists that he no longer knows about right and wrong, "sin" and "virtue"; " 'There's just stuff people do,' " he says. The social outrage that underlies *The Grapes of Wrath* comes back again and again to impersonal "conditions"; but in *East of Eden,* people make their own fate, if they choose to; and if they choose not to, the responsibility is their own. Yet this formulation, moral fulcrum of the whole book though it be, fails to account for the character of Cathy Ames. Cathy — Kate, as she becomes — seems meant to serve as the embodiment of evil in the book's world, evil made tangible, visible, assailable. Cathy, suggests the author, is some kind of "monster," a "variation from the accepted normal"; in this case, "born without kindness or the potential of conscience." As a moral "cripple," with "tendencies, or lack of them, which drove and forced her all of her life," Cathy is introduced to the reader as a genetically conditioned freak whose apparently motiveless evil, a wielding of power for its own sake, recalls the non-moral world of de Sade and seems increasingly at odds with an orderly morality predicated upon man's capacities for choice. One of the book's important sources of energy derives, that is, from the tension set up between the force of Kate and the force of the characters who, in their various ways, choose among the different options open to them. This second force, that of the freedom to choose, echoes explicitly through the book via the Hebrew word "*timshel*," "which has been variously translated 'do thou,' 'thou shalt,' and 'thou mayest,'" Steinbeck wrote exultantly to his editor.

Steinbeck's own excitement over the implications of the story of Cain and Abel does shape the book, to be sure. The title itself apparently came to him only after he had copied out the 16 verses from Genesis, and the repeated structure of sibling relationships, the rounds of rejection, guilt, anger, and retribution, and the closing scene of the book, all communicate, as clearly as the words Lee uses, the crucial importance of choice, of choosing, if one is to be fully human. But in the letters to his editor (published as *Journal of a Novel* in 1969), written as a way into each day's work on the novel, Steinbeck comes back again and again to Cathy. "She is a fascinating and horrible person to me," he says on March 30, 1951. And two months later: "I think you will find that Cathy as Kate fascinates people though. People are always interested in evil even when they pretend their interest is clinical. And they will mull Kate over. They will forget I said she was bad. And they will hate her because while she is a monster, she is a little piece of the monster in all of us. It won't be because she is foreign that people will be interested but because she is not." Often, he mentions that the time has come to get back not to the book but to Cathy, and once he refers to this monster of evil as "my dear Cathy."

Behind the intellectual structure that would isolate Kate from the human condition, this more profound, because empathetic, response to her gradually overtakes the reader. In her total irresponsibility to the humanity of all around her, Kate both attracts and repels; as daughter, mistress, wife, mother, and prostitute, her view of people limits itself to how they can be of use to her. Her evil takes on at least two meanings. The less interesting, but probably the more universally human, shows itself in her infantile retreat into the small, grey lean-to toward the close of her life. Like Alice, she would become tinier and tinier, disappearing into the womb of death in retreat from a world that fails to grant her the central, all-powerful position that an infant's megalomania demands. She must be in total control of all people and situations, else she is nothing. But it is another, less case-book, sort of meaning that makes Kate's pattern interesting as well as fascinating. Again and again, one sees her act in total emotional isolation; except when she feels threatened by the imperviousness of others to her venom — as happens with Sam Hamilton, finally with Adam Trask, and with her son Caleb — she shows no sense of connection with another human being and never does her behavior suggest a sense of responsibility, of human community. Unlike the other "Cain" figures in the novel, Cathy never asks, no matter how derisively, if she is her brother's keeper. The question would not occur to her, for she knows no brother. Her evil, from this perspective, becomes less a matter of monstrosity, or of psychopathology, than of total estrangement from Preacher Casy's "one big soul," or from the more modest sense of brotherhood and responsibility that gives direction to the lives of the characters who choose to act with the sense that they are responsible for what they do and that their actions concern the lives of others.

This is a very mild sort of meaning when baldly stated. As the felt core of a major novel, however, it takes on considerable power. "I know [*East of Eden*] is the best book I have ever done," wrote John Steinbeck when a little more than half finished with its creation. Most critics, while agreeing that this is Steinbeck's most ambitious novel, have disagreed with the author's evaluation, a not uncommon phenomenon. The question of absolute excellence is probably best left to distant posterity. It does seem, however, that the characters' capacity to live on in a reader's imagination is great; one remembers Sam Hamilton, Adam Trask, Caleb, Cathy, and Lee — and others — almost as one remembers memorable people one has known. And one remembers the story, what happens to them. And one remembers the conflicts and issues that tear them apart. But this "remembering" is at a lower pitch than the kind of independent existence that the people of *The Grapes of Wrath* come to. Does this make the one less alive than the other? Not to this reader, obviously, but the question brings one to the difficult problem of the relationship between philosophical vision on the one hand and creative vitality on the other. As Henry James said in another context, what an author CAN do he MAY do; some ideas, however, conform more closely to the curve of a particular artistic bent than do others. It may be that in moving from what have been called his transcendental under-pinnings (see especially Frederick I. Carpenter, "The Philosophical Joads," *College English*, January, 1941), John Steinbeck encount-ered difficulties that he could not completely dominate.

If evil in the book emerges as a failure to accept any sort of responsibility for one's brothers, then the social distance between *The Grapes of Wrath* and *East of Eden* clearly is not great. In the destroying of food to keep the prices up, Steinbeck presented and denounced the evil that an irresponsible society perpetrates in denying men the right to live. Although the book emphasizes ignorance more than evil — " 'You don't know what you're a-'doin',' " laments Casy as he is struck down, a paraphrase that Tom Joad repeats later on — the point remains that the removal of ignorance would make for a sense of responsibility, of one man's involvement with his fellow humans. Lee, in his excited outpour-ing to Sam Hamilton of the fruits of his pondering over the Cain and Abel paradigm, and over the implications of translating the crucial word *"timshel"* as "thou mayest," says, " 'You can call sin ignorance.' " Because he so firmly believes that man can choose, Lee discovers that he has " 'a new love for that glittering instru-ment, the human soul. It is a lovely and unique thing in the universe. It is always attacked and never destroyed — because "Thou mayest." ' "

Part of Samuel Hamilton's unique loveliness lies in his capacity to choose to tell Adam the truth about Cathy, taking upon himself the responsibility if his news of her viciousness as a Madam prove too much for Adam to withstand. And it is this personal sort of responsibiilty that differentiates the concerns of *East of Eden* from those of *The Grapes of Wrath*. In both books, a kind of "ignor-ance" — of irresponsibility for fellow men — is seen to lie at the root of evil-doing, but the ignorance in the earlier book is not the sort through which people can break by deliberate choice. Experi-ence, as in the case of Tom Joad, or inspiration, as in Casy's solitary wandering " 'into the wilderness like Him, without no campin' stuff,' " can break down the walls that separate a man from knowing true things about the human condition, but the kinds of changes that Steinbeck makes vivid concern attitudes toward the way men live together in groups rather than in the ways they feel about each other as individuals. Human dignity derives from the satisfactions of work well done, not from the consciousness of being able to choose one line of action rather than another. "For man, unlike any other thing organic or inorganic in the universe, grows beyond his work, walks up the stairs of his concepts, emerges ahead of his accomplishments." The sin, or ignorance, of the larger society is, in a sense, "invincible" ignorance; "they don't know what they're doin'." Separated by machines from the feel of the land — and by affluence from what it feels like to be human — the great owners are victims as much as they are victimizers. The forces in *East of Eden,* however — for all that the book is a social chronicle of changing America, the author finding both the school system and "the whorehouse situation" important to his narrative — lie within individuals rather than outside of them. This drift toward the psyche signals not so much a loss of social interest on the author's part as a growing commitment to individual men as opposed to a generalized "Manself."

The difficulty of the shift comes, in part, from the very nature of fictional art itself. As many mid-century authors have been rediscovering, the process of creation is essentially a process of making order, pattern, meaning. When the largest meaning that one perceives in life is that of the glories of human freedom to choose, then the creator of fictional reality must encounter resistance in the very shaping of his art. In *East of Eden,* no one — except for Cathy early in the book (the later Kate seems, if one looks closely, a slightly different creature) — no one absolutely has to do evil. Neither heredity nor conditioning compel behavior; a man can choose. As Caleb comes to see and to say triumphantly to his mother, Kate, " 'If I'm mean, it's my own mean.' " Human freedom suggests a kind of randomness that social determinism does not. The sequences of fiction impart a quality of cause-and-effect relationships, especially when the narrative adheres to a chronological line. In this sense, conventionally organized fiction is "naturalisitic" in its thrust, for the reader feels the weight of forces beyond the control of any one character. By retaining a sense of motive, John Steinbeck complicates the problem of presenting human freedom; the strategies by which he tries to resolve the difficulty give the novel much of its strength.

Most important are the interweaving of the personal with the fictional and the larger interweaving of the Hamilton with the Trask family. Not only do these allow for the fracturing of the time line, important though that be, but they also give the effect of "documenting" the unpredictable variety with which human beings respond to circumstances; the reader perceives in this variety the very kind of freedom that the discussion of *"timshel"* postulates. Hamiltons and Trasks, children and adults, grow in their individual directions; because the characters through whose eyes — or, rather, over whose shoulders — the reader perceives events are themselves the ones who attain to the greatest freedom (Sam Hamilton, Adam Trask, Caleb Trask), one becomes persuaded that the freedom is real. Because the author, as narrator of the Hamilton-Steinbeck family history to his own sons, at times moves freely across the decades, a further sense of non-determined selection emerges. Certainly a careful look at just how narrative point-of-view is handled in *East of Eden* could carry one very far into the aesthetic and psychological problems of presenting a sense of fredom in art.

And the other major strategy — although "strategy" is not the right word — operative here, and in all of Steinbeck's late fiction, is, quite simply, a focusing upon the family and its relationships. (Even *Sweet Thursday* suggests, though unconvincingly, that Doc and Susie will find in marriage all the satisfactions that their lives have come to lack.) In the arena where people are most compulsively driven, Steinbeck develops with paradoxical fullness and complexity the kinds of familial freedoms that signify responsibility freely accepted or rejected. Although other works would be to the point, *East of Eden* by itself establishes "the matter of the family" as successor to "the matter of the land" in John Steinbeck's myth of life in America. Whether he would have been able to move beyond the dualistic denial of simple monism that his strong aesthetic commitment to the issues of choice and responsibility led him to we cannot know. Perhaps a larger synthesis would have invigorated his further fiction; perhaps his preoccupation with Malory's *Morte D'Arthur*, important in his work from *The Cup of Gold* (1929) and *Tortilla Flat* (1935) on through *Travels with Charley* (1962), would have carried him, through the modernized version to which he devoted so much time in the late 50s, to a way of combining a sense of passionate commitment with an equally passionate sense of freedom.

But such speculation is relevant only in so far as it leads one to a savoring of what John Steinbeck did in fact achieve. *East of Eden* marks a deliberate shift of philosophical vision by a writer whose greatest strengths lay in his capacity to present non-intellectual people in their deepest relationships to their land and to the conditions they confront. By turning to the creation of deliberate choosers in a morally weighted world rather than of mystically integrated seers in a unified and amoral ecology, John Steinbeck risked his power to make life upon the page to a greater extent than has any other novelist who comes to mind. How successful he finally was, how much vitality his fiction gained or lost, will become more apparent as the immediacy of his social issues yields to the long-range relevance of his moral concerns. This reader suspects that there has been a profound underrating of Steinbeck's importance as an American novelist, although these words would make John Steinbeck himself very uncomfortable. He would want simply to be read, and I think that he will be.

Norman Mailer:
Advertisements for Myself

or

A PORTRAIT OF THE ARTIST AS A DISGRUNTLED COUNTER-PUNCHER

by WILLIAM HOFFA

The breadth and interest of Norman Mailer's writing during the 50s can perhaps be best indicated by a brief noting of the widely differing modes and manners of his work in both the preceding and following decades. During the 40s (or what was left of them after he had earned his Harvard degree in aeronautical engineering and spent three years as a G.I. fighting in the Pacific) his most significant and characteristic literary achievement had been the best-selling war novel, *The Naked and the Dead* (1948). This impressive first (published) novel, then and since judged to be the best written out of the experience of World War II, is a dramatic chronicle of the daily psychic anxieties and physical ordeals of soldiers and officers engaged in an unceasing "battle" as much against each other and the natural elements as against the enemy Japanese. While it has symbolic undertones — Mailer later said that *Moby Dick* lay just beneath its surface — the dominant mode of *The Naked and the Dead* is realism, if not naturalism: events are rendered objectively and dramatically; the inner tensions of the characters are balanced by a detached 'point of view' against the outward particularities of their environment and the larger social forces which committed them to battle. Dos Passos and Farrell, Malraux and Hemingway appear to be the dominant literary progenitors. Critics were thus justified in expecting Mailer's future development to be in this inherited realistic-naturalistic vein.

But the work of the 60s, so surrealistic in both subject and expression, suggests that the intervening decade was one of severe re-examination, experiment and, ultimately, transformation. For in the 60s Mailer's most worthy achievements were his subjectively rendered books of "journalism" — *The Presidential Papers* (1963), *Cannibals and Christians* (1966), *The Armies of the Night* (1967) and *Miami and the Siege of Chicago* (1968) — and only secondarily his two novels, *An American Dream* (1965) and *Why Are We in VietNam?* (1967), both nightmare-ridden monologues of anxiety and compulsion. Gone is any purport of objectivity and detachment and in place of the formerly restrained and tautly paced prose style of the 40s we observe a flamboyant rhetorical idiom, fervid and relentless, nurtured on outraging social event and the outrageous metaphor which tries to constrain it.

That the 50s are to be seen as years of transformation is made clear by Mailer's last and certainly most important book of the decade, *Advertisements for Myself* (1959). This self-compiled anthology of his experiments in fiction, the essay, poetry and drama, during the 50s, is a well-illustrated, step-by-step, account — a "nonfiction novel" as one critic called it — of Mailer's slow and painful emergence into a "style" of his own. And, as he said in a recent interview, "A really good style comes only when a man has become as good as he can be. Style is character." The work of the 50s, then, begins with Mailer's own admission that the huge success of *The Naked and the Dead* was somehow irrelevant to his ambitions to become a "genuinely disturbing" writer, one who would be able "to alter the consciousness of his time." It ends in the candid confessions and reappraisals of *Advertisements for Myself*, in which he assesses how far he has moved toward that goal and how far he has yet to go.

Strictly speaking the story of the 50s, the biography of both a literary and a 'life'-style, which is summed up by the table of contents in *Advertisements*, extends backwards to the early stories of the 40s. These pieces, some of which are included in the

"Beginnings" section of *Advertisements*, reveal Mailer's profound debt to writers such as Fitzgerald, Hemingway, Farrell, and Steinbeck, but also show that he was often capable of assimilating their lessons without being totally inhibited by them. Still, a short novel like *A Calculus at Heaven* (1942) does little not done more smoothly and successfully by Hemingway in *For Whom The Bell Tolls* or Malraux in *Man's Fate*. As Mailer himself admits, except for its mature sense of realistic detail and well-paced narrative, this story of the 'last stand' of a group of ambushed soldiers "was an attempt of the imagination (aided and warped by books, movies, war correspondents and the liberal mentality) to guess what war might really be like."

By contrast the stories of the early 50s *do* appear to have grown out of Mailer's personal experience (usually in the war) and in their emphasis on the 'quiet desperation' of soldiers away from home entangled in realms of experience which daily frustrate and dispirit them, they show that he had left behind the heroic fatalism at the center of many of his earlier stories and, more importantly, shed many of the inherited stylistic mannerisms of his literary forebears. But, while there is a welcome detachment in the narration of these stories — due perhaps to the assurance gained through the success of *The Naked and the Dead* — there is also, as Mailer himself has noted, a sense of "sadness" in the prose, a mood of "retreat" in their resolutions. This mood, unassuming and restrictive, is apparently an accurate measure of Mailer's own personal situation at the time, depressed as he was over his too easy early success, yet inhibited by it, so that he was afraid to try for new effects and new themes. "The Paper House," put with two other War Stories in the "Middles" section of *Advertisements* is the best and most representative of these stories. In it Mailer's unique insights into the sex-scarred consciousness of the G.I. abroad emerge effectively through the story of a selfish, frightened, and headstrong soldier whose refusal to admit his complex love for his Japanese Geisha forces this anguished girl into dishonor and revenge. The success of this poignant and often humorous story is largely due to Mailer's decision to narrate it through the eyes of another soldier who is sympathetic to both, yet confused by the dialectics of their motivation.

Barbary Shore, written at this time and published in 1951, is too obviously the ambitious second novel of a young novelist straining to repeat the effect but not the substance of his first success. Mailer's imagination, while obviously in a state of turmoil during these years, was too much nurtured on the present to revert for its inspiration to the past. But the story of the novel's composition indicates just how complicated was its author's motivation: it was originally a study of the effects of the war on the American woman and was first titled, *Mrs. Guenivere*. Then, under the influence of Jean Malaquais, Mailer's political mentor, it was to have become a "labor" novel. In the end it became a kind of *bildungsroman*, in which the ostensible interest ultimately focuses on the political maturation and consequent dedication to revolutionary socialism of its young narrator, Mikey Lovett. Mailer claims that the novel "wrote itself," that he often felt "no conscious control over it" — a claim which obtains some currency when we note its strange transformation and its many places of composition, which include Paris, Crawfordsville (Indiana), Jamaica (Vermont), and finally Hollywood. However if the short stories of the early 50s are to be considered "retreats" which succeed because of Mailer's full psychological and technical mastery of his subject, *Barbary Shore* must assuredly be seen as an "advance" in scope and intention which, nevertheless, does not quite live up to its author's fullest new ambitions.

These ambitions were to capture "the air of our time, authority and nihilism stalking one another in the orgiastic hollow of this century" and to do so by peopling a shabby and claustrophobic Brooklyn rooming-house with "Stalinists, secret policemen, narcissists, children, lesbians, hysterics, and revolutioniaries." As a dramatic focus Mailer chose a young writer *manqué*, Lovett, suffering from amnesia, who *thinks* he was in the war and who only vaguely recalls until the end, his own youthful Trotskyist zeal. As a reflector of the main psychological and intellectual stresses of the novel, Lovett is perhaps too much a *voyeur* and not enough a participant; certainly his blank presence at the central debates of the novel between McLeod — the treasonous double agent who betrays himself, his wife Guenivere, and the *true* Marxist Revolution — and Hollingsworth, his CIA-prototype prosecutor, seeking a "secret package" McLeod has mysteriously retained, does little to dramatize this ideological conflict. Nor does he claim our interest later when he inherits the "secret package" (which allegory identifies as "hope" for individual freedom and economic justice) and escapes.

Nevertheless, *Barbary Shore* nearly overcomes its most obvious limitations: the frequent bumptious vacuities and vanities of its narrator, the demeaning melodrama of its plot, and the strained garrulousness of Mailer's prose. Its dispirited secondary characters are finely drawn: Mrs. McLeod (Guenivere of the original novel), unable to live up to the self-advertized sexual prowess of the past, an unfaithful pawn with an empty sense of humor; Monina Mc-Leod, screaming elf-like register of her parents' anxieties, resembling no one so much as Hawthorne's Pearl, in *The Scarlet Letter*; and Lanie, homeless, bisexual young woman whose sanity and honor have long since been destroyed by the tortures she has witnessed. These portraits are among Mailer's best; taken together they represent the disfigured and distorted surface of Cold War American society beneath which Mailer was to delve for the remainder of the decade. *Barbary Shore* thus represents the first full indication that Mailer's heritage of realism and naturalism was fast crumbling in the early 50s. To the extent to which the fates of the individual participants in the drama of *Barbary Shore* are *determined* by environmental forces — social, political, economic — the novel can still be seen to be in the inherited tradition; but the motivations of most of these characters and the values which guide their separate quests for fulfillment, are far more elusive, shifting, and mysterious than realism generally allows. Lovett's final "escape," while it seems to us contrived for *him*, is really a symbolic act, undertaken as an expression of the collective *free will* of the rest of the characters. His act is decidedly Romantic, and it shifts the final allegiance of the novel perceptibly away from the dominant mode of Realism. But this final gesture at the conclusion of *Barbary Shore* must still be seen against the compromised and wasted lives of the rest of the characters, caught up in the swirl of inevitable historical change. It was more than a decade before Mailer in *An American Dream* could plan a whole novel around propulsive and (in its own terms) successful anti-social behaviour.

The fiction of the remainder of the 50s, however, continued to focus on the "quiet desperation" of men who had made too many "dreary compromises" with life. Both Mailer's best short story of the decade, "The Man Who Studied Yoga" (1954) and his most interesting novel, *The Deer Park*, are primarily concerned with middle-aged men who are unable, ultimately, to replenish their lost creative and sexual energies. Charles Francis Eitel, a formerly successful Hollywood director of documentary films in the 30s, the central figure in *The Deer Park*, struggles valiantly to regain his former integrity and potency, and with the help of his complexly passionate and often pitiable mistress, Elena Esposito, almost does. But in the end, he too (like Sam Slavoda in "The Man Who Studied Yoga") realizes, because his manuscript for "new" films is symbolically incomplete and his love life a mess of contradictions and neuroses, that he can no longer maintain the will and strength to recover. Eitel's unsuccessful and ultimately *pathetic* (as opposed to *tragic*) quest is closely watched by the novel's narrator, Sergius O'Shaugnessy, guilt-filled, drifting, ex-Air Force hero (and first cousin to Mikey Lovett), who then escapes to the more fundamental passions of bull-fighting and the search for "the good orgasm" — some of the "new circuits" Mailer's own private meanderings were leading him through in the middle 50s. As a narrator O'Shaugnessy provides a more full-bodied center for the novel than Lovett does in *Barbary Shore,* but his "escape" still does not seem a dramatically appropriate conclusion to the novel.

Originally *The Deer Park* (called then *The Idol and the Octopus*) had centered much more on Eitel's *public* conflicts, those with Congressional Investigation Committees and with his producer, Herman Teppis — in other words, with the fate of the creative person in America, trying to put forth his "vision" untrammeled by censorship or the immutable laws of the marketplace. But Mailer's conviction, growing throughout the decade, that public morality and political ideology had their bases in the health of man's deeper, more irrational drives, led him finally to focus *The Deer Park* rather on Eitel's quest for psychic and sexual vitality and personal integrity.

Moreover, the novel is not the "Hollywood Exposé" some of its advertisers claimed it to be. Its "boldness" lies not in the breadth of its social satire of the polychrome and plastic world of Desert D'Or, a kind of WasteLand West, or of the public fantasies launched from there to the movie screen and into the lives of the rest of America; instead it lies in Mailer's insight that the *private* fantasies of America, the images by which it lives and nurtures its own identity, are merely more exposed and apparent in Hollywood than elsewhere, and that "the film colony" is just as much victimized by these evasive images of identity and purpose as anyone else.

The most frightening figure in *The Deer Park* is Marion Faye, a filmland pimp, who refuses to accept the hypocrisy and denatured illusions of those around him. Unlike the neurotic Eitel or Teppis, the insensitive mogul, Faye refuses to compromise or accept weakness in himself or in others. Yet in his search for "pure emotion," often induced by drugs, Faye is subject to both *melancholia* and *paranoia*, and his actions toward others often reveal a sinister sadism; his freedom from the illusions of others only brings a perverted and empty illusion which is himself. By contrast, Sergius O'Shaugnessy is a vapid, vain, and passive agent throughout. He is both attracted and repelled by the deceit and ruin he sees around himself in the surrealistic mixture of Hollywood's public fantasies and private drives, the "orgy, murder, rape, and prostitution," which Mailer says was his constant preoccupation during the composition of *The Deer Park*. But O'Shaugnessy's reflections on the infertile scene of Desert D'Or during the first fifty pages of the novel contain some of Mailer's best impressionistic prose — and are precursors of his later depictions of "the American Scene" in his political reporting of the 60s.

As noted above both *Barbary Shore* and *The Deer Park* contain a wealth of ideas, frequently fine portraiture, and vivid depiction of scenes, and yet both are somewhat marred by a misplaced narrative center. Mickey Lovett and Sergius O'Shaugnessy are essentially *voyeurs* and while this is part of Mailer's theme (i.e. they are both supposedly *hurt* into a protective inaction and insensitivity by the violence and injustice of the world), their passive presence at the center of the novels they narrate is too frequently irritating, dulling, and misleading. Likewise, their "escapes" into less-tainted existences seem too much like conveniences to the novelist rather than inevitable resolutions to the drama of which they are a part.

This dilution of dramatic intensity is perhaps in part attributed to three causes, all of which affected Mailer's consciousness during the 50s: first, his preoccupation with subconscious obsessions, compulsions, and anxieties and his own indulgence in alcohol and narcotics as a means of exploring these areas of irrational human experience; second, his feeling that "the best way to grow, as a novelist and man, was not to write one novel after another but to move from activity to activity, a notion that began with Renaissance man," the result of which was both the expense of great intellectual energy and much time on non-fiction writing projects and the inclusion of many new and often extraneous dimensions in the fiction itself; and third, a long-suppressed desire to write openly about the intellectual and emotional nuances of his *own* consciousness, or at least to use this *own* subjective ego as a basis for registering the shocks of the wider social drama, rather than inventing "characters" to do this in his fiction. These varying demands put undue strains on the texture and form of both his fiction and non-fiction. But in his next published book, *Advertisements for Myself* (1959) resourceful Mailer found a means of reconciling and uniting these disparate demands.

Advertisements for Myself, with its multiple tables of contents which provide a shifting framework for the varied selections of Mailer's fiction, literary and social criticism, poetry and drama of the 50s and the candid autobiographical commentary that provides a unity of presence and theme for the whole, is certainly Mailer's most inventive and satisfying book of the decade. For in this remarkably honest "non-fiction novel," he has provided a portrait of the artist (as a disgruntled counter-puncher?) which is dramatically convincing as a whole, despite the disjointedness and uneven quality of its parts. Mailer emerges through this unique conception of himself and his work as a courageous and original writer who just *might* (his own valuation, too) write the "Big Novel" he has aimed himself toward from the start of his career. Contrariwise, though this is of small consolation, he leaves the reader thinking that if he does not some day succeed, the story of his failure might be as disturbingly interesting as his success.

For the uniqueness of *Advertisements* does not reside simply and solely in the relative or collective merits of the assembled pieces of writing or in the fact that they were written by one man. This is perhaps made clear initially in the two tables of contents, the first based on chronology, the second on genre — frames of reference easily dismissed by the "Biography of a Style," which succeeds them in the front of the book, as it obliterates their too rigid control throughout. Mailer's challenge to the reader is clear: against the relative merits of his previous work in all genres, he is wagering that his present consciousness of that varied achievement will provide the basis for new work, richer, broader, and more interesting. Thus, against *our* judgment of his writing he places his *own* judgment, in nearly every instance outdistancing us in severity and humility. But at the same time by his candor and his nakedly stated ambitions, Mailer involves us in the *dynamic* inner process of his own growth, so that in the end our judgments on his work do not really seem to matter any more than, say, the judgments we make upon Stephen Dedaelus' writing and posturing in Joyce's *Portrait;* here as there, the *process* of growth is far more appealing as a subject than its penultimate products.

The first table of contents, for instance, breaks the book into five distinct parts, each corresponding to a phase of Mailer's life in the past decade. "Beginnings" contains the early short stories discussed above. "Middles" contains excerpts from *Barbary Shore,* the three "war stories," and "Yoga" and three political pieces, all of which reveal his faltering socialism and literary realism. "Births" furnishes essays on marijuana, homosexuality, excerpts from *The Deer Park,* and columns from *The Village Voice.* "Hipsters" offers his essay "The White Negro" and various expositions on "Hip." Finally "Games and Ends" contains some "Hip"-inspired stories and essays, poems, excerpts from the stage version of *The Deer Park;* a very bristling story, "The Time of Her Time," and a long prologue to a novel. As biography, these parts emphasize the growth of Mailer's thinking from his early liberal socialism to the later espousal of existential-Hipsterism. They also show how these ideas were increasingly expressed in expository rather than dramatic terms. In the second table of contents, which arranges the various pieces of writing according to kind, Mailer seems to be inviting the reader's judgment as to whether he is a *better* writer in one genre than another or even challenging the reader to compare him with other practitioners of a particular genre — in which case his efforts as poet and dramatist might be seen as non-competitive. But in both cases, these frames of reference are misleading and unsatisfying; they fail to control and contain that elusive spark of writing genius which is uniquely Mailer's own and which is spread throughout his own reflective "advertisements."

Worries expressed throughout the 50s that the "promising young novelist of *The Naked and the Dead*" (to quote a haunting and irritating phrase which has greeted Mailer in nearly every critical review of his work since 1949) would dissipate this genius by spreading it too thinly on the jagged surfaces of his multiform interests or by his over-indulgence in a dangerous and flamboyant life-style, have now proved groundless. Mailer's often demonic and many-faced muse has continued to provoke him to prolific and varied artistic activity — activity, unlike that of most of his contemporaries, directly inspired by and grounded in the significant political and social events of the day. Moreover, it is this firm basis in a 'common experience' which has given concreteness and substance to his work since the middle 50s and which keeps it at least partially indebted to the heritage of Realism in American literature — with its emphasis on the faithful reproduction of physical, social, and psychological realities. But there is another, even deeper and older, tradition in American literature to which Mailer's subjectivism in *Advertisements for Myself* admits him: the tradition of William Byrd and Jonathan Edwards, Franklin, Emerson, Thoreau, and especially Walt Whitman, writers whose own "advertisements" turn inward upon the naked self in order to see the outside world — of nature or metaphysics, politics or art — reflected in it. The excitement which Mailer's positioning in both these traditions brings is owing to the hope that in the time to come he will, like Melville, James, and Faulkner before him, be capable of again fusing them in novels of formal beauty and significant truth.

The Disappointments of Maturity: Bellow's The Adventures of Augie March

by DAVID R. JONES

"I know I longed very much, but I didn't
understand for what."—Augie March (84) *
" . . . while they're looking for the best there
is — and I figure that's what's wrong with you —
everything else gets lost. It's sad, it's a
pity, but it's that way." — Simon March to
                                        Augie March (199)

Augie March recounts his adventures while living in Paris
during the late 1940s. Because he often travels about the continent
on business, he composes at cafe tables, on trains, any of the available places in his desultory life. He writes "as I have taught myself,
free-style" (3), and the subject, despite the continental setting, is
his youth in Chicago during the 1920s, his early manhood, and the
reverberations of his experience. The shadows from those twin
catastrophes — Hiroshima and Auschwitz — have not reached out
to disturb his labors. The austerity of post-war Europe is not his

*Quotations from the text (New York, The Viking Press, 1953)
are followed by page citations in parenthesis.

concern, nor is the incipient boom at home. Senator McCarthy is still looking for a passage to fame. Augie is "an American, Chicago born" (3), and on the threshold of the 50s, but for the moment he is on vacation and reflecting on the past.

Saul Bellow, who was born in Quebec but always "a Chicagoan" in his own view, wrote *The Adventures of Augie March* under nearly identical conditions. Living in Paris during 1948 on the support of a Guggenheim grant, he was working hard at a third novel. The first two — *Dangling Man* (1944) and *The Victim* (1947) — had been slim, tightly constructed stories of modern despair. The new novel, tentatively called *The Crab and the Butterfly,* was another essay in the same style; Bellow's own word for it was "grim." When this work depressed him, he treated himself to a "fantasy holiday," a new piece which drew him from the present to a more exotic locale, "Chicago before the Depression." After 100,000 words, *The Crab and the Butterfly* was "junked," and Bellow abandoned himself to his "favorite fantasy." Here there was no grimness, no pain, no depression. For a change, the characters ran away from him, "demanded to have their own existence." Material came fast, in quantity, and in strange places — Italian cafes, the Borghese Gardens, Salzburg, the Princeton library, and Penn Station, among others; the final two paragraphs were composed on a typewriter in the publisher's office. Not a single sentence was written in Chicago. At one time, thinking that he would not finish for many years, Bellow contemplated publishing a "Part I." But in 1953 it came to rest, and the novel once called *Life Among the Machiavellians* was issued with considerable fanfare as *The Adventures of Augie March.* The Book-of-the-Month Club offered it as an alternate selection and the National Book Award was only a few months in coming. Bellow, nearly forty, was cover material for the literary magazines and an established author.

Despite its initial success, the novel has not worn well. Some of Bellow's later critics have even preferred the slight *Seize the Day* (1956), a direct successor of the first two novels, to Augie's robust and episodic adventures. Professors, looking for a label, have been torn between calling *Augie March* a *bildungsroman* and accepting Bellow's own word "picaresque." Both classifications admit the work under severe strain, and we do not, in any case, know a thing by labeling it. But more difficult questions continue to disrupt considerations of the novel. Bellow's strategy here is a reckless one, to fling an individual out across the surface of a very large work. Any such book depends for its success on the resiliency of that individual, on his ability to become, like a new coat, comfortable with time. There is also a problem of focus, for Bellow parades American types and deformities past the reader in considerable number, and we often have to peer over their heads to get a glimpse of Augie. As if to complicate matters, we must continually adjust our register to accommodate the two Augie Marchs, narrator and actor, an adjustment which is not always easy. And after we have resolved these problems, how are we to take this expatriate American, disenchanted Chicagoan, non-Jewish Jew, and unadventurous adventurer? Is he, unlike Bellow's earlier heroes, a proof that modern society can bring to maturity a man who affirms — by his words and his presence — the brutish, glorious, squalid, monumental, and petty life of men? Or is he an example of our society's ability to make all motion circular, to reduce men to demented jabbering in the face of its alternating demands and rejections? Finally, and more important for the reader approaching the book for the first time, does the style of Augie's reminiscences bear enduring? The pitch of the writing here is more extreme than anything else Bellow has attempted in his career. Augie's prose is either daringly successful or very aggravating, and more than one reader has put the novel aside because he could not tolerate its surface.

Augie tells us at the first that "a man's character is his fate" (3), and if this is true, we need to know who and what Augie March is. He introduces himself with a naive bluster which is neither informative nor encouraging, and the initial words, "an American, Chicago born," are most helpful to the hunter of allegories. We find out a great many irrelevancies in the next pages (to be exact, in the first half of the book), but we still do not know the answer to this question. His particular Chicago runs from Humboldt Park, a west-side Jewish neighborhood ringed by Poles, north to the wealthy suburb of Evanston and south to Hyde Park, an area in which he diligently skirts the civilizing influence of the University of Chicago. But Augie, a free soul, will not be defined by neighborhood. Neither can we place him by occupation. Though his first action is to lie to the welfare authorities and though we leave him conducting shady business activities in Europe, his occasional criminality is no more than a sign of his social indirection. In between, he holds various jobs, in a department store (as a Santa's helper, with some theft on the side), a flower shop, pool room, luxury dog service, and coal yard, among many. He helps manage a bum fighter, steals books for university students, organizes unions for the fledgling C.I.O., hunts iguanas in Mexico with a manned eagle, acts as servant or research assistant to several strange men, and barely escapes a role in an effort to protect Trotsky from Russian assassins. Throughout, rich women are constantly present, and only his particular sense of himself saves Augie from becoming a gigolo. No, we will not find him out there.

We begin to discover Augie in the reactions he provokes in others. He is "the by-blow of a traveling man" (125), for the family has been deserted by the father and is now tended by a Russian emigré grandmother, Mrs. Lausch. If his father's desertion makes Augie a casually "disinherited" modern hero, it also gives rise to the book's dominant action. His grandmother, his older brother Simon, the neighborhood magnate Einhorn, and the wealthy Renlings all try unsuccessfully to "adopt" Augie, for his character is "adoptional" (151). But the matter is more serious, and Augie soon realizes it. He was born under "the sign of the recruit" (508), is always "under an influence and not the carrier of it" (244), and his elders are constantly trying to "recruit" him to their "version of what's real" (402). By his character rather than his will, he is thrust into the middle of a philosophic battlefield.

Clem Tambow tells Augie, "The trouble with you is that you're looking for a manager" (203), but that is exactly the delusion under which all the "Machiavellians" of the early title operate. The world, like the March family, is broken down into the managers and the dumb brutes (Grandma Lausch and Simon against Augie's simple-minded mother and idiot brother George). Life is the swindling of the brutes by the managers, the trade of advantage for pain. In the middle stands Augie, the free agent, the "man of feeling" (434). Urged to find a profession and become "a specialist" before the world closes up, he vacillates. Overpowered by his opponents, he wiggles away and strikes off on his own. Mired in inaction, he is called "fool" (29), "mushhead" (94), and "too dumb to live" (275). Mrs. Renling in particular is convinced that without her tooth-and-claw tutelage, Augie will be stamped out in the life struggle. But Einhorn cannily sees that Augie is not completely passive: "All of a sudden I catch on to something about you. You've got *opposition* in you. You don't slide through everything. You just make it look so" (117). Unlike Mimi Villars, another resister, Augie has not the temperament to be "an attacker" (209). His form of "opposition" is to duck a shoulder under the outreached arm and sidle off into another chapter, another adventure. He admits his own "larkiness," but knows that it is in the best cause, the search for a "worth-while fate" (432).

In the middle of the book, while Augie is peacefully down-and-out, Thea Fenchel appears. She met and chased him unsuccessfully years before, has made and broken a marriage since, and is now ready to capture both young March and giant iguanas. Thea is among the most savage of the Machiavellians, for her dominant idea is that there is something better than reality. In the throes of the most violent love he has known, Augie capitulates to this vision, but the narrator's voice carries broad irony: "Oh, well and good. Very good and bravo! Let's have this better, nobler reality" (316). Predictably, Augie has an accident while hunting and their trained eagle proves a coward; Augie soon works his way out from under this velvet yoke.

But when the affair with Thea begins, the novel, like the glue on its binding, cracks in half. First, the style alters considerably. Augie leaves Chicago for the first sustained period, and the bursting descriptive passages which had dominated the novel disappear entirely. So does Augie's basic preoccupation with others. From the opening battles of the book, we have a very difficult time learning anything about the young Augie March. The principles behind his actions are obscure. When he is asked to commit a robbery, he "didn't say no" (114), and when another friend asks if he is honest, he answers, "not completely" (190). Larger issues are explained with equal vagueness, for the older March, the writer of the memoirs, is usually as mystified as his readers. At the beginning of the Renling episode he remarks, "From here a new course was set —by us, for us: I'm not going to try to unravel all the causes" (125). What little we learn about Augie himself is drowned in the descriptions of his surroundings and recruiters. At the beginning of another new adventure, the narrator alludes to the difficulty which bothers his readers: "All the influences were lined up waiting for me. I was born, and there they were to form me, which is why I tell you more of them than of myself" (43). The book, however, is about his submission and resistance to these influences, and we should know more about the character which determines his fate. A *bildungsroman* is usually about somebody, and Augie March seems suspiciously, at times, like nobody. But in the latter half of the novel, as if to reward us for our patience, he turns what was a trickle of self-reflection into a torrent. The collapse of the affair with Thea is the signal for his incessant gabbing to begin. By the end of the novel, when he meets an old friend in Paris and refuses to discuss his accumulated ideas, we gasp in relief.

More important, the disintegration of his love for Thea provides the emotional climax of the book and his first significant insight. At the beginning of their trip, he tells her of his opposition to others and that he "had looked all [his] life . . . for a fate good enough." The new love affair has changed all that: now, he says, "I understood much better what I myself wanted" (318). But Augie is wrong about both his new understanding and his old quest, as he comes to realize when he has drifted from Thea: "I thought that my aim of being simple was just a fraud, that I wasn't a bit goodhearted or affectionate" (401). His "simplicity" is an invention, and this "devising" costs him dearly in his "secret heart." He too is creating a "someone who can exist before" external life and is advertising, if only to himself, a "version of what's real." "Personality," he moans, "is unsafe in the first place. It's the types that are safe" (402).

This is an important and pertinent revelation, that even those who resist the "versions" of others do so by creating their own fictions. But it would have had more force if the novel had not lapsed back into another series of bouts with the Machiavellians. Augie returns to Chicago and is interrogated in turn by nearly all his acquaintances there. Clem Tambow is treated to a long disquisition on the theory of "axial lines," Augie's latest maneuver in his "campaign after a worth-while fate" (432). The outlandish Robey, who intends to write a book on human happiness, and the maniacal Basteshaw, a biochemist in search of the cure for boredom, are nothing but pale, insane shadows of the early figures in his life. By this time, we are onto the trick and little interested in more of the same. And at the end, having wed Stella, the woman who would put an end to his "trouble and hankering" (474), he is no more at peace than before. Their marriage is troubled by memories of Stella's past affair, her career as a screen actress, and her refusal to divulge her inner life to him. This "Columbus of those near-at-hand" (536) has sailed through storm to find that he was, all the time, half-way down on the side of the whirlpool. The novel has long since begun to sputter.

The principal difficulty in approaching Bellow's third novel, then, is in getting to know Augie March. At first he tells us too little about himself as he piles up the remarkably detailed picture of Chicago. Later, by talking compulsively, he tells us nothing. And as a narrator, he becomes increasingly ponderous, as one short example will perhaps show. Augie rescues Stella from her underworld lover in Mexico and takes an impassable mountain road, stranding them for the night. Though strangers, they lie in one another's arms, and sex is only a touch away. At this critical moment, the narrator takes over:

> I suppose if you pass the night with a woman in a deserted mountain place there's only one appropriate thing, according to the secret urging of the world. Or not so secret. And the woman, who has done so much to be dangerous in this same scheme, the more she comes of the world the less she knows how to vary from it. I thought that in the crisis that seems to have to occur when a man and a woman are thrown together nothing, nothing easy, can happen until first one difficulty is cleared and it is shown how the man is a man and the woman a woman; as if a life's trial had to be made, and the pretensions of the man and the woman satisfied (390).

The thought is interesting, but on the brink of passion, we expect something else. Stunned by long, repeated attacks of this kind, by whole chapters of cracker-barrel philosophising, the reader may be excused if he begins to find Augie a verbose bore.

Aggravations multiply. As he ages, Augie becomes surlier, and the negative facets of the poolroom wise-guy show more frequently. But nowhere is he more tiresome than in his prose. He describes his method of writing as "free-style," and it is, in fact, as simple and repetitive as the freestyler's crawl. Augie's stroke is the simile, a device he almost invariably secures with the debris of his self-education. The following items represent half of those used in similes in the first hundred pages of the novel: Heraclitus, Machiavelli, Zeus, Ophelia, Napoleon (several times), the Leaning Tower of Pisa, Georges Dandin, Belshazzer, Cato, Jonah, the Rosetta Stone, Danton, Chevalier Bayard, Cincinnatus, the Congress of Vienna, Nero, Fouché, Talleyrand, the Gioconda, Louis

XIV, Pope Alexander VI, Sardanapalus, Hephaestus, Christopher Wren, Robinson Crusoe, Empedocles, Origen, Charlemagne, and the fact that a law still exists which allows British aristocrats "to piss, if they should care to, on the hind wheels of carriages" (65). The similes continue. Augie and Mrs. Renling are like "Moses and the Pharoah's daughter." A boarding-house room is "like the Baths of Caracalla," Simon like Alexander, Commodus, and Caracalla, his wife like Lady Macbeth. The eagle in Mexico at first "looked to be close kin to the one that lit on Prometheus once a day" (331), then flew "like a Satan" (338), then "like an Attila's horseman" (348). Fittingly, it is named "Caligula," and Augie himself is dubbed "Bolingbroke" by acquaintances in Mexico.

Besides appearing on nearly every page, the similes become long, mixed, and wildly inappropriate. On the occasion of the Depression, Augie glosses Einhorn with a two-hundred word comparison to Croesus, and a later friend is compared at similar length to Clemenceau's statue in the Champs Elysées. A brief term with a dog service brings forth mention of Xenophon's Ten Thousand, Cerberus, the Escurial, Marcus Aurelius, and Pompeii in rapid succession. The young Simon, in one paragraph, reminds Augie of Danton, Napoleon, Chevalier Bayard, and Cincinnatus. Stella's former lover was "built up to be about like Jupiter-Ammon, with an eye like that new telescope out at the Mount Palomar observatory, about as wicked as Tiberius, a czar and mastermind" (524). In one of the book's most startling collection of phrases, Grandma Lausch sits "beside the Crystal-Palace turret of the stove" in her "starched dress with hem as stiff as a line of Euclid" (93). Both Augie and his supporters justify the displays of learning as proof that modern man is not altogether unlike his large, heroic ancestors, that Einhorn, for instance, truly resembles Croesus in many things. Perhaps so. But, in contrast with the use Joyce makes of such parallels in *Ulysses,* Bellow's devices seem undirected, superficial, and wearying — in short, a self-indulgence.

In general, the prose is a child's wildest ice-cream sundae dream. Augie prefers verbs and adjectives six or eight in a row. The historical material shoulders its way among slang (*hipped, dough, piker, dinky, quiff, gizmo, the clink, the riot act*), eminent people of the time (Senator Borah, Big Bill Thompson, Samuel Insull, Julius Rosenwald) and the familiar objects of life (dixie-cups, crackerjax, Castile soap, Jewett Sedans, Bisodol, Ceresota sacks, alpacuna coats, and bulldog editions). Mayors and ward-healers live comfortably with Dave Apollon and his Komarinsky Dancers, Rose La Rose, Sophie Tucker, and a nearly complete collection of Chicago gangsters. To fortify the Runyanesque flavor, names of minor characters are ethnic and vivid: Moonya Staplanski, "Five Properties" Coblin, Nails Nagel, Manny Padilla, Kayo Obermark, Nosey Mutchnik, Dingbat Einhorn. At its best, the prose is like the city, a pile of objects and people. A short example concerns the City Hall elevator:

> In the cage we rose and dropped, rubbing elbows with bigshots and operators, commissioners, grabbers, heelers, tipsters, hoodlums, wolves, fixers, plaintiffs, flatfeet, men in Western hats and women in lizard shoes and fur coats, hothouse and arctic drafts mixed up, brute things and airs of sex, evidence of heavy feeding and systematic shaving, of calculations, grief, not-caring, and hopes of tremendous millions in concrete to be poured or whole Mississippis of bootleg whisky and beer (39).

Particularly in the opening pages of the book, every new place or event sets off a jam-packed, Babel-and-babble, no-holds-barred stem-winder of a description, the best sustained example being Chapter V, our introduction to Einhorn. When successful, this prose is among modern America's finest. We forget the "etceteras," the "whatnots," and the "who-else-nots" which dangle on the ends of clauses and the "kind of's" which are liberally sprinkled throughout. All too often, however, the prose is simply elephantine or uncomfortably limp and soggy: "He said he'd be at the Pump Room, than which few places were considered niftier in the city" (445).

These things said, the vital failure of *The Adventures of Augie March* is still not explained. If we dislike Augie himself (some readers find him "masochistic"), his occasionally bloated prose, and his speeches with their air of old theatrical rant, we can find convincing rationalizations. Structural flaws, of themselves, do not consign works to the categories of "interesting" and "little read." *Huckleberry Finn,* a book very like *Augie March* in obvious ways, is broken in the middle but still entrancing. There is something else wrong here. What? The question arises at many points in discussing the book, and the answer may lie not in its imperfections, but in a quality which it lacks.

The holiday nature of the book's composition is an attractive, if vexed, answer. Favorably inclined, we could say that Bellow returned from *The Crab and the Butterfly* to a central, important concern; most authors, after all, write best about what they *must* write about. But the exuberance between the novel's lines often resembles the cry of a boy let out from school, and simple "liberation" (a word Bellow used for the writing of *Augie March*) is not necessarily a ticket to success. In his rejection of polish and tight, clear structure for episodic jaunting and steam-powered prose, Bellow obviously found this a delightful book to write. It has, in addition, many of the material ingredients of a great novel. But at that place in its creation where the imagination should have fired the material into life, a vagueness crept in.

If this vagueness is the problem, it surely must trouble our impressions of the novel's two central characters, Augie March and the city of Chicago. In the case of Augie, the borderline between his "opposition" and sheer passivity is too cloudy; his adventures all too clearly happen *to* him. The definition of character by negative action ("opposition" or passivity) leaves Augie uncertain about himself in very many ways and frustrates our search for that character among the details and behind the talk. The same can be said for Bellow's Chicago. He has said that, while writing the book, "Chicago itself had grown exotic to me," and the word "exotic" illuminates the difficulty we encounter. For all the portraits, caricatures, massive detail, and inside knowledge, his Chicago is not alive, like Dickens' London or Joyce's Dublin. The picture of the city is taken from a fascinated traveler's notebook.

Unfortunately — for the novel has many successes and spectacular potential — the man and his city have become their superficies.

Finally a Lady: Mary McCarthy

by ELEANOR WIDMER

The difference between the Victorian novelist George Eliot (Mary Ann Evans) and the mid-twentieth century Mary McCarthy is that the former was a literary lady, while the writing of the latter reveals her as a sometime broad. The comparison is not meant frivolously. Both women had formidable powers of intellect, both could give any man a run for his philosophical money, both lived advanced lives that went against the convention of their respective periods, and both were concerned with psychological and social dramas that transcended the domestic. But whereas the first commanded a nation-wide reputation, the second remained, for two decades at least, a coterie writer, restricted in her following to the New York intelligentsia and to literary academicians. Although George Eliot lived with a married man for over twenty years — a state so shocking that Queen Victoria could hardly be persuaded to meet the famous author — she kept her personal life out of her writing, was chaste and impeccable in choosing the broadest moral themes for her work. With Mary McCarthy, the exact opposite prevailed. Her own best heroine, she utilized her immediate experiences as the basis of her writing, intent on displaying her awesome erudition, her sexual emancipation, her political astuteness and her cultural significance.

Nor was it, with McCarthy, merely a case of *épater le bourgeois.* Far from it. She wrote about a restricted circle of New York friends, presumably for these friends, and while totally obsessed with them she sought nevertheless to shock and to violate, to mock and to undercut them. Adored and made much of, rising to power with the help of well known literary figures, she savaged them in her writing while waiting to be congratulated for her clever-ness. Though an anti-establishment writer in the 40s and 50s, her primary target was rarely other than her own group, and the thrust to her writing derived from biting the very intellectual hand that fed her. Always at the center of her own dramas, she saw her cosmopolitanism and the irony for which she was much praised, as pitted against that of her male friends, and in the struggle she did not mean to fail. Not even the rousing Norman Mailer with his advertisements for himself could outdo Miss McCarthy in the realm of taking such a narrow self as cynosure.

Yet, were she all brilliance and all self-chronicler, she would not have survived three decades of hard writing. Her appeal lies in her over-weening pride on the one hand and her genuine humility on the other, in the strange revelations of her guilt and inadequacies along with her monstrous desire to show-off. Essen-tially a girl from the provinces, she worked consistently at polishing her image as the sophisticate, indeed making a profession of it. And, just as her novels often fail from an almost suffocating cleverness, she evokes our sympathy for trying too hard to succeed at too little.

Which is not to say that her powers are not formidable. In an essay, "The Fact in Fiction," she stated that she conceived of the novel as 'news" similar to eyewitness journalism and concerned with the actual, with verifiable realities. Like Gautier, she believed that *"le monde l'exterieur l'existe,"* and in setting about to delin-eate this world she managed to reflect the never-ending shifts in a coterie intellectual and artistic climate, as well as to define the new left-wing politics of the decades following the second World War — anti-Stalinist, though with traces of sentimental Marxism — and anti-orthodox society, at the expense of individual art and justification. In retrospect, her political postures, like her sexual revelations, appear tame. But in the late 40s and mid-50s they created considerable tremors.

Some clues to the McCarthy stances can be found in her most admirable work, *Memoirs of a Catholic Girlhood* (1957), which explores without her usual overlay of forced sophistication, her early, and almost theatrically paradoxical, years. Born in Seattle in 1912 of wealthy, indulgent, capricious parents, she was orphaned by the flu epidemic of 1918. Though each set of grandparents had considerable wealth, she and her three brothers became the wards of an incredibly repressive great-aunt Margaret and a German-born uncle Myers in Minneapolis, whose portraits border on Gothic horror. When the 11-year-old Mary won a prize essay contest for the topic, "The Irish in American History," her uncle "silently rose from his chair, led me into a dark downstairs lavatory . . . and furiously beat me with a razor strop — to teach me a lesson, he said, lest I become stuck up. Aunt Margaret did not intervene."

This regime of terror came to an end in 1923, when Mary returned to the home of her Presbyterian grandfather and her Jewish grandmother in Seattle, where once again she enjoyed the privileges of the wealthy. Strangely, her three brothers were dispensed to Catholic boarding schools while Mary alone received preferred treatment — no doubt a factor that contributed to her concept of herself as her own best heroine. This dramatic notion of herself is equally evident in her break with Catholic dogma; for while seeking to gain the attention of the local bishop by saying she had lost her faith, she discovered that what had been a pose constituted her reality. During her drab days in Minneapolis, Catholicism proved her one source of elitism, defining and enhancing her role as pariah. Once she became the center of an adoring household, rebelling against the church proved more satisfactory than being a penitent.

It is both too facile and dangerous to draw parallels between the guilty and punished child and the attention seeking overly confident one of Miss McCarthy's later life. But an element of this child always remains to seek recognition and to shock, to cry simultaneously *mea culpa* and "How great I am," in a fusion of personal attitude and public image. Where one began and the other left off became increasingly hard to say, particularly as her writing career progressed.

Few women writers had such an easy time of it, though in a restricted fashion, as Mary McCarthy. Her Victorian counterpart, George Eliot, had to take refuge in a male pseudonym and to keep her identity secret for years. McCarthy did exactly the opposite. While still at Vassar she managed to obtain a job at *The New Republic* and later *The Nation,* and during the paralyzing Depression, when many men and her betters sat scraping

their feet waiting for a paltry book to review, she had the opportunity to do battle with established writers. Moreover, when she
became associated with Philip Rahv, editor of *Partisan Review*,
which dominated the political and literary avant-garde scene in
New York, she began, not only to make a reputation for herself
as the magazine's theatre critic, but, under Rahv's guidance, to
move into the left-wing politics noted for its ferocious reaction
against the Moscow trials. As if the sponsorship of Rahv were not
enough, she soon married Edmund Wilson, eighteen years her
senior and a noted critic, thus appearing to fulfill her precocious
promises.

As an ironist, Miss McCarthy could not have missed the mock-
ery of this marriage. Corruscating on the surface, it festered underneath, and far from being liberated she found herself the victim
of Wilson's harsh imperiousness. Nevertheless, Wilson provided
the change in her literary fortunes. Insisting that she could write
fiction, he more or less commanded her to do so, and she obeyed.
The result was a series of linked autobiographical sketches, barely
disguised as fiction, *The Company She Keeps* (1942).

Satirizing Miss McCarthy in his academic novel, *Pictures from
An Institution* (1955), Randall Jarrell wrote, "How can we expect
novelists to be moral when their trade forces them to treat every
end they meet as no more than imperfect means to a novel?" This
applied most aptly to McCarthy's first book of fiction. She had an
eidetic personal memory, and she used it; she also had colorful
friends, some mildly famous, some eccentric, but passionately dedicated to New York Bohemia, and she used them. The book is a
veritable catalogue of the "things" which define her fellow members, from their possession of Archipenko heads and Harold Cash
sculptures to their literary and political attitudes. It is also an
account of her role as Bohemian Girl.

In the opening chapter, entitled "Cruel and Barbarous Treatment," the author-heroine, alienated from her first husband and
in the throes of an affair, comments on her attitude toward men,
"It was a pity, she reflected, that she was so sensitive to public
opinion. 'I really couldn't love a man,' she murmured to herself
once, 'if everybody didn't think he was wonderful.'" But this
desire for approval is coupled with a form of self-willed degradation. In the most vivid episode in the book, "The Man in the
Brooks Brothers Shirt," she describes her brief affair with a salesman on a train en route to her Reno divorce. From the embarras-

sing safety pin in her underwear to the dirty words he asks her to repeat during her copulation, to the literal vomit in her mouth the next morning, to the bath he insists that she take because she smells, Miss McCarthy spares the reader nothing. Is she shocking us or revealing her own shock. Is her easy virtue to be held for or against her? We must keep in mind that the gains of the sexual revolution of the 60s had not permeated the 40s and 50s and that McCarthy ran the risk of appearing as a loose woman, for all that her action was disguised with intellectual and political talk. But for McCarthy, rather that calculated risk, rather the clucking of tongues, rather the outrage than mere conventionality. At the end of the episode when the salesman sends her a telegram whose sentiments she regards as gauche, the heroine "did not file it away with the other messages, but tore it up carefully and threw it in the wastebasket. It would have been dreadful if anyone had seen it." Style, then, is the primary reality.

This almost fanatical insistence upon appearing properly advanced and *au courant* is one of the flaws, not just of *The Company She Keeps,* which contains the best and worst of her mannerisms, but of the succeeding works as well. So eager is McCarthy to appear as a rebel among the Philistines, with Philistinism defined as last year's intellectual ideology, that she over-emphasizes fashionable details at the expense of either character development or narrative line. Incisive memory and cosmopolitan detail lend candor to her work; at the same time they generate the anxiety that if removed, nothing would remain. Or, as Randall Jarrell notes in parodying her later academic novel, "All clichés, slogans . . . turns of speech, tunnels or by-passes of ideology, gravestones of rationalization and cant lived in [her] as though in nutrient broth; and [she] nourished them unharmed, knowing all, believing none." Whether Mary McCarthy believed in them or merely in their evocation, she managed, by the initial display, to set up the same kind of ricocheting reaction that a gossip column does after a major ball. The seemingly tough minded intelligentsia tittered hysterically, not at what had already been committed to paper, but at the prospects of exposure to come.

The Oasis (1949) consummated the fears of her circle by satirizing some of the men who had been closest to her. A tale about the foundering of an ideal community called Utopia in the Taconic Mountains of New York State, it posits the factionalism of the contending groups, the "purists" and the "realists," representing two rather abstract and vaguely post-Marxian views of the New York literary intellectuals in the post-World-War-II years.

Macdougal Macdermott (the critic and essayist, Dwight Macdonald) leads the purists while Will Taub (Philip Rahv) centers his activities among the realists. Amidst the jockeying for position, the misunderstanding in rhetoric, and the inability of their concepts to meet stress — the entire community becomes immobilized when no one is capable of ordering off some stray pickers of wild strawberries — Utopia collapses. So does the novel. The use of caricature for character and the hastily sketched-out events for a drama that does not exist, limits and defines this work as a curiosity. To say, as McCarthy does, that it is a *conte philosophique* (with its vestiginal traces of Voltaire) does not dismiss it from the responsibilities of content; presumably a novel of ideas, it holds both factions up to ridicule and then makes a hasty retreat from what should be the broader implications of the heartbreak and pitfalls of community living and of sectarian ideologies. Moreover, while Philip Rahv threatened to sue for Miss McCarthy's damaging portrait of himself as Will Taub, she managed little more than one dimension. Rahv deserved better than to have himself written off for his obsessive abstractions as did Dwight Macdonald, for the sake of his cigarette holder, his high nervous laugh, and his love of economy-size packages. Though purportedly serious, the novel offers no glimpse of possibilities for alternate choices, and by reducing everyone to his common foible, it lacks any tragic quality. To those uninitiated in McCarthysim, the brevity, lack of sufficient narrative, and the general torpor of the denouement (the episode with the strawberry pickers), must have made the book merely trivial.

Several years later, Miss McCarthy attempted to break with the New York ambiance as well as to produce a fully achieved novel with a recognizable plot and more subtly drawn characters. With her unfailing ear for the fashionable, she selected the popular subgenre, the academic novel, using her teaching experiences at Bard and Sarah Lawrence Colleges as material.

The Groves of Academe (1952) was most relevant to the 50s for its use of the academy as a microcosm of the increased conservatism amidst intellectuals who flocked to college teaching as a means of partial retreats and for its play upon the "witch-hunting" and anti-Communist nastiness that hit the colleges during the reign of Senator Joseph McCarthy. The anti-hero of this novel, Henry

Mulcahy, a "tall, soft-bellied, lisping man with a tense, mushroom-white face, rimless bifocals, and greying thin red hair," deliberately fosters the impression that he was once a Communist in the attempt to rouse the sympathy of the libertarians on the staff to fight his dismissal. As Mulcahy shrewdly anticipates, several of the idealistic faculty members, including the black-haired beautiful heroine, 23-year-old Domna Rejnev, daughter of a Russian emigré, come to his ardent defense. The president, Maynard Hoar, rescinds Mulcahy's dismissal. Despite or because of his deceitful pose, Mulcahy thrives and organizes a poetry conference during which the "proletarian poet" (Kenneth Rexroth?) reveals that Mulcahy never was a Communist. Mulcahy, who has consistently identified himself with "the sacred untouchables of modern martyrology," terms this mild inquest a witch-hunt, and rather than again fire Mulcahy for what was the original issue — bumbling incompetence — the president himself resigns.

The Groves of Academe poses a series of antinomines: how to distinguish the hunter from the hunted, how to establish truth when everyone practices self-justifying falsehoods and — most important — how to cope with scruples when outward circumstances and inward frailty combine to compromise the absolutes. In Mulcahy, Miss McCarthy has produced one of her more obnoxious male characters — in her hagiology, males are either weak, confused, ineffective, brutish, or simply stupid — and he represents the standard moral trimmer, in the liberal world at large as well as in the academic. And what of the exotic heroine-author, Domna Rejnev, who constantly asks herself, "What would Tolstoi say?" She is far too judicious, far too moral, far too advanced for her years and hence more of a symbol than a human being, patently sexless while representing the good and the true. Surely a reversal from the more autobiographical narrator in *The Company She Keeps,* this heroine points to a weakness in conceptualization when McCarthy is not putting herself personally on the literary line. But as a novel, and especially to those in the academic world, *The Groves of Academe*, with its erudition, its acute references to modern literature, its allusions to martyrdom, and its usual dalliance with real poets and people, provided an advance over her earlier work and a more fitting vehicle for in-group revelations and ridicule.

Perhaps Miss McCarthy's most successful novel during the 50s is *A Charmed Life* (1955), in which she is again on the solid ground of projecting herself as the heroine. Several years after her divorce from Edmund Wilson, Mary McCarthy married for the third time and returned with Bowden Broadwater to Wellfleet, where she had lived with Wilson. This situation, the return of a newly married heroine to the scene of her former marriage, is the basis of *A Charmed Life*. Speaking of Wilson, Mary McCarthy had said, "He was two people. One is this humanistic Princetonian critic and the other is a sort of minotaur, really, with his terror and pathos." Of his fictitious self, Miles Murphy, she wrote, "Nobody, except Miles had ever browbeat her successfully," and "with Miles she had done steadily what she had hated, starting from the moment she married him, violently and against her will." In Martha Sinnott, Miss McCarthy finds an appropriate voice for herself. This heroine is beautiful in the McCarthy fashion, with hair pulled to the nape of her neck, a one time actress now attempting to write a play, a woman with a love of modern values and ancient houses, an expert at *pot de crême* (Miss McCarthy uses recipes as an iconography of the female character) and a person who dotes upon being petted by her new husband and old friends.

The title underscores the irony: her personal and intellectual gifts notwithstanding, the heroine is barren. She cannot conceive either a child or a finished play. Inevitably, though she resists meeting her former husband Miles Murphy, Martha does. At a play reading of Racine's *Bérénice* (characteristically for Miss McCarthy read in the original French and with veiled hints at the personal conflict between domestic love and literary duty) they both became drunk. Since her husband is out of town, Martha allows Miles to drive her home and to make love to her. Later, when she discovers she is pregnant, and with no way of determining the real father, she decides upon an abortion as the moral choice. Reflecting upon her evening with Miles, Martha chastises herself for her major failing, "She ought to have thought. This failure to *think* was what she could not forgive herself." The ability to search for the truth, to reason, to think, the heroine puts above all other attributes. Indeed, she sees the abortion as a means of re-establishing her relationship with her husband, of restoring "the truth between them."

On the eve of her abortion, "happy that she had changed," that "she was no longer afraid of herself," she drives away from her friends' house, only to have another car crash into her. "She knew in a wild flash of humor, that she had made a fatal mistake:

in New Leeds, after sundown, she would have been safer on the wrong side of the road. 'Killed instantly,' she said to herself regretfully, as she lost consciousness." By not thinking that the right side may also prove the wrong side in a topsy-turvy intellectual world, the heroine forfeits her life.

A Charmed Life is noteworthy for probing the truth for its characters, for its authentic portrayal of the advanced woman-heroine, Martha, its acidly accurate one of the writer-critic, Miles Murphy, and for its unerring description of an artistic community — the paternity trial of the irresponsible Sandy Gray, which brings together the town Bohemians, becomes one of the defter episodes of the novel. Miss McCarthy's reliance on her own experiences, and perhaps even the symbolic death of her old self, provides a surety and certitude to *A Charmed Life* that sporadically asserts itself in her academic novel. Writing about herself, Mary McCarthy's style soars, her insights are perceptive and the work transcends mere narcissism to attain an almost objective lyricism. This lyricism applies equally well to her non-fictional account of herself, *Memoirs of a Catholic Girlhood,* one of the most sustained good pieces of writing in the McCarthy canon, where an essential honesty supersedes the necessity to be the devastating cosmopolite.

Yet, in the 50s, the image of the brazen Mary McCarthy remains untarnished. Though no sale of any individual book goes beyond 17,000 copies, she is regarded by her fellow craftsmen with a mixture of awe and fear for her ability to "cast a cold eye" upon all she surveys, including herself. It is not until the 60s, with the publication of *The Group,* a story of several Vassar women from the Depression to the second War, that she achieves not only national, but world fame. One of the chapters, "Dottie Makes an Honest Woman of Herself;" had appeared in the 50s in the pages of the *Partisan Review,* causing an enormous stir for its graphic description of then modern birth control — the obtaining of a pessary. A decade later, incorporated into *The Group,* its clinical details, far from shocking, appear woefully dated, as does its basically conservative heroine. Indeed, it is by casting down her savage trappings and by relying on more conventional attitudes that Miss McCarthy arrives at her major triumph — a "ladies' novel." As an author, she could not have envisioned a more delicious reversal for herself.

In his incisive essay, "The Case Against McCarthy: A Review of *The Group,*" Norman Mailer summarizes her work, "She failed out of vanity, the accumulated vanity of being overpraised for too little, and so being pleased with herself for too little . . . she has failed by an act of imagination . . . finally she suffers from a lack of reach. Mary's vice is her terror of being ridiculous."

If then, Mary McCarthy has played the brittle, deracinated game of the American intellectual, now tough contentious broad, now precocious little girl, we must admire this intense pose for all of its occasional desperation. And, if the assertiveness, the knowledgeability, the sophistication finally turn quaint, we must grant her the rather hollow victory of at last becoming a sometime lady.

The Voice at the Back Door:
Elizabeth Spencer
Looks into Mississippi

by DAVID G. PUGH

Fiction often enables the reader to look into the workings of another society which he feels is a little different from his own or gives him pleasure in recognizing aspects of his own social group, even though there are some dangers in equating the real society with a literary look into it. As one Yale-educated young lawyer comments in Elizabeth Spencer's novel, *The Voice at the Back Door* (1956), all that he knows (of lynching) is what he reads in William Faulkner. The novel's title refers to the male southern Negroes' custom of approaching only to the back doors of white folks' houses, not knocking, but just calling for attention. To interpret Miss Spencer's selection of incidents set in the eight months up to the August Democratic primary election in 1952 requires only a little data from the political almanac (Truman, MacArthur, Korea) but a powerful lot of awareness of what is left unsaid (but calling for attention) in the narration, and especially in the dialogue, concerning the motives and occasions for hypocrisy, for saying what one does not believe. Hortense Powdermaker's autobiographical commentary on her anthropological field work, *Stranger and Friend* (1966), describes the patterns she observed in this culture in the early 30s and gives some feeling for the social fabric and customs, for the significance of the small commonplace detail. However, the novel is shaped by literary as well as cultural conventions, so a reader also has to remember what he has read in William Faulkner.

This mixture of the conventions of the social fabric and of literary conventions is exemplified in one small bit of Jason Hunt's conversation with his daughter Marcia Mae (always called by both her names, naturally). He is saying that what her friend, Acting Sheriff Duncan Harper advocates "is something that's going to come, but can't be spoken out for. I reckon that makes me a hypocrite. But I don't want you around where there's any trouble." Stripped of its context, this paternal admonition is not peculiarly Southern, peculiarly from the fifties, or even peculiarly American. Nor is most of what Jason has just said before it: "None of this counts with you. I've made money out of this county for forty years, given jobs to everybody worth a plugged nickel, kept this house up and you children fed, clothed, and flying around in automobiles. I reckon this makes me a crook. . . ." Except for the rural overtone of 'reckon', this passage would probably speak to (and for) middle-age urban and suburban America of the 50s and even of the present. Heard of a generation gap lately?

It is easy enough to ignore the word 'county' or think it is a misprint for country'. Jason, though, *means* 'county'. He reflects a culture which takes pride in being a Winfield County boy, even though he wants Marcia Mae to keep away from where there's any trouble, caused no doubt by men who would be labeled (and call themselves, too, for that matter) "good ol' Winfield County Boys." By the time this passage occurs, the reader has been given several biographical details which place him in the social fabric and give insight into Hunt's reaction to "hypocrite" — which is what Marcia Mae has just accused him of being. (Does that sound familiar?)

Now near sixty, he has shut up his office in town, still dabbling in business from a side room in his home; having been in almost every type of local commercial venture in the county at one time or another, he now takes summer afternoon naps with an afghan over his stocking feet, enjoys the quiet of his relationship with his mother-in-law, and endures his wife and two daughters, thirty-ish, war-widowed Marcia Mae, and Cissy, nineteen; having married well (Judge Standsbury's daughter recognized the go-getter in him), he is still drawn to the countryside where he grew up, can still lapse into metaphors of 'trace chains tight and the single-tree riding high,' and, beyond that, knows that there are people in town still very much aware "that in the old days the Hunts used to come to town on Saturday in a wagon, wearing shoes for the first time that week."

What difference does that make? The George F. Babbitts of the Middle West would still admire the man. But that creaky wagon and those stiff shoes both bear a lot of weight, even when mentioned fully a hundred pages earlier in the novel. Although wagons were used everywhere in the 1890s, even in the alphabetical towns strung out every dozen miles along the Northern Pacific Railroad, what the mention of that creaky wagon of his leaves unstated (but calling for attention) is the way social class is valued in, among other places, Yoknapatawpha County as well as in Winfield County. The Bundrens, or the Snopes, conventionally occupy the wagon seats.

A second mingled thread of social fabric and literary convention lurks in Jason Hunt's name: Hunt is monosyllabic, Anglo-Saxon, and appropriate to his character, driving for success, hunting a place in society through marriage. But Jason? There may be some shrewd overtones of the hardware store in Faulkner's *The Sound and Fury* and of the classical hunter of the Golden Fleece, although as a literary convention such classical non-biblical nomenclature is more likely to be used for ante-bellum established families. Old Testament names and first names derived from the mother's maiden name are more prevalent for families of his background.

A Hypocrite. About what? Something that's going to come, but can't be spoken out for. The good ol' boys of Winfield County might make it dangerous, even for adult, widowed Marcia Mae to go to a public gathering. Quite possibly, northern readers of the 50s could react smugly to this point, in a way no longer possible today. The reviews of the novel, after the Supreme Court decision on school desegregation, emphasized this theme of Civil Rights, indicating that the novel offered a cautious hope for tomorrow and a contemporary sermon to the hoodlums blocking the schools in Little Rock. As Louis Rubin pointed out later in *South: Modern Southern Literature* (1961). "Miss Spencer is also aware that, important though the race problem may be, most people, even in the South, do not spend every waking moment thinking of it." Nash K. Burger, writing at some length in the *South Atlantic*

Quarterly (1964) about the Mississippi background for all of her first three novels, indicates the pervasive contest between two white social classes and the energy focused on what is 'the respectable thing', buttressed or shored up by whatever means necessary to maintain it. To use his phrase, "Miss Spencer has much that is true to say to both North and South."

A closer examination of what is left unspoken, conveyed only by costume or gesture or setting, often sharpens the effect of this sense of family or respectability, leaving the theme of Civil Rights, topical though it was (and is), submerged in the evocation of mores and morals which in themselves frame accusations of hypocrisy much more fundamental to the social fabric than even the admittedly powerful taboos regarding race. Consequently, the "moral" which the author puts into italics to highlight her climactic scene (when the Acting Sheriff tells the Negro he is taking into protective custody to sit in the front seat of the car, next to the Sheriff's wife, while two good ol' country boys look on infuriated), bears wider application, as a 'moral,' than just to racial relationships:

> So it comes down to this, Duncan thought. To the tiniest decision you can make. To the slightest action. In front of people daring you to do what you believe in and they don't. "There's plenty of room in front." he said.

Beck Dozer doesn't get in, however, until Mrs. Harper says, sliding over, "Of course there's room." Although the sheriff's action, a high point in the literary fabrication, the structure of the novel, can seem incredible, unreal, whether South or North, now or in the 50s, many other actions in the novel, particularly those revealing the pressures of the "respectable thing" and the patterns of saying what one does not believe have "much that is true to say to both North and South."

The classic paradigm for this is the form of addressing Whites used by Southern Negroes. The Whites' view of the Black as Step'nfetchit, clownish, wall-eyed, "acking dumb," keeping his true face only for his own race in order to avoid being "uppity," has been a widespread one, not limited to the South, and we are beginning to get some measure of its psychic costs for both parties involved. An aged colored auntie who has nursed white folk, infant and sick, can "sass you to your face" as old Aunt Mattie says in this novel, since the establishment of a very personal interaction bends the customary racial taboos, allowing real feelings to be uttered.

Saying what one does not believe is often associated with politics, especially in a State where prohibition laws were still "enforced." Some understanding by the reader of the unspoken alliances of beer dealers and Baptists to keep out legal whiskey will sharpen his skill in watching the pattern of the tactful hypocrite and the influence it has on the aspiring young politician, causing him to wave the Confederate flag on the stump in the tradition of Vardaman and Bilbo, whatever his personal beliefs. The epilogue at the end of this novel, however, treats not the public political stance of smart, clever, state representative Kerney Woolbright, 25, recently of Yale Law School and now running for State Senator. It examines instead the reactions of the Hunt family (into which he is marrying) to a different hypocrisy, a more private one.

Kerney, after identifying himself closely with Duncan Harper, has publicly divorced himself from the position of "equal rights before the law, as the Constitution guarantees," which the Sheriff has taken, convinced that no one can get elected by speaking out in favor of it, even though he believes the time is coming. His private lie involves a telegram for Harper given to Kerney, containing proof that Beck Dozer is innocent. Kerney kept it, but is asked by Jason if he had read it before making his break with Harper known. Jason's attitudes we have seen; Marcia Mae sides with Harper (her lover, who has just gone back to his wife — another area of tactful hypocrisy); Mrs. Hunt, the true Southern Belle, tells Kerney to follow the impulses of his heart, not Jason's reasoning or rationalizing — a tactic that indirectly convinces him to do the opposite. *Reason* is more trustworthy than *trust* or *faith,* concepts often invoked in the appeal for equal rights. Duncan Harper, after all, *trusts* Beck Dozer's innocence.

Before Kerney is able to come clean, admitting that he knew the contents exonerating Beck, Cissy, his 19 year old fiancée, interrupts, saying she saw him hand it to Duncan *unread.* In agreeing with her, Kerney lies again, but as Marcia Mae points out, the whole family knows it, although they will continue to lie for him: "They will organize themselves for evasions and excuses . . . for your sake and their own." They will all act on the fiction, as if his lie were truth, all hypocrites, all mistrusting each other. Why would Cissy step in and lie? Did Kerney Woolbright pull the wool over her eyes? What threads in the social fabric and in conventional literary characterization motivate her actions? The shielded young Southern belle, placed on a pedestal, attentive to the appearance of things, is a second classic paradigm, both literary and cultural, for putting on a different face, for saying what is expected but not necessarily believed.

A subtler reflection of the expected behavior for a young woman is encapsulated in Marcia Mae's actions walking to a lovers' rendezvous with Duncan at an old deserted Negro cabin. Before she had walked out of the screened side porch where she and Cissy had taken refuge because their mother had a caller (they weren't dressed to receive company), she had tucked her shirt into her shorts and grabbed up a wrap-around skirt. (Properly brought up young women don't go out in shorts, even on a walk where they intend not to be seen; it's probably like not wearing unmended lingerie in case you're in an auto accident.) As she came "from the woods into open pasture, she took off the skirt that had shielded her legs from scratches and some idea of snakes, and threw it over her head for protection against the July afternoon sun." (Expected respectable behavior — to shield the delicate white skin, the attractiveness of surface — even shielded from some *idea* of snakes. What 'snakes' had Cissy's upbringing given her any ideas about?

Cissy's mother had often commented that some girl (and by implication, Marcia Mae) had not married well "because she didn't play her cards right," that she should "keep Kerney guessing," that "if you gave a man what he wanted he wouldn't want it any more." Intense concentration on doing her nails or fussing about her clothes could be approved and going on for hours saying "what a silly, silly old boy you are" pleased men immensely. At one point, however, she does react bluntly, "I don't like the way you're doing me, Kerney. . . . All I'm supposed to do is talk baby talk to you. I do it when I don't feel like it one bit. I think it's the silliest thing I ever heard of. . . . You're treating me the way Daddy treats Mother. He never tells her anything. . . ."

After she had found the undelivered telegram on the seat of the car as they drove away from Kerney's speech repudiating Harper, Kerney pleaded with her, parked near a country cemetery, to deny to anyone that she knew anything about the telegram (which she really didn't care about, anyway). Then, when she said she'd have to ask Papa, he had forced her down on the car seat, which "posture she had for some time been dreaming about in bed. 'Oh', she kept saying in various ways until his mouth stopped her. She discovered she had been absolutely right in thinking how boring most things were." Later, discovering that "her pretty cotton eyelet underthings were dragged awry, she did not mind; this was why they were so pretty." She promised never to tell — about the telegram, either. That afternoon, she and her mother slowly turned the big slick pages of the June magazines that her mother had saved, "leaning together near the corner of the sideboard where the light came in strongest through the bay window." So much for Southern belles, and some idea of snakes.

As Kerney tells Cissy at one point earlier when she observes that all the men like to protect Tinker Harper, but she doesn't seem to have any girl friends, "You women are all snobs. . . . You think, Oh, Tinker *Taylor*. The one that chased Duncan Harper till he finally married her. . . . She's nobody but old Gains Taylor's daughter." And Marcia Mae, who had been Duncan Harper's fiancée in 1940 until she had run away, "retained a satisfying impression of Tinker too carefully matched in navy and white, even to navy and white pumps. You would wonder perhaps if in her navy bag there was not a white handkerchief with a navy figure." What is the respectable thing? "It comes down to this. . . . To the tiniest decision you can make. . . ."

Dorothy Van Ghent, reviewing this novel with many others in the *Yale Review* (1957) under Taine's concept of Race, Moment, Milieu, referred specifically to Miss Spencer's power to create "the illusion of life lived," even though she treats of clichés in the actions and attitudes of her central characters. "Cliches wouldn't be cliches if they didn't have truth in them, as perhaps every insight of literature is insight into a cliché, a vitalization of the formally given. . . ." The unobtrusive use of the conversational cliché, possibly freighted with more than one meaning, is deftly handled when Jimmy Tallant (who has loved Tinker unsuccessfully these many years) calls up, knowing that Tinker has been low because of Duncan's renewed affair with Marcia Mae, his pre-war fiancée. At a natural pause in the small talk, he asks, "How are things, Tink?" To her reply, "Everything's okay," he immediately responds, "Then I guess Harper must be home." Duncan is in the house, overhearing the non-committal conversation, but also home, back at his hearthside, the pull of Marcia Mae over and done with. This plays off two levels of meaning for the unwary reader, vitalizing what would otherwise be a cliché quickly skimmed over. Most of us know of conversations which have that two-level quality.

To gain "the illusion of life lived" in the following situational cliché, you surely don't have to have already looked into an anthropologist — or into William Faulkner. Not only in a southern Sheriff's office would two men, hovering near the gas heater on a just-freezing February day, watch the young secretary, wrapped up good in her coat, leave on her coffee break and cross the courthouse square, and then speculate whether the bare space between a girl's stockingtops and her pants would get cold — that is if she was wearing any. "You think Miss Mattie Sue wears pants?" "Never looked into it," said Jimmy Tallant. "Have you?"

Flannery O'Connor's Vision: The Violence of Revelation

by KENNETH FRIELING

*From "The Teaching of Literature" as reprinted in *Mystery and Manners* (New York: Farrar Straus & Giroux, 1969), p. 124. All future references to her essays will be to their location in this collection of her occasional writings; all references to her stories will be found in *A Good Man Is Hard to Find* (New York: Harcourt, Brace & World, Inc., 1955).

Paradoxically, Flannery O'Connor's themes are so traditional as to make her fiction seem unique within the context of the 50s. During a period in which regionalism was becoming suspect, O'Connor rooted her hilariously — often painfully — textured concrete reality in the regionalism of the Georgia sector of the Bible Belt. In a time whose literature still avoided absolutes in its various existential stances, she presents an anti-existential vision of a world offered the mystery of grace, the possibility of redemption through violent revelation. While always aware of being a practicing Catholic in the Protestant South, O'Connor is most fully aware of her challenge as an artist in a much broader area: "the business of fiction is to embody mystery through manners, and mystery is a great embarrassment to the modern mind."

A facile explanation of her reputation would be to ignore her fusion of Catholic mystery and Southern manners and point rather to the extraordinary verve of her brilliant style by which she presents grotesque characters experiencing horror coalesced with dark comedy, as in this brief scene in "A Good Man Is Hard to Find":

> . . . [the mother] was sitting against the side of the red gutted ditch, holding the screaming baby, but she only had a cut down her face and a broken shoulder. "We've had an ACCIDENT." the children screamed in a frenzy of delight.
> "But nobody's killed," June Star said with disappointment . . . (19).

Much attraction lies in O'Connor's ability to depict her characters' shallowness in one adroit comment ("Mrs. Hopewell had no bad qualities of her own but she was able to use other people's in such a constructive way that she never felt the lack" — 171), to expose their love of possessions as thoroughly alienated from what is natural (Sally Poker gushes that her corsage "was made with gladiola petals taken off and painted gold and put back together to look like a rose. It was exquisite" — 158), and to present the characters' self-parodies through an outrageous image (the American patriot's self-designed advertisement for his cafe ironically smacks of Commie commercialism: RED SAM! THE FAT BOY WITH THE HAPPY LAUGH. A VETERAN! RED SAMMY'S YOUR MAN!).

Yet one cannot stop at this point, for her portraits of the physically grotesque reflect the spiritually distorted. Flannery O'Connor's tragi-comedy exists somewhere between Nathanael West's black humor and what Melville called the "blackness' of Nathaniel Hawthorne. Thomas Mann's observation that modern art no longer recognizes the categories of comic and tragic but "sees life as tragi-comedy, with the result that the grotesque is its most genuine style" is reflected in the concluding tableaux of most O'Connor stories (this is hardly unique — but again in the tradition of the greatest of religious literature, such as the *Divine Comedy*). Furthermore, as she emphasizes in her essay, "The Fiction Writer & His Country,"

> The novelist with Christian concerns will find in modern life distortions which are repugnant to him, and his problem will be to make these appear as distortions to an audience which is used to seeing them as natural; and he

may well be forced to take ever more violent means to get his vision across to a hostile audience. (*M & M*, 30) .

Just as her readers must recognize the grotesque as something other than horrific sensationalism, O'Connor's characters must recognize through violent revelation the grotesque as ugly, as unnatural distortion, and thus achieve the possibility of grace. In its basic form her grotesque is not a Gothic extravagance, but is as real and subtle as Mrs. Sortley's reaction to the family of the "displaced person" in the story of that title: "The first thing that struck her as very peculiar was that they looked like other people" (198). Most characters are unable to achieve a complete recognition, a revelation with the force of violence such as that exploding from the confrontation of the Misfit and the Grandmother in "A Good Man Is Hard to Find."

As the Misfit proceeds to kill her son Bailey and his family even while wearing Bailey's parrot-blue-and-yellow shirt, the benignly bothersome grandmother switches from the cliché of the story's title to another, "You should pray." His response to her pleading admonition explains his emblematic name and its cause, the terror of free will, man's agony of choice:

> He [Jesus] thrown everything off balance. If he did what he said, then it's nothing for you to do but throw away everything and follow him, and if He didn't, then it's nothing for you to do but enjoy the few minutes you got left the best way you can — by killing somebody or burning down his house or doing some other meanness to him. No pleasure but meanness (28).

His twisted face (and her son's shirt) next to her wrenches a violent recognition from the grandmother, " 'Why you're one of my babies. You're one of my own children! She reached out and touched him on the shoulder." She has seen her own self as one of the spiritually grotesque, as the mother of misfits, and thus achieves grace even as the anti-prophet Misfit shoots her "three times through the chest" so that her body forms an inverted crucifix in her own blood, her "face smiling up at the cloudless sky."

But the Misfit's violence is also self-revelatory, for, although his immediate reaction to her epiphanic gesture is to spring back "as if a snake had bitten him" and shoot her, he recognizes the real significance of her cliché ("She would have been a good woman . . . if it had been somebody there to shoot her every minute of her life"). As he senses her body's symbolic death gesture, he is prepared for his moment of grace in his next revelation, the story's last line: "It's no real pleasure in life" (29).

This recognition of the grotesque is accomplished through a violent displacement unleashing epiphanies with elemental religious force. The very violence of this epiphany and its accompanying potential of grace demands a vehicle which is brief, which is emphatically personal, which illuminates rather than explicates. Thus Flannery O'Connor most successfully presents mystery through manners within the structure of the short story.

This violence of revelation is artistically presented by O'Connor in her first collection of stories *A Good Man Is Hard to Find* through four interrelated techniques or "experiences," here artificially distinguished in order to discuss their function: (1) the recognition of an emblem's full significance, (2) the realization of a cliché's true implications, (3) the emerging epiphanic gesture indicating the recognition of humanity and the acceptance of grace, and (4) the violently catalytic effect of the presence of a prophet figure, typically an anti-prophet. Thus, the primary force of the title story, as mentioned above, emerges from the recognition of the emblematic significance of the name "Misfit" and the son's shirt, of the realization of the "good man" cliché's actual meaning, and of the gestures of the grandmother's touch and the Misfit's shot of recognition — all fused by the catalytic presence of the anti-prophet, the Misfit.

These artistic techniques — which are not merely extraneous stylistic tricks but the mode of revealing characters' interreacting experiences — are the basis for Flannery O'Connor's transcendence of the facile tags "religious writer" and "regionalist" in their pejorative sense, and further elucidate her success with the briefly illustrated (rather than novelistically resolved or explained) tableaux of the short story form. Nevertheless, the stories of *A Good Man* do comprise a related whole. This larger unity is not only one of a common thematic vision but also one of technique, as each story presents variation of the interrelationships of the four basic experiences which violently jolt the character into a realization of the possibility of grace.

Often the recognition of an emblem's significance is the most important experience of the character (and concurrently, the technique of the author). When the shirt of her son is later worn by the Misfit, it helps, emblematically, the grandmother recognize the Misfit of her "son"; in "A Stroke of Good Fortune," Ruby, fearing pregnancy and having ominous fainting hallucinations of being in a cavern, is violently approached by a neighbor's child, Hartly Gilfeet, whose Christ-suggestive name is further emphasized by his pet name, "Mister Good Fortune." After her gesture of taking away his prophetic phallic pistol when she realizes it is not a threat, she will recognize humanity by having her baby. Thus the implication of the cliché of the title are realized.

However, the emblem and clichés true significance are not always recognized. In "A Good Man is Hard to Find" the anti-prophetic Misfit's final decision is ambivalent and unresolved, while in "The Life You Save May Be Your Own," the one-armed drifter, Mr. Shiftlet, cannot recognize distortions for what they are because of his self-blinding penchant for moralizing.

The Misfit's choice — to follow Jesus, or to deny Him and destroy — is paralleled by the Manichean split that distorts Mr. Shiftlet's pseudo-spiritual view: "The body, lady, is like a house: it don't go anywhere; but the spirit, lady, is like an automobile: always on the move" (63). Like the Misfit, Shiftlet is presented with an extraordinary experience, but Shiftlet seems immune to revelation. After leaving his newly-wed idiot wife Lucynell Crater in the significantly named Hot Spot Diner (having recognized the "luney" but not the "knell" of her name as an emblematic "angel of Gawd"), Mr. Shiftlet ignores the billboard clichés of the road, "the life you save may be your own," as well as the gesture of outrage in a hitchhiker's violent reaction to Shiftlet's insincere eulogy to motherhood. Yet Shiftlet's own fusion of the inanimate (in the auto-spirit metaphor) with the spiritual is inverted as he drives his car to Mobile while "there was a guffawing peal of thunder from behind and fantastic raindrops, like tin-can tops, crashed over the rear of Mr. Shiftlet's car" (68). Evidently he is to be offered yet another chance for revelation.

A true revelation is experienced by Mr. Head and his grandson Nelson as they are jolted into a recognition which heals the one's betrayal and the other's pride by an outside object, the emblematic plaster "Artificial Nigger," in which they recognize themselves as truly grotesque. They are not like the vital Negro woman met earlier, but like a fake Negro that is a plaster statue. Further, since Mr. Head had denied kinship to Nelson after the boy had knocked down a black woman carrying groceries, the statue becomes an emblematic "monument to another's victory that brought them together in their common defeat" (128).

At this story's conclusion Mr. Head's violent epiphany of the emblem's significance made his name now inappropriate as he "felt the action of mercy touch him . . . he knew that there were no words in the world that could name it. He understood that it grew out of agony." Finally, he realized that "no sin was too monstrous for him to claim as his own, and since God loved in proportion as he forgave, he felt ready at that instance to enter Paradise" (129).

More typically, the emblem of potential revelation is somehow a physical part of the character whose moment of grace is made possible by recognizing the actual significance of that emblem. Thus, although Powel's sweatshirt with its faded destroyer print in the "Circle in the Fire," like Bailey's shirt, is an emblem outside the body of the person given the chance for grace; in "Good Country People" Joy Hopewell's sweatshirt with its faded cowboy on a horse, like her wooden leg, is the emblem demanding her self-recogniztion. She must see these as well as her "weak heart" and her Ph. D. in atheism for the grotesque emblems of her spiritual state that they truly are. Joy had changed her name to "Hulga," an act embracing what she sees not only as her most creative gesture, but as an ugly joke symoblizing the disgust and constant "outrage" she experienced at home. Her plan to seduce an uneducated, itinerant Bible salesman, Manley Pointer, seems to succeed for her at first as she manages to entice him to the loft in a deserted barn, especially when he voices what she is so proud of, "you ain't like anybody else."

However, this is a false recognition which denies all bonds with humanity — it is like the subsequent false seduction in which lust and love are both noticeably absent. Relying on Manley Pointer's being "good country people," but forgetting that the best representative of this cliché is Mrs. Freeman whose interests center on lingering illnesses and on the mechanics of the sex act in an iron lung, Hulga (Joy no longer) is unprepared for the violence of her recognition when Manley disengages her wooden leg (emblematic of her wooden soul), shouts to her "you ain't so smart. I been believing in nothing ever since I was born," and in a scene of supreme black humor, leaves her stranded, legless, in the barn loft (195).

But Manley Pointer, the Christ-dutied anti-prophet whose name indicates his function, has jolted Hulga into seeing her present state as hopelessly grotesque; he has pointed her back to her true state as a part of mankind and also to her state of Joy as he leaves with her wooden leg — an obvious symbolic gesture. In her final violent revelation she seems to see him emblematically as Christ on the waters: "When she turned her churning face toward the opening, she saw his blue figure struggling successfully over the green speckled lake" (195).

The symbolic name change and the importance of the regenerative water image is even more significant in "The River," in which ignored, unloved, city-bred Henry Ashfield is taken by his rough day-sitter to her rural home where he violently confronts an ugly hog, then is told that the man "wearing a white sheet" in a picture is the Jesus Christ who is depicted elsewhere as a "carpenter driving a crowd of pigs out of a man" and finally is taken to the river to a healing service being held by Reverend Bevel Summers, who calls people to lay their pain in the "River of Faith, in the River of Life, on the River of Love, in the rich red river of Jesus' Blood" (41). As he is baptized, Henry Ashfield's gesture is a cry, "my name is Bevvvuuuuul." After another frightful experience in the city wasteland the renamed boy returns to the river to carry out his final gesture of revelation, the realization of his new name as he makes the "inclination" from his past life as Ashfield by walking out into the river. The catalyst of Bevel's final gesture is the doubting Mr. Paradise (the anti-prophet as emblematic pig-devil) who storms after Bevel in an ironic attempt to save him from physical drowning:

> Then he [Bevel] heard a shout and turned his head and saw something like a giant pig bounding after him, shaking a red and white club [a peppermint stick] and shouting. He plunged under once and this time, the waiting current caught him like a long gentle hand and pulled him swiftly forward and down. For an instant he was overcome with surprise; then since he was moving quickly and knew that he was getting somewhere, all fury and his fear left him (52).

Bevel's revelation is parallelled by that in "A Late Encounter with the Enemy," of 104-year-old General Sash, who after hallucinating his daughter's graduation procession of B. S. candidates into the procession of the past, of words, and then the "black procession" of death, finally "made such a desperate effort to see over it . . . that his hand clenched the sword until the blade touched bone" (167). The sword of God seems to free the General as he dies just as the river of the Blood of God frees Bevel from life.

The violent revelation of grace relies often on a particular type of grotesque — the freaks which Reverend Summers mentions, "I read in Mark about an unclean man, I read in Luke about a blind man" (41). These New Testament freaks, who appear in these stories as such persons as Hulga Hopewell and Mr. Shiftlet, are, says Flannery O'Connor, "images of the man forced out to meet the extremes of his own nature"; they are figures "for our essential displacement" (M & M, 45).

In "A Temple of the Holy Ghost," the young girl, a self-prophet who — in contrast to Shiftlet — realizes her own shortcomings in that she "could never be a saint, but she thought she could be a martyr if they killed her quick," is at first obscenely interested in a circus hermaphrodite who is described to her by two cousins. While these two anti-prophets consider a Temple of the Holy Ghost to suggest a tasteless sexual joke, the young girl is awakened during a violent nightmare to the true significance of the religious cliché and eventually becomes that temple in which the epiphany of God's forms are seen: "When the priest raised the monstrance with the Host shining ivory-colored [as the sun had earlier been described] in the center of it, she was thinking of the tent at the fair that had the freak in it" (100). As in the last story in *A Good Man Is Hard to Find,* Christ is, like the freak, displaced in his human condition; however, he is also, in his Godly condition, the Son. Indeed, the final scene presents a Stephen Crane-like image in which "The sun was a huge red ball like an elevated Host drenched in blood" (101).

Thus, although the prophet's — as well as the anti-prophet's — vision usually jolts others into a violent recognition, the self-prophet who is honest may also achieve this epiphany by the paradoxical denial or questioning of self. The import of the prophet's function is continually stressed by Flannery O'Connor, who even uses his vision as a metaphor for the vision of the writer of fiction: "prophecy is a matter of seeing near things with their extensions of meaning and thus seeing far things close up. The prophet is a realist of distances and it is this kind of realism that you find in the best modern instances of the grotesque" (*M&M*, 64).

This necessity of man's recognizing the grotesque in others and in himself in order to experience the revelation of grace, the revealing of God as spiritual Sun, is brilliantly depicted in "A Circle in the Fire." The title refers to purification in purgatory as well as the visible presence of the Holy Ghost. Like women in other stories (Mrs. Crater, Mrs. Hopewell, Mrs. McIntyre, and the mother in "Temple"), Mrs. Cope is symbolically without a husband (Christ) and thus the family, usually representing firm religious faith, is incomplete. Mrs. Cope's reliance on the platitude "Everyday I say a prayer of thanksgiving" is as meaningless and impotent as the grandmother's admonition to the Misfit that if "you should pray . . . Jesus would help you." The prayer has to be acted, not voiced. In "The Circle in the Fire" the sun, becoming an omen for the issuing experience, "was swollen and flame-colored and hung in a net of ragged cloud as if it might burn through any second and fall into the woods" when Mrs. Cope is no longer able to cope with the three destructive boys who arrive ominously with a pig-shaped valise, refuse to leave, and further refuse to recognize the possibility of human ownership of nature such as Mrs. Cope's ownership of her precious woods. Naturally, the violent revelation follows.

When Powell and the other two boys talk of building a parking lot where the emblematic woods are, Mrs. Cope's daughter felt "some new unplaced misery" (153); when the three boys, catalytic prophets, set fire to the woods, Mrs. Cope discards her grotesque platitudes and violently experiences the new misery which allows her face to look "as if it might have belonged to anybody, a Negro or a European or to Powell himself" as she hears the three boys' shrieks "as if the prophets were dancing in the fiery furnace, in the circle the angel had cleared for them" (154). Obvious are the cross-references to the peacock's tail of suns in "The Displaced Person" and to Mr. Head's experience in "the Artificial Nigger" when "the action of mercy covered his pride like a flame and consumed it."

The very sudden violence of the epiphanies — the strain of the interaction of the characters functioning as prophets; the revelation of the significance of an emblem; the cliché's explosion of meaning; and, the final gesture either of freedom from life (Bevel, General Sash), or the recognition of fellow humanity (the grandmother, Mr. Head, Ruby), or the revelation of the presence of God (Joy Hopewell, Mrs. Cope, the girl in "Temple") — necessitates a brief, terse form of presentation. Flannery O'Connor's ability to illustrate the presence of the Mystery of grace through the violent fusion of image and gesture into a concentrated revelatory illumination explains her success with the short story form as well as her success in presenting her religious vision, the "sense of Mystery," to a contemporary audience which would probably be offended or bored by a more expanded explanation or apology, more typical of the novel. Her characters' epiphanies must be illuminated as the extremely personal individual experiences they are; the tendency toward the more general in the novel form would possibly destroy this sense.

A Death in the Family:
Agee's "Unfinished" Novel

by GENE W. RUOFF

"It is very remarkable . . . that the last works of celebrated artists, which they left imperfect, are always the most prized. . . . These are valued even above their finished productions. The broken lineaments of the piece, and the half-formed idea of the painter, are carefully studied; and our very grief for that curious hand, which had been stopped by death, is an additional increase to our pleasure."

Pliny the Elder, *Natural History*,
xxxv, 145, tr. David Hume

There are not many important unfinished novels in American literature. Those which do command our attention, such as *The Ivory Tower* and *The Sense of the Past* by Henry James, or *The Last Tycoon* by F. Scott Fitzgerald, do so more through their authors' stature than their intrinsic merit. We discover in these fragments the marks of their writers' past greatness, and perhaps, through a process of sentimentalization that is hardly escapable, we read into them as well the signs of potential triumphs which might have eclipsed even their earlier accomplishments. James Agree's *A

121

122

*Death in the Family,** published in 1957, two years after his death, is an exception. First, because Agee's work cannot trade on interest accrued by preceding masterpieces; if he ever achieved greatness, it is here. Second, because the novel is not nearly so unfinished as it has been made to appear by its publisher's decision to release it as an anthology rather than a work of fiction. Introduced by the famous lyrical prose reminiscence, "Knoxville: Summer, 1915," and larded with two lengthy narrative sequences of limited internal coherence, a novel that can stand comparison with any written this century lies buried and splintered between the covers of the volume. The hidden novel may be found in pp. 11-79, 115-212, and 249-339; the rest of the book — regardless of the quality of the writing — belongs with Agee's collected prose.

How *A Death in the Family* reached us in its present state can only be guessed. Apparently the story proper was contained in a continuous manuscript, divided into chapters and three basic sections by Agee himself. It concerns four days in the life of the Follett family: three consecutive days relate Jay Follett's last evening at home, his departure to visit the bedside of his father, who has suffered a heart attack, and his family's discovery of and response to Jay's own death in an automobile accident on his way back home. Separated by a short but undetermined space of time, the final day of the novel concerns Jay's burial. The editors who prepared the manuscript for publication acknowledge in their prefatory note the wholeness of the narrative of Jay's death: "The ending of *A Death in the Family* had been reached sometime before Agee's death." Still, they felt that certain editorial decisions had to be made: "The only editorial problem involved the placing of several scenes outside the time span of the basic story. It was finally decided to print these in italics and to put them after Parts I and II. It seemed presumptuous to try to guess where he might have inserted them. This arrangement also obviated the necessity of the editors having to compose any transitional material. The

---

*Parenthetical references to Agee's works are to the following editions: *AD*: *A Death in the Family* (New York, 1957); *AF,* I: *Agee on Film, Volume One* (New York, 1967); *LF*: *Letters of James Agee to Father Flye* (New York, 1962); *LU*: *Let Us Now Praise Famous Men,* with Walker Evans (Boston, 1960); *SP*: *The Collected Short Prose of James Agee,* ed. Robert Fitzgerald (Boston, 1968).

short section *Knoxville: Summer of 1915,* which serves as a sort of prologue, has been added. It was not a part of the manuscript which Agee left, but the editors would certainly have urged him to include it in the final draft." Those "editorial problems" have, in short, been created by the decision to include the extraneous episodes. However, the assumption that Agee himself would have included them may well have resulted from a baffled devotion to the author, since the completed manuscript which he left is wholly unlike any of the previous work which had brought him his small following. The last thing anyone might have expected of the writer who had published *Let Us Now Praise Famous Men* in 1941 and *The Morning Watch* in 1951 as his only book-length prose work, is a simply conceived, classically controlled piece of narrative fiction. Agee's previous marks as a prose artist had been made, to use Thomas Wolfe's terms, more as a "putter-inner" than as a "taker-outer."

Agee's first book of prose, *Let Us Now Praise Famous Men,* was a natural outgrowth of his schoolboy love of Walt Whitman, expressed to his former teacher and lifelong friend, Father James Harold Flye, in 1927: "I've been reading *Leaves of Grass* since I came back. You know, since last winter or so I've been feeling something — a sort of universal — oh, I don't know, feeling the beauty of everything, not excluding, slop-jars and foetuses — and a feeling of love for everything — and now I've run into Walt Whitman — and it seems to me as if I'd dived into a sort of infinitude of beautiful stuff — all the better (for me) because it was just what had been knocking at me unawares" (*LF,* p. 34). *Let Us Now Praise Famous Men* is almost literally an infinitude of beautiful stuff. In its own way as baffling as *Finnegans Wake,* Agee's piece of reportage attempts to tell the whole truth about the situation of the southern farm worker, while proclaiming at the same time that language is incapable of telling even a part of the truth about anything. Indeed, Agee claims that he would rather not even have written the work: "If I could do it, I'd do no writing at all here. It would be photographs; the rest would be fragments of cloth, bits of cotton, lumps of earth, records of speech, pieces of wood and iron, phials of odors, plates of food and of excrement. Booksellers would consider it quite a novelty; critics would murmur, yes, but is it art; and I could trust a majority of you to use it as you would a parlor game. A piece of the body torn out by the roots might be more to the point" (*LU,* p. 13) . In *Agee*

(New York, 1966), the first full-length critique of the writer, Peter Ohlin tries valiantly but vainly to describe the book's structure, because the book is a verbal collage. Detailed, objective description is juxtaposed against fierce self-laceration, prose is intermixed with verse, and appendices throw together fragments of newspaper columns, page-long lists of words and names, and a selection from William Blake's "Proverbs of Hell." Agee can allow no structure, not only because to organize would be to sell out life to art, but also because in this omnivorous account nothing is more important than anything else. Because Agee will let nothing be alien to his sensibility, everything is, or could be, incorporated in his book.

In direct contrast, *The Morning Watch* follows one of the main-streams of modern fiction in its attempt to extract the utmost psychological and symbolic significance from the most limited narrative material. The religious passion of the twelve-year-old protagonist, Richard, is balanced against the passion of Christ on Maundy Thursday and Good Friday. Driven to self-flagellation and crucifixion fantasies in his desire to imitate Christ, the boy is torn by an equally compulsive need to fit into the vulgarly human world of his schoolmates. Richard is confused about God's demands of man, and finally and most crucially, about the role of God in the death of his father. Agee's novella is almost imitative of James Joyce's presentation of Stephen Dedalus's religious crisis in *A Portrait of the Artist as a Young Man*. However, Agee's work is even more intense in its portrayal of the agony of the youth's spiritual failure, for he does not see it as adolescent crisis to be outgrown. The books are most similar, though, in their attempts to define a personality through the entire range of its emotional responses. *The Morning Watch* is set in Richard's consciousness, and Agee attempts to capture the total personality of his protagonist, past, present, and future, through one day's Gestalt of sensory responses and reflections.

The prose interpolations in *A Death in the Family,* all of which cover episodes in the life of Rufus Follett before his father's death, attempt to re-create the boy's sensory life in a manner close to that employed in *The Morning Watch*. Almost invariably they are more lyrically evocative and symbolically charged than the narrative into which they have been inserted. Read as a part of the novel, they move Rufus toward its center, turning the story of Jay's death into the central crisis of the boy's growing up. In reviewing the book,

Leslie Fiedler noted its internal contradictions, sensing a not wholly constructive tension between the narrative of Jay's death and the larger family saga suggested by the italicized passages. Although Fiedler was divided in his response to the work, he seemed to value the lyrical passages more highly than the narrative core: "The point is, I think, that Agee's talent is peculiarly *visual*, that the world comes to him in sharp fragmented sights — all detailed foreground" *(New Republic,* Dec. 9, 1957, p. 25). If one agrees that description is Agee's greatest gift, *A Death in the Family* could hardly do without its added passages; as almost everyone has remarked, they contain some of the most brilliant writing in the book. For example, the scene in which Rufus kisses his hundred and three (or four) year old great-great-grandmother, is almost unbearably realized: " 'Now kiss her,' his father said, and he drew out of the shadow of her bonnet and leaned far over and again entered the shadow and kissed her paper mouth, and the mouth opened, and the cold sweet breath of rotting and of spice broke from her with the dry croaking, and he felt the hands take him by the shoulders like knives and forks of ice through his clothes" *(AD,* p. 240). To have reproduced so intensely this moment of sheer physical sensation may well be a mark of descriptive artistry at its highest level. To have omitted such a moment because in the end it did not fit with his narrative intentions, is a mark not just of artistry but of moral character.

Agee did change his mind about what *A Death in the Family* was to be. When he first mentioned the project to Father Flye in a letter of March 2, 1948, he envisioned it as a chronicle of his early life: "I think I'd better not talk much about the piece of writing. A novel, short but longer than I had foreseen or thought best for it, about my first 6 years, ending the day of my father's burial" *(LF,* pp. 170-171). *The Morning Watch,* one might recall, had been set at age twelve and had flashed back to the father's death at its conclusion. In his final version Agee has settled on a presentation of the pivotal event itself, which does not evade or dilute its significance by turning it into the final epiphany of a bildungsroman. A recently published prose fragment of Agee's, which Robert Fitzgerald has been unable to date but takes to be the indication of a fresh start on the autobiographical novel, may point toward the ultimate form of *A Death in the Family*: "This book is chiefly a remembrance of my childhood, and a memorial to my father; and I find that I value my childhood and my father as they were, as well and as exactly as I can remember them, far beyond any transmutations of these matters I have made, or might ever make, into poetry or fiction" (*SP,* pp. 125-126). Agee's renunciation of poeticizing or fictionalizing in his story is far removed from his shrill outcries against art in *Let Us Now Praise Famous Men.* It announces instead a dedication to an older, perhaps more difficult, kind of art: that which represents reality in terms of a continuous action rather than as the reflection of a sensibility.

Still, to speak of even the central account of *A Death in the Family* as a representation of an action requires some elaboration, because many of the novel's most sympathetic reviewers objected particularly to its lack of narrative movement. Richard Hayes said the work had "no movement through that stream which is the medium of the great novels: the stream of time" (*Commonweal,* Sept. 12, 1958, p. 591); David L. Stevenson complained that "it lacks narrative thrust" (*Nation,* Dec. 14, 1957, p. 461); and in a long, loving essay, Dwight Macdonald remarked that its episodes "are often vividly rendered, in novelistic terms, but there is no plot, no suspense, no development, and thus no novel" (*New Yorker,* Nov. 16, 1957, p. 226). What these critics seem to be expecting from any novel that is not overtly experimental is a narrative of character conflict and development, laced with motifs which converge in some final dramatic resolution: at best a well-made novel, at worst first-class melodrama. Tad Mosel play-doctored Agee's narrative to inject just such excitement, and came up with *All the Way Home,* a stage version pretentious and phony enough to take two major Broadway awards in 1961. If this were what Agee had wanted, he could have done it handily. His 1950 script for John Huston's *The African Queen* demonstrates that he could stage-manage melodrama admirably, even if he never brought himself to think highly of it as a form.

However, Agee was after something else in *A Death in the Family.* He wanted not the kind of action through which character is suddenly and dramatically changed and shaped, but the kind through which character is simply revealed. In his character portrayal he aims not at the eccentric but at the ethical: "that which reveals moral purpose, showing what kinds of things a man chooses or avoids" (Aristotle, *Poetics,* vi, 16). Or, on a level less exalted but more in line with Agee's enthusiasms, the kind of action he found so characteristic of the silent movies he loved — Rufus' trip to the movies with his father begins *A Death in the Family.* Agee was struck with the way in which Charlie Chaplin's slightest, most individual movement could become a representation of general humanity: "At the end of *City Lights* the blind girl who has regained her sight, thanks to the Tramp, sees him for the first time. She has imagined and anticipated him as princely, to say the least; and it has never seriously occurred to him that he is inadequate. She recognizes who he must be by his shy, confident, shining joy as he comes silently toward her. And he recognizes himself, for the first time, through the terrible changes in her face. The camera just exchanges a few quiet close-ups of the emotions which shift and intensify in each face. It is enough to shrivel the heart to see, and it is the greatest piece of acting and the highest moment in movies" (*AF*, I, 10). Agee's novel is filled with such quiet gestures of character revelation. Stopping off for a drink after the movies, for example, Jay lifts his son onto the bar: " 'That's my boy,' he said warmly, 'Six years old, and he can already read like I couldn't read when I was twict his age.' Rufus felt a sudden hollowness in his voice, and all along the bar, and in his own heart. But how does he fight it, he thought. You don't brag about smartness if your son is brave" (*AD*, p. 16). Later in the night, when Jay is roused by his brother Ralph's drunken phone call to go to his father's bedside, his wife goes downstairs to fix a full breakfast for him: "Well, he thought, I can do *some*thing for her. He put his things on the floor, smoothed the sheets, and punched the pillows. The sheets were still warm on her side. He drew the covers up to keep the warmth, then laid them open a few inches, so it would look inviting to get into. She'll be glad of that, he thought, very well pleased with the look of it" (*AD*, p. 31). The small episodes convey economically Jay's character and the nature of his relationship with his family; he is proud of his son but awkward in expressing it, because Rufus' accomplishments fall outside the accepted masculine values of his Tennessee heritage. Uneasy in the presence of Mary's quiet, automatic devotion, he attempts to compete with her in considerateness; his inordinate pride is not just in having done something for her, but in having done something she will interpret as an act of love.

Of course, the novel does not rest principally on subtle gestures of character revelation. Its major action portrays the responses of Jay's family, first to the fear, then to the fact of his death. The most agonizing section of the book is the period of suspension in time between Mary's receiving the terse phone call, telling her Jay has been involved in an accident but relating no details, and the return of Mary's brother Andrew with the news that he had been killed instantly. Mary is caught between two conflicting needs: she must hope for the best for everyone's sake, yet she must anticipate the worst in order to prepare herself for what she instinctively knows has happened: " 'That's what I think,' Mary said, 'and that's what I'm ready for. But I'm not going to say it, or accept it, or do my husband any such dishonor or danger — not until I know beyond recall that it's so' " (*AD*, p. 138). Mary is joined in her vigil by her aunt Hannah, who is in some ways the most striking character in the novel. Throughout the wait, the burden of ethical decision is chiefly placed on Hannah: her every action must be weighed as to its effect on her niece. Her desire to reach out to help Mary is balanced by her knowledge that nothing she could do could help, that the best she can accomplish is to be there and to avoid hurting her. It is in the pain of Hannah's participation in Mary's emotions, feeling with and for her while at the same time weighing and judging the younger woman's actions by her own in a similar tragedy thirty years earlier, that we get the full sense of Agee's belief in the inherent goodness of humanity, a goodness which lies in nothing more than man's ability to act right in the fact of enormous pressure, or at least to want to act right. Although Hannah is afraid that Mary will fall into an unearned triumph of too-easy religiosity, towards which she has a natural tendency, she firmly keeps her fears unvoiced. Above all, Hannah's accomplishment as a human being is in her ability to forego lecturing on the basis of her own experience.

Hannah's impulses are not all noble: she is capable of a selfish exultation that someone else is now suffering what she has suffered. However, Agee will not allow her to be judged on her worst impulses. Throughout the novel he holds people responsible not for the possibilities for action they reject, but for the actions they undertake. Agee's belief in the sufficiency of functional goodness can hardly be over-emphasized. Readers miss the point who find in the obvious divisions between Mary and Jay — her orthodox piety, his non-belief; her urban refinement, his sometimes boisterous rusticity; her dislike of alcohol, his affection for it — indications of a marriage that would eventually have disintegrated. Whatever Mary's wistful hopes for Jay's conversion, whatever Jay's feelings of living under constraint, they had made the marriage work through the simple compromises, conscious and unconscious, that Agee establishes as the fundamental ground of human society.

In the long family conversation that follows Andrew's revelation of Jay's death, the family's unified spirit is earned rather than automatic, for its members are not in religious agreement. Joel, Mary's father, is a cynical humanist; Andrew tends to be a self-indulgent romantic agnostic; and Hannah's orthodoxy is far less securely optimistic than Mary's. The freakish cause of Jay's accident, a cotter pin lost from the steering assembly, with death itself resulting from one sharp blow to the chin, invites all manner of cheap irony and pious nonsense. The death can be viewed as anything from a malicious quirk of fate, one chance in a million, to a mercifully quick escape from lingering pain and invalidhood. Indeed, in the ensuing philosophical exchanges there is an occasional angry flurry. But basically the disagreements are muted by the individuals' awareness of responsibility to one another. In this section the work becomes a novel of ideas as well as human interaction, encompassing what Kenneth Seib calls, without exaggeration, "almost the entire range of human speculation about . . . that sense of the absolute which we must all confront sooner or later" (*James Agee: Promise and Fulfillment*, p. 76). However, in marked contrast to common practice in novels of ideas, the concepts here are generated by the action; they never take over its direction, and the characters never become ciphers for philosophic positions. What is more unusual, though, the novel's ideas are not really placed in dramatic conflict. Because the characters are working toward the common goal of understanding and accepting the death of Jay, their views are more complementary than contradictory. Agee wrote in *Religion and the Intellectuals,* a forum in *Partisan Review,* XVII (1950), that his own beliefs were inconsistent: "I veer between belief in God, non-belief, and a kind of neutrality. In all three frames of mind I keep what I believe is meant by the religious consciousness" (p. 112).

Such a unity within diversity holds the family together when Mary senses a mystical visitation of Jay's spirit within the house. Both Hannah and Mary are convinced of Jay's actual presence. Mary to the point of speaking to her husband, while Andrew can only say, 'No, I had no idea *what* it was. But I know it was *something*" (*AD,* p. 188). Even Mary's mother Catherine, who is so deaf the others must speak directly into what she fondly calls her good ear, is certain she heard footsteps. Although Joel himself is confused and embarrassed, he tries to understand: "The least I can do is accept the fact that three people had a hallucination, and honor their belief in it" (*AD*, p. 188). The quiet ease with which Agee introduces the supernatural into the novel may reflect his reading of Charles Williams, which he mentioned to Father Flye in October 1952: "one of the very few contemporary religious writers who moves and interests me to read. . . . He takes the supernatural for granted, rather than semidoubtfully or on trust, let alone in any shading of agnosticism or atheism; and has a wonderful gift for conveying, and dramatizing, the 'borderline' states of mind or Being" (*LF*, p. 203). Jay's visitation evokes all these shades of response; Hannah particularly tries to understand the phenomenon in terms recalling Williams' characteristic descriptions of souls in mid-passage between the mortal and immortal regions, while Mary exhibits utter contentment in unrationalized experience.

The inclusiveness of Agee's religious values enables him to embrace even Father Jackson, the inhumanly frigid priest who begins his visit of consolation by lecturing the anxious and disturbed children, Rufus and Catherine, on the ill-breeding of staring at one's elders, and later infuriates Andrew by refusing to read the complete burial service over Jay's unbaptized corpse. When Father Jackson prays with Mary and Hannah, though, the ritualistic act becomes invested with a transcendent spirit apparent even to the uncomprehending, hostile ears of the children: "They realized that there was something to which their mother and their great-aunt were devoted, something which gave their voices peculiar vitality and charm, which was beyond and outside any love that was felt for them; and they felt that this meant even more to their mother and their great-aunt than they did, or than anyone else in the world did. They realized, fairly clearly, that the object of this devotion was not this man whom they mistrusted, but they felt that he was altogether too deeply involved in it" (*AD*, p. 298). Although neither the children nor Andrew can disentangle their personal dislike for Father Jackson from their evaluation of him, Agee makes it clear that for Mary and Hannah the unworthiness of the priest does not hinder the effect of the sacraments. Agee seems to have reached such a point of toleration in his own religious views, when in his response to the *Partisan Review* forum he finds the institutionalism of the Father Jacksons as necessary as any other aspect of religion: "Prophets, institutionalists and the neutral mass are as mutually indispensable as they are inevitable. Christian values, social and otherwise, have endured (insofar as they have), thanks to the interaction upon them, and upon each other, of the three" (p. 111). Within the novel, Agee accepts all humanly useful actions or attitudes as at least partial truths, perhaps even as parts of the same truth.

In terms of Agee's fictional achievement, to the extent that it is separable from his moral and philosophical achievement, his greatest triumph may lie in his presentation of the children of the household. They remain totally credible, bickering and fighting in the midst of events they only begin to understand. Agee's portrayal of himself as Rufus is almost ruthlessly exact: he wants to go to school on the day his father died, because he has a new yellow cap to wear and because having a dead father would make him important, just once, in the eyes of the older boys; he also wants his sister and him to be orphans, because, as he explains to his mother, they are something special: " 'Like the Belgians,' he informed her. 'French. When you haven't got any daddy or momma because they're killed in the war you're an orphan and other children send you things and write you letters' " (*AD*, p. 287). Rufus never takes over the center of the novel; he grows up no more than is appropriate to his age and understanding. More importantly, Agee somehow manages to keep Rufus-Agee, the adult artist, from entering into his portrayal of the child. This, I suppose, is what he meant by having come to value his childhood as it was.

The novel's concentration on its central action may explain some of its seeming fictional shortcomings. There is no consistent point of view, because at different times different characters assume predominant roles. As a character Rufus is obviously an incompetent vehicle through which to view the events, and even the sensibility of an adult as centrally concerned as Mary would distort them to some degree. Certain themes suggested early in the book, such as differences between Jay's and Mary's families, are dropped simply because subsequent events render them negligible. Background description of the characters is minimal, because everything really important about them is conveyed by their actions during the four days in question. The narrative itself is chronologically episodic rather than causal in structure, because that is the way in which the significance of the events is best revealed. Agee's fictional framework is the barest imaginable; only the content is rich, and the famous Agee prose rises as a tool to meet the richness of the revealed humanity.

In reviewing *A Death in the Family*, Dwight Macdonald commented that Agee needed a "sympathetically severe editor" (p. 232), such as Thomas Wolfe had in Maxwell Perkins. Ironically, Agee had finally found such an editor within himself. His success in narrative control within his novel has, I think, been fully recognized only by his friend Robert Fitzgerald: "Jim arrived at his austere style fifty years and a torn world away from Edwardian Dublin and Trieste; if it took him twenty years longer than it took Joyce, who else arrived at all?" (*SP*, p. 55). Perhaps we will be given in the 70s an edition of *A Death in the Family* that will make Agee's final destination and accomplishment less obscure. The novel can do very nicely without the consideration accorded "unfinished" works.

From Bernard Malamud, with Discipline and with Love

by WILLIAM FREEDMAN

Ah yes, the Fifties. Who can forget them? That was the Eisenhower decade, the decade before Civil Rights, before Viet Nam, before Berkeley, before The Living and naked theaters, the decade when presidents knew their places, Blacks and dissenters knew theirs, students, actors, and audiences theirs. In the Fifties if you didn't like what was going on — if indeed you were sufficiently awake to know what was going on and to know you didn't like it — you muttered something about next year and reported for work the following morning — ten minutes early. It was the decade of discipline; and art, doing its duty, reacted to life, whether through confrontation or self-conscious rejection and recoil. Discipline was one of the principal items on the literary menu, the specialty of the house if the restaurant happened to be kosher.

Discipline is no recent visitor to the house of fiction. It comes with the artist's territory; it is the architect as tenant. When Voltaire advises the cultivation of our gardens, Conrad the salvatory attention to busy work, Hemingway the stoic code, they speak of what they know. Each is translating out of his own creative experience and the recommendations are translatable back to their probable source: the disciplined business of authorship.

133

But during the Fifties we had something else to keep the subject dangling before us like a grotesque puppet. We had the lingering memory of the War, the War to end all thought of the end of war; and we had the bomb. The thought of recent past and likely future sent us scurrying in several directions. To some it suggested the need for a tighter leash on the not-so-latent beast. Human beings, even the most cultivated and sophisticated, were capable of savagery to which cannibalism was cycling in the park. Beneath it all we were fiends and we had better do what we can — all we can — to keep the fiend beneath it all. To others — we call them Beats — it suggested an Epicurean indulgence of the moment, each of which threatened to be the last. And it sent others — the overwhelming majority — back to the mindless absorption in the task of simply getting on, to the business of sweeping past and future under the rug of real and invented need. One way or another the questions of discipline, restraint, and self-control were on our minds, even if only, like the white bear we challenge ourselves not to think about, in the futile attempt to force them off.

Some read the Holocaust more closely and read more. They saw in the examples of Nazi and Jew a mad paradox of discipline. On the one hand discipline, a vital acquisition in our drift from caves to cities, was put at the service of our most atavistic instincts. If the Nazis used discipline, presumably the mark and tool of civilization, as an instrument of savage massacre, the Jews, contrary to its preservative function, seemed to use it in the passive acceptance of their own annihilation. Discipline to destroy others. Discipline to facilitate one's own destruction. Neither could be allowed again and the thoughtful, many of them writers, many of them Jewish writers, began to look harder for alternatives.

The artist who is also a Jew has a historical step on the field. His preoccupation with discipline is as much a part of his racial as of his professional heritage. According to the legend, before God gave his Law to the Israelites he went among all the other nations and asked of each, "Will you accept my Torah, my Law?" All refused it. At this, God came to Israel and asked, "Will ye accept the Torah?" They inquired, "What is written therein?" He answered, "Six hundred and thirteen commandments." And they replied, "All that the Lord has spoken we will do and we will hear." As Morris Bober would say, others had more sense; the Jews accepted. They were "The Chosen People," a very mixed blessing indeed, for it meant that in exchange for the most precious gift in God's possession, "the future world," the Jews had bound themselves to the 613 commandments — ethical rules, social duties, religious beliefs, dietary regulations, etc. And as Mark Zborowski points out in *Life Is with People*, his classic study of the East European shtetl (the smalltown Jewish community), "All life was oriented toward rigorous fulfillment of the commandments." Freud offers in *Moses and Monotheism* another explanation for the renunciatory character of Judaism — penitential submission to the hated father, "the consciousness of guilt because of that hostility, the bad conscience because one had sinned against God and continued so to sin." But the result is the same, and the consequences, though less prominent, are still very much in evidence. Judaism is a religion of what Freud calls "instinctual renunciation," and Jews pride themselves on their restraint, their self-control, their future-orientation that enables them to abstain from immediate gratification in the interest of long-range goals. In exchange for the blessings of "the future life" they will accept the Yoke of the Law or any other yoke that promises a brighter future, particularly *fur der kinder*. Those who seek to understand, like Jesus Ortiz, the assistant to Edward Wallant's Pawnbroker, the secret of Jewish worldly success, must begin here. The Jew will prepare, principally with education; he will endure, and he will wait. He will complain interminably about the yoke of his endurance, but he revels in the yoke as he revels in his complaints, for he interprets his renunciation as a mark of higher spirituality; and in terms of success as we habitually measure it, it pays off.

This is the heritage of the Jew and the Jewish author, and Jewish fiction is a window to it. Andre Schwarz-Bart's *The Last of the Just* (an unhappily forgotten book) logs the shamanic initiation of a latter day Just Man in search of his soul and his mission. Wallant's *The Pawnbroker*, tale of a concentration camp survivor, studies a defensive renunciation of feeling tantamount to death. Bellow's "heroes," particularly Joseph (*Dangling Man*) and Henderson, grope their way out of chaos toward order, accommodation, and discipline. "Hurray for regular hours!" shouts the no longer dangling man in the book's last lines. "And for the supervision of the spirit! Long live regimentation!" And Philip Roth, the hopelessly exceptional rule-maker, brings the tradition — along with a variety of others — to a delightfully agonizing (what could be more Jewish?) counter-climax in *Portnoy's Complaint*. Having lived through the 50s, not to mention the 40s and part of the 30s, with his eternal Jewish earth mother, goddess of fear, inhibition, repression, and constipation, Portnoy has had it up to there (yes there!) with restrictions, and with the orgiastic fury of the rebel he lights out for the territory of the female crotch: he ain't been there before.

But among Jewish writers none is more provocatively or more habitually concerned with the subject of discipline than Bernard Malamud. And the two novels he wrote between 1950 and 1959, *The Natural* (1952) and *The Assistant* (1957), bear the still tender scars of World War II. Both probe the animal nature of man, reveal a fearful mistrust of instinctual behavior, and struggle toward an answer in discipline and love. Discipline not at the expense of others, not at the price of self; but discipline in the service of others and toward a fuller realization of self.

The Natural is a baseball story, but beneath the uniform it is a mythic tale of pride, impulse, guilt, self-destruction, and the failure of self-control. Roy Hobbs is a congenital bad-ball hitter, a Knight who chases the wrong women and the wrong ideals even more persistently than he chases the wrong pitches; and though he gets away with both pursuits for a while, in the end, as inevitably he must, he pays. Roy's sin is hubris. He wants too much and he wants it for himself. His ambition, as he audaciously announces on his "Day," is "to become the greatest there ever was in the game." His fans feared the brash proclamation "might tempt the wrath of some mighty powerful ghosts," as ultimately it does, but his dream is more than audacious. More damagingly it is aggressive, a goal reached over the fallen bodies of competitors, each of whom looms not as a man but as an obstacle, and each of whom is clearly associated with the figure of the father, whom Roy did sometimes "want to skull." The inevitable litter of the parricide dream are guilt, self-hatred, and the impulse to self-destruction, and the habitual accidents and blunders that trip the questing Knight at the door of every chapel are not the inexplicable mysteries he imagines. Nor are they the fortuitous agents of a hypostatic fate. Ultimately we make our own fate, and Roy makes his of the symptomatic "accidents" that cloak his deepest needs. The premature celebration of the pennant is an act of hubris that tempts fate, but fate is inert. It will not respond to mere temptation; it must be met. The compulsive gluttony with which he "celebrates" and which cuts him down just before the crucial last series with the second place Pirates is pathological. It at once feeds his craving for self-annihilation and serves as a misguided attempt to satisfy still another buried hunger, a longing for expiation and purification. What Roy has not yet learned is that love and dedication to the needs of the larger group — the family, the team, mankind — are the true grail, not the triple devils of fame, wealth, and beauty he self-destructively pursues.

In the end he does locate the true grail in the person of the unbeautiful Iris and his child inside her, but it is too late. Although at last he has glimpsed the proper dream — "suffering," Iris had told him, "teaches us to want the right things" — he lacks the discipline, the habit of renunciation that builds a future and separates the successful grail Knights from those who strew the way. And that same failure obscures the dream itself. Roy is, at the end as at the start, a bad-ball hitter, a man who in his crying need for redemption cannot escape the impulse to overreach. Midway through the final game of the season, the playoff on which all depends, he moves to renounce the sellout he had agreed to in exchange for the temptress Memo Paris and the financial security she demands. We pay for our sins, however, often and ironically in the very act of inadequate atonement, and Roy, who should have been content with the fourth ball that would have kept the team alive, lunges for it instead — and strikes out. Hubris has to an extent yielded to redemption as his principal motivation, but bad habits, like corrupt goals, do not die with an expiatory gesture of the will; they must be gradually and painfully burned away. Even at the last he was thinking of himself — "only a homer with himself scoring the winning run would truly redeem him"; still he lacked the discipline to moderate his goals and to subordinate personal gain to larger dreams. The result is as familiar as it is inevitable: symbolic murder of another father figure, Pop Fisher, the team's manager to whom the pennant is almost literally a matter of life and death, and for Roy failure on triumph's edge.

What we need are the right goals, "the right things" which suffering teaches us to want, possible, non-destructive things like love and service and self-sacrifice. The price is discipline, self-control, the capacity for renunciation, for we live in a world where homemade fate smacks its lips around the corner and where our own aggressive impulses, plaguing guilt and self-hatred chase us up the street, our heads turned back, stumbling into its arms. Roy Hobbs learns the lesson too late, and when his sellout is exposed and the newsboy begs him to "Say it ain't true, Roy . . . he wanted to say it wasn't but couldn't, and he lifted his hands to his face and wept many bitter tears."

Only the most obstinately literal-minded will deny that *The Natural* is deliberately patterned along the lines of the mythic grail quest. It is Sir Percival at the bat. Roy plays, appropriately, for the Knights, and wields a phallic bat affectionately dubbed "Wonderboy," with which, in his first professional game he knocks the cover off the ball and brings the rain to the drought-parched stadium. This is good clean academic fun, but at times the mythic trappings become somewhat cumbersome, weighing the characters down, obscuring their humanity, and occasionally pulling the story in embarrassingly unplotted directions. Malamud's next and probably finest novel, *The Assistant*, likewise shows the author's unashamed familiarity with the stuff of myth and ritual: it is a fusion of initiation rite and initiatory quest. But Malamud is more at home in a Jewish grocery store than he is on the ballfield, and the dressing is mixed to suit the salad, not the other way around. What Malamud wants to say determines how, when, and whether he will employ the materials of rite and myth; there is little if any pull in the opposite direction.

"Initiation lies at the core of any genuine human life," writes Mircea Eliade in *Rites and Symbols of Initiation*. "And this is true for two reasons.

> The first is that any genuine human life implies profound 'death and resurrection.' The second is that, whatever degree of fulfillment it may have brought him, at a certain moment every man sees his life as a failure. This vision does not arise from a moral judgment made on his past, but from an obscure feeling that he has missed his vocation; that he has betrayed the best that was in him. In such moments of total crisis, only one hope seems to offer any issue — the hope of beginning life over again. This means, in short, that the man undergoing such a crisis dreams of new, regenerated life, fully realized and significant. . . . Such a renewal is the result of every genuine religious conversion.

Eliade's description of the initiate's crisis reads like the constitution of a club to which we all belong, but Frank Alpine, the Assistant, could make just claims to chairmanship. The account fits him with uncanny precision but for one point: his vision of failure does arise, at least in part, from a moral judgment on his past. Frank is trapped in an endless circle of uncertain origin but proved result. Like Roy Hobbs he wants too much too soon. Lacking a clear sense of where he is going, he is afflicted with a compulsive over-eagerness to arrive. He is the drowning man who, by lunging at what at least may be driftwood, only succeeds in pushing it further away:

> I work like a mule for what I want [he tells the Jewish grocer, Morris Bober], and just when it looks like I am going to get it I make some kind of a stupid move, and everything that is just about nailed down tight blows up in my face. . . .
> With me one wrong thing leads to another and it ends in a trap. I want the moon so all I get is cheese.

Alpine's trap is a fatal circle of guilt, recrimination, and failure. An impatient, often criminal act leads to guilt. Self-hatred born of guilt demands punishment in the form of another self-destructive gesture which adds to the weight of guilt, renews the demand for punishment, engenders another crime, and so on.

The only way out of the trap is through the definition of clearer and nobler goals and the acquisition of the eminently Jewish talent for renunciatory staying power, for the self-discipline that makes such goals attainable. The book plots the assistant's initiation under the tutelage and guidance of Morris Bober, the aging, and chronically suffering Jewish grocer, and of Bober's daughter Helen, the guilt-ridden dreamer with whom he falls in love (The story of Jacob and Rachel floats just beneath the surface). Frank begins to work in Bober's dismal store as an act of expiation. In a mad vision he had imagined himself destined for greatness in a life of crime, and the paupered Morris Bober, as both their lucks would have it, had been his first victim. Service in the store, then, begins as atonement — twelve hours a day, seven days a week virtually without pay — but it gradually develops into something more. The store is in effect the cabin, or cave (it is variously described as a "cave" and a "tomb"), where the tribal initiate dies out of the old life in order to begin a new one as a full-blown member of the tribe. The "tribe" in this case is of course the Jews, the Rabbi or priest is Morris Bober (a bobo

Moses or Martin Buber), the store's ledgers the Holy Books, and the inevitable apron the prayer shawl. There is no need to insist on these parallels. The point is unmistakable. Frank Alpine, the restless Italian drifter, undergoes through the imposed discipline of the store, through conversations with and the example of the infinitely enduring grocer, and for the love of his employer's daughter, a process of initiatory *re*discovery. "The perilous journey [of the hero]," observes Joseph Campbell in *The Hero With a Thousand Faces*, "was a labor not of attainment but of reattainment, not discovery but rediscovery. The godly powers sought and dangerously won are revealed to have been within the heart of the hero all the time." Frank Alpine undergoes the painful process of rediscovery, of locating that better self he knows lies buried inside him beneath the dirt of his compulsive behavior. He does not become a Jew so much as he discovers what Malamud elsewhere affirms: that in an important sense "all men are Jews."

The store confines him, restricts his movements, and inhibits his impulses. The grocer teaches him the habit of endurance with hope, interprets for him the Law his people received on Mt. Sinai (Morris is the English equivalent for Moses, and the name Alpine may be intended to suggest that Frank too must climb a mountain to make his Covenant). He teaches him the duties and ethical strictures that separate man from beast (Bober from Alpine at this point) and for which we must suffer; to suffer for the Law is to suffer for others. "What I like to know," demands Alpine almost defiantly, "is what is a Jew anyway?" "The important thing," replies Bober, "is the Torah. This is the Law — a Jew must believe in the Law. . . . This means to do what is right, to be honest, to be good. . . .

'I think other religions have those ideas too,' Frank said. 'But tell me why is it that the Jews suffer so damn much, Morris? It seems to me that they like to suffer, don't they?'

'Do you like to suffer? They suffer because they are Jews.'

'That's what I mean, they suffer more than they have to.'

'If you live, you suffer. Some people suffer more, but not because they want. But I think if a Jew don't suffer for the Law, he will suffer for nothing.'

'What do you suffer for, Morris?' Frank said.

'I suffer for you,' Morris said calmly.

Frank laid his knife down on the table. His mouth ached. 'What do you mean?'
'I mean you suffer for me.'
The clerk let it go at that.

Alpine is at this point still in darkness, but he is brought nearer the light by the grocer's daughter. Helen provides the assistant with a more specific goal, with something to suffer for — herself and her love. And she offers more specific instruction, bred of her own torment, on the question of means. Helen had yielded her body without love to another man. The price, paid and repaid daily, was guilt and self-hatred, but unlike Frank she knows the way out of the encircling trap of transgression and self-hatred.

She tells him he must develop discipline. The idea fascinates him; it touches the root of his need:

> Often since the time Helen had been in his room he had recalled her remark that he must discipline himself and wondered why he had been so moved by the word, why it should now bang around in his head like a stick against a drum. With the idea of self-control came the feeling of the beauty of it — the beauty of a person being able to do things the way he wanted to, to do good if he wanted . . .

But instruction alone is not adequate to the needs of conversion. Frank Alpine is, as he repeatedly insists, not the man he once was. He has changed; but not completely. He is not yet in control of his urges, his hungers, his aggressive and self-destructive impulses. The lessons of *The Natural* are the lessons of *The Assistant*. Habits nourished a lifetime do not readily loosen their bite. Nor can past sins be brushed away with a flick of the will; as Roy Hobbs learns to his grief, they may begin to draw blood in the very act of imperfect atonement. Ironically, the grocer catches Alpine with his hand in the till not when he is stealing but when he is borrowing back a fraction of the money he has finally begun to repay in a futile attempt at absolution.

To die out of the old life and be reborn is not the work of days; "to do what he had to do he needed years." But Frank is at once a wiser and a more fortunate man than Roy Hobbs. He learns what he must do and he is given the chance to do it. In Malamud's world, however, full recognition and reversal come only after all external supports have been removed; they come when the assistant has lost all outward assistance and is thrown back entirely on his own resources. Instruction is a necessary first step, but ultimately the initiate must face the dark alone. Not until his theft is discovered and he is evicted from the store like Adam from a dubious Eden, and not until his importunate love drives Helen all but irredeemably beyond his reach does he arrive at a full understanding of the tragic pattern of his life and the basic goodness — and Jewishness — of his buried self. This is the hero's moment of reattainment, of rediscovery.

When Bober's death removes another prop, Alpine has his chance. He has worked his way back into the store during the grocer's illness; Morris had never mentioned the thefts to either his wife or daughter, and the store is the family's only sustenance. It is also Frank's only hope, and his use of it indicates that like the initiate he is, he has found his personal identity in the identity of the tribe. Alpine, like Yakov Bok, the hero of Malamud's *The Fixer*, discovers himself through the private recapitulation of the sufferings, trials, and history of the larger group. And like Bok he discovers that his personal identity is indistinguishable from his group identity: one is discovered — or rediscovered — in the process of discovering the other and is in fact the other. But he can touch his tribal and thereby his personal soul only when forced back entirely upon and into himself, for the group soul sleeps in the private spirit and is discovered only in the ordeal of isolated responsibility. When everything else is gone, we discover ourselves and our intimate connection with, and responsibility to, everything else.

Morris Bober has died, his dream of a college education for his daughter apparently buried in his plain wooden coffin. To give his life meaning, Helen knows she must in some way, though it will take years, earn her degree. By quietly and self-effacingly dedicating himself to the realization of that dream, by working day and night, without encouragement but with discipline and with love, to send Helen through school, Frank breaks out of the circle of his personal hell and enters the divine circle of service. Morris gave to Frank his virtually barren store and the invaluable tradition of suffering for others with discipline, endurance, and with hope. With these gifts Frank will see to Helen's education, one purpose of which is to give posthumous meaning to the grocer's pathetic life. Thus each life gains meaning by what it gives to the next, and the divine circle of the Law, of doing for others, curves back on the point of its origin: the meaning of Morris Bober's life.

When at the end Frank is circumcised and becomes a Jew he ritually confirms the completed act of psychic conversion. But the event is more than mere ritual confirmation. The fact that it takes place in April, and that he becomes a Jew "after Passover" is particularly meaningful in the context of the season symbolism of the novel. The psychic and seasonal setting of the action is winter, the Sacred Time of the initiation of novices, and the eager anticipation of spring, the season of life, of renewal, weighs heavily on everyone's mind. To Helen it represents the season of fulfillment through love, release from the winter of her sexual guilt; and it is on a "warmish" "spring-like" late February night that Frank precipitously takes her on the grass. It is also a premature celebration of spring that kills Morris Bober who insists on shovelling snow without a coat on the last day of March and contracts pneumonia for his lone impulsive gesture. "Tomorrow is April," he reminds his wife. "What kind of winter can be in April?" The last of March is not April, but when Frank converts it is April, the season of renewal, and it is after Passover, the season of deliverance. The act is as appropriate as its timing. The circumcision is the mark of the Jew's covenant with God — his acceptance of the Yoke of the Law and his submission to a disciplined life dedicated to the fulfillment of God's commandments. And it is also a painful "ceremonial mutilation," a symbolic substitute for castration that, in Freud's view, signalled the initiate's submission to the father's will. Frank Alpine has submitted to the father's will, to the will of Morris Bober and to the will of his own conscience — the father as superego. What Roy Hobbs childishly destroys, Frank Alpine maturely accepts. But perhaps most importantly, he signals his acceptance in an act symbolic of sexual renunciation. He has been painfully transformed from "uncircumcised Dog!", from undisciplined beast, to circumcised Jew, the "man of stern morality."

James Purdy:
Shaman in Nowhere Land

by Donald Pease

In the United States there is even a pathos of inverted
emphasis: the goal is not to grow old, but to remain young;
not to mature away from Mother, but to cleave to her. . . .
Apparently there is something in those initiation images so
necessary to the psyche that if they are not supplied from
without . . . our energies should remain locked in a hard,
long outmoded toyroom at the bottom of the sea.

(Joseph Campbell, *The Hero With a Thousand Faces*)

Color of Darkness appeared in America in 1956. The book
presented eleven close-ups of very still-lifes and one novella, *63:
Dream Palace*. Purdy himself has summarized the message behind
this work along with his view of America in the 50s:

. . . my work is a criticism of the United States, implicit not
explicit. . . . This is a culture based on money and competition.
[It] is inhuman, terrified of love, sexual and other, obsessed
with homosexuality and brutality. Our entire moral life is
pestiferous, and we live in a completely immoral atmosphere.
. . . I believe the human being under capitalism is a stilted, depressed, sick creature, that marriage in the U. S. is homosexual-

145

ity and homosexuality a real disease. . . . (All quotations from Purdy appear in Webster Schott, "James Purdy: American Dreams," *The Nation*, March 23, 1964) .

The method for the stories involves an unreal emotional dialectic between friends or among members of a family. Each confrontation results in a revelation of mutual desperation rather than resolution.

The collection takes its title from the story of a man whose wife has deserted him. He suffers from an inability to remember the color of his wife's eyes, or, indeed, those of his maid, Mrs. Zilke, or his son, Baxter. Existential darkness does not facilitate color discrimination. But more importantly this amnesia characterizes what I believe to be the keynote of Purdy's work in the 50s — the impossibility of a rebirth in America. Ernst Cassirer points out that memory is "not simply a repetition but rather a rebirth of the past; it implies a creative and constructive process" (*Essay on Man*) .

In order to have a memory in any authentic sense, it is necessary to have grown up, to have undergone an initiation into the human community. Just how inaccessible this state is for the father in "Color of Darkness" becomes evident in his rumination:

She [Mrs. Zilke, the maid] was his "mother," he supposed.
And the boy [his son] was an infant "brother" he did not know too well, and who asked hard questions, and his "wife," who had run off, was just any girl he had gone out with. He could not remember now at all.

American dreams replace initiation rituals. As a result, American society stagnates in what Géza Roheim describes as "a huge network of more or less successful attempts to protect mankind against the danger of object-loss, the colossal efforts made by a baby who is afraid of being left alone in the dark" (*The Origin and Function of Culture*) . As Purdy states, "There don't seem to be any men or women in America; there are those who are young and have something before them—and then there are the others, mostly dead."

The ten other tales present a litany of freaks. A boy's loss of a father image compels him to eat his absent father's photographs. A black mother wishes her son in the "perfect" state of death rather than apart from her. A mother feels threatened by the appearance of her bearded son. Her dilemma increases when he sunbathes in the nude. "She wanted to call a friend and tell her but she had no friend to whom she could tell this." A wife wishes her husband dead so she can include him in her "memory book." A woman tortures her crippled husband with the fantasy of a raven who cries, "George is dead." A homosexual confesses his weakness for boys to his manly wife but promises, "I will always stand by you anyhow, Peaches Maud." A womanish man bitches about his office-mates' muscle-building program.

Despite the desperate denunciation in the themes of these stories, a promise remains in their method. In order to present his vision, Purdy had to perform some magic with technique. The actions proceed within the crucible of irony. In each of these stories, Purdy grounds the decaying spirits of the characters in an animistic world. His stay in Mexico supplied him a sense of primitivism he delicately balances with America's cultural decadence.

A businessman's lunch becomes an "offering." Perhaps too nascently, the "shrine" a widow builds for her husband is decorated with "toilet articles." An invalid's suffering "would make him swell in the chair until he looked like a god in ecstasy," but this was "just a man practicing for death, and the suffering illusion." After his parents' prolonged intimidation, a youth scrapes off his beard with a hunting knife. Purdy proffers, "his sacrifice had been in vain." A schoolmate remarks that a forty-year old "child" "looked so much like God or something mythological." A hen-pecked husband feels his wife's anger "covering him and glancing off like hot sun onto the wallpaper." After a boy sees the horrors of the city, his youth becomes "superfluous, as age to a god." A profane world encloses the sacred like a skin. When the reader almost despairs of life, Purdy suggests a pulse.

Purdy's best effects necessitate a primitive response from the reader. Consider his favorite device for gaining sympathy for a character, "He no longer looked like a child, but in his small un-mended night shirt like some crippled and dying animal running hopelessly from its pain." Purdy invests characters with therio-morphic qualities to suggest an almost totemic identification. Words themselves assume their original magical power. Before Peaches Maud pronounces Lafe a "queer," she listens for "any sound that might perhaps rescue them both together." When a crossword puzzle demands "clandestine," an invalid's wife realizes, "It was

148

a word which she had never said to anybody and it described her and haunted her like a face you can't quite remember the name for which keeps popping up in your mind."

An initiation rite united primitive man with nature, presented him with a sense of his place and destiny in the world. The absence of any contemporary equivalent alienates man from nature and himself. A disjointed nature encourages gratuitous brutality and violence—sad travesties of a longed-for adulthood. Man's mind darkens with irreconcilable dualisms. In this twilight world a face can look "grave, but at the same time amused," a room "both severe and cozy."

In such a world, there is no possibility for a viable marital relationship. A wife becomes either something to show off to "the boys" or a cover-up. In order to survive, American womanhood clandestinely becomes more of a man. Whenever a crisis arises, Lois McBane's husband disappears, "like a boy, without any sense of responsibility." The war of the sexes reflects the universal infantilism. In "A Good Woman," a plump housewife squares her bill for a month's supply of chocolate sodas by flirting with a divorced and aging druggist. After this conquest, she daydreams of strolling with her mother, "not like mother and daughter but like two good girl chums away at school."

Purdy's first attempt at a panoramic view of this nightmare world was *63: Dream Palace*. Perhaps contempt for a multiplying reading public that "can't bear to hear about anything that ain't human" led to the creation of Fenton Riddleway (see an oblique play on Holden Caulfield). Fenton, "wild as West Virginia," is very unlike Salinger's eternal pre-pubescents or Capote's anthropomorphic insinuations. He and brother Claire arrive at rat-infested, metropolitan "63: Dream Palace" after the death of their mother. American myths to the contrary Fenton and Claire have the same difficulty in the city as on the frontier, "Claire when West Virginia was bad, why did we come clear over here?"

Writer Parkhearst Cratty discovers Fenton lost in a park and offers him a "new life" as a replacement for "the greatlady" Grainger's late husband.

Fenton's louse-riddled brother is a threat to this "new life." He has visions of God, dreams of joining their mother on a star and sees through Cratty, the "greatlady" and Fenton. Society requires Fenton murder him. The presentation of their conflict — that between the profane and sacred — indicates a problem endemic to America, past and present. Their plight supplies an emblem more honest than Salinger's *unintended* absurdities or the Beats' ethereal masturbations. Zen saints perform about the same function for Americans in the 50s as morphine does for a corpse.

Fenton completes the ritual murder after smoking pot, exchanging borrowed clothes, and beating up a homosexual. His failure to remember the act underscores the futility of any rite of passage. Fenton begins his day, as usual, wakes up, greets Claire, gets the morning communion of coffee and donuts. But Holy Eucharist becomes Extreme Unction as Fenton watches the coffee dribble down Claire's neck "broken softly like a small bird's, the hair around his neck like ruffled young feathers, the eyes had come open a little and seemed to be attempting to focus on something too far out of his reach."

Fenton allays his guilt by initiating a ceremony without substance. As rats attend the viewing, he places Claire in a box with a bridal veil under a picture of Christ among thieves. Claire becomes a bride of Christ in death. Fenton kisses Claire's coffee-stained lips and picks up the box with the words. "Up we go then motherfucker." A sense of recurrent evil and loss pervades these words of endearment — a perfect ending.

That's the difficulty. The ending is too perfect. In the land of the dead, Apocalypse is a comforting illusion. Purdy's stories properly deal with the last things before the last. As Nera says in the play *Cracks*, "The world does not come to an end, no matter how great the pain or the loss." Purdy had not yet found a vehicle strong enough to carry his vision. The picaresque form properly conveys a sense of homelessness in a world of strangers, but at the expense of almost becoming a romance. Claire's death assumes too much weight. He becomes a martyr-saint in a world too late for saints. Purdy inadvertently sentimentalizes an absurdist vision. Also, Purdy's preoccupation with the "immortal fruits," Bruno Korsawski and Hayden Banks, becomes a sideshow late in the novel, causing the reader to lose sight of the Grainger-Cratty circle completely. And obviously all the characters are overshadowed by Claire's death.

Purdy had not yet learned to use a young man as a controlling metaphor. He was still groping for a structure to support his ironic vision. He found one in the world of *Malcolm*:

Everywhere in the house, no matter at what hour, one felt

that it was afternoon, late afternoon breaking into twilight, with a coolness, too, like perpetual autumn, an autumn that will not pass into winter owing to some damage perhaps to the machinery of the cosmos.

However, *63: Dream Palace* did supply Purdy the archetypes for *Malcolm*. Malcolm is Fenton Riddleway without Claire. The novel grounds the mannered world of such as Grainger's social circle in a fairy-tale setting. Purdy presents the fable of a fertility god who comes into a twilight world, America. The name "Malcolm" means a follower of St. Columba (Mother Columbus?).

When he lands in one of the "most palatial hotels in the world," this "foreigner" appears to be neither too short nor too tall and appears as though he would always remain the same.

Mr. Cox, astrologer-pederast, "recognizes" the bench Malcolm seems "wedded" to and considers him an "augury." Purdy plays a delightful word game with the image of the bench. "Judge," "recognize" and "addresses" assume a double significance to suggest that Malcolm is the son of man come again to judge the living and the dead. He comes too late for the gods and too early for man.

The work is a sustained ironic comedy. The characters and actions imitated are those of the fairy tale or romance. But Cox's "addresses" and the actions they perform are caricatures. Purdy causes laughter by brushing a world of "ormolu clocks," "kinkajous" and "Japanese temples" against one who seemed to "belong nowhere and to nobody."

This cyclical odyssey of a youth in search of security and identity is perfectly structured. Cox, instead of helping Malcolm find himself, feels threatened. He gives the boy "addresses" he hopes will transform him into a thing, a role. Purdy divides *Malcolm* into three stages defined by three Blacks, like Malcolm social outcasts. Each Black has a special way of coping with reality and each reminds Malcolm of his father.

Malcolm begins by harrowing puce-jacketed Estel Blanc's Empire Mortuary. Here he seems too detached and proceeds to the house of the first of three unhappily married couples, Laureen and Kermit Raphaelson. Kermit and Laureen establish a pattern by competing for Malcolm's affection. Kermit is a midget — an appropriate image for truncated humanity. He is also Malcolm's alter-ego. No one has informed him of the fact that he is a midget. After Laureen leaves him, Kermit seem "suddenly to have reached

[a] majority in age" and realizes that he was "beginning life at last. Alone, as everybody is."

But the Raphaelsons are mere bourgeois "break-in" men for the Girards, the "real equipment." When Madame Girard receives Malcolm he quickly becomes "a real prince" in her eyes by naming Mr. Cox "pederast." The Girards wish to adopt him.

But Malcolm finds the Girards too imposing. Cox, in a desperation move, sends him to the home of artists Jerome and Eloisa Brace. Malcolm suppresses the advances of ex-con Jerome, a Genêt caricature, who comes on in Caulfield's vernacular, "I'm not a queer or anything. . . . You do something to me because I guess you just seem like the spirit of . . . life, or something, and I wouldn't have said anything so corny before in all my life. But hell, you do." Whereas Salinger's Holden runs away from "flits," Malcolm understandably falls asleep.

A nude Malcolm awakens the next day to find himself in bed with the second Black, pianist George Leeds, whom he associates with his father and Estel Blanc. But Malcolm's life fails to change direction, for Leeds tells him he can't help because he tends to let the rest of the world go by.

In a modern inversion of the original sin, Jerome forces Eloisa to eat a check for $10,000, Madame Girard's payment for a painting of Malcolm. Naturally, Malcolm eats an apple while watching the scene. Jerome's action strips Madame Girard of her power — money. Girard Girard leaves his "greatlady," but she keeps her name, her only real identity.

Girard Girard also abandons Malcolm — on a stone bench in the Horticultural Gardens. The attendants shut the boy outside the gates in this strange re-enactment of the myth of the original Fall.

Here "Gus or Brownie," the third Black, takes Malcolm for a "contemporary," an identity validated by *chanteuse* Melba, who decides to marry Malcolm. She tells Malcolm that Brownie will be "like a father" to him. Gus and the intended walk out of a door marked "Authority" and Malcolm begins and ends.

What follows is a reversal of what happened under Cox. Pederast-tattooist Robinolte replaces the pederast-astrologer. Prostitute Madame Rosita replaces Madame Girard. A tattoo palace and whorehouse replace Malcolm's palatial hotel and the Girard chateau.

Malcolm is screwed and tattooed. But Gus's "de-coration" kills him. After Gus's death, Malcolm cries a torrent of tears for the first time since his father's disappearance.

Marriage with Melba is all "peaches and cream." Malcolm's "one little thing" satisfies her "one solid piece" until one night when drunk he recognizes his father in a nightclub restroom. The man promptly calls Malcolm a pederast, a role he accepts by saying "Blow my father" repeatedly.

He undergoes a metamorphosis which calls to mind the salient verbal and physical characteristics of some preceding characters. He gets Cora Naldi's white hair, uses Eloisa's and Melba's favorite punctuation, "O.K.," agrees with Madame Girard's dictum that his father never existed. Before his death from "acute alcoholism and sexual hyperaesthesia," he claims a dog bit him — calling to mind Kermit's early threat to turn him into a cat. He sees Estel Blanc on a pale horse and says "Hurrah" for the third time in the novel. Each "hurrah" celebrated his following in his father's footsteps. Now Malcolm is a perfect imitation of his father.

In typical anti-apocalyptic fashion, Purdy ends with a catalogue of where they are now. Madame Girard prepares the funeral amidst the saccharine smell of ketchup. Malcolm receives a spray of flowers in the simulacrum of a bench. And of course everyone wonders whether Malcolm was buried or whether he existed at all.

This skepticism is defensive. None of the characters in *Malcolm* enjoys an authentic existence. Cheap imitations of bad art result. Everyone undergoes "a lifetime of melodrama." The "greatladies" take "half-falls," make exits and entrances, await "signals and cues." *Malcolm* evokes a sense of watching a silent movie with misleading subtitles. Sometimes Purdy even achieves a form of verbal slapstick: " 'You hit a wrong note,' she explained, and they both knew she said this as a lie, even though he *had* hit a wrong note."

Laughter is possible. Purdy's technique affords the reader perspective. The gestures and exclamations of the characters stand out. Purdy puts on their histrionics. Madame Girard's reminiscence of her betrothal comes to her "with kind of feathered softness, like that of a poisoned arrow," and Mr. Cox goes "to the bottom of Malcolm's psychology of the moment." On occasion Purdy even completes the characters' expressions: " 'What are you saying?' she wanted to know." This technique sometimes fails. Malcolm eats a "Delicious apple." Among other fragrances, a prostitute wears "bay rum (domestic) ." After Eloisa's rude push,

Jerome "laughed superior to this comment." Purdy can cross the line between preciousness and bitterness.

But while the surface caricatures describe a broad social satire, a subtle subterranean comedy recurs throughout the work. Purdy reworks the surface tapestry to evoke finally the presence of substantial forms. The interplay forms suggests the mystery of good and evil. Strong medicine subverts nature to the extent that art seems more alive than life:

> The drawings of Negroes looking out from their pale eyes, of strange perhaps non-existent animals gazing at him from canvases everywhere. . . . The mythological animals will move their eyes slightly for the last time as they fade into indistinction.

The spiritual sometimes intrudes into the material like the face of the Cheshire cat, "Malcolm protested against the *all,* which sounded to him both complete and frightening."

Purdy's vision possesses a constant angle of refraction — as if he watched the proceedings through a glass-bottom boat. His imagery can enable the reader to accompany him. Estel Blanc can look "at Malcolm with as firm a scrutiny as if he had held a monocle, or even a telescope to his eyes." And Madame Girard can raise a hand "with the pistol like one who may command an entire army to extinguish itself."

Purdy becomes doubly oblique in indirect quotation. Professor Robinolte warns Malcolm "not to expose the tattoos to the unprotected sun." Malcolm waits for the tattoo to be "perpetrated on him." This technique fails Purdy when the metaphors cut away from their grounding. The epicene detachment of his ironic vision succumbs to a somewhat heated bitchery, "There was a faint smell from her like that of an uncovered cistern when she put on the robe."

While Purdy's work is involved, it is also involving. Unlike Parkhearst Cratty, the reader must be prepared to be involved "in more than a story." To get with Purdy, the reader must imitate the action of comedy — break out of the bonds of social infantilism and emerge an initiate. This is comedy in its original sense, the rite of passage from the stasis of winter to the full life of spring. Purdy describes America in the winter of its life—nowhere and coming to nothing.

When Purdy says, "I am not even writing novels . . . I am

154

writing me. I go on writing to tell myself at least what I have been through," he proposes not autism but the original duty of the artist. He fights the demons of a society of sleepwalkers to evoke the real.

Purdy emerges from his struggle with the nothing that is America with a vision of promise. Most importantly, he challenges his readers to do the same.

The Beat in the Rise of the Populist Culture

by KINGSLEY WIDMER

I. The Rebellious Movement

Few commentators on the "Beat Generation," as it was formally
called in the 50s, saw it as part of an enduring cultural movement. But in the 70s they should be able to recognize the Beats
as parcel as well as part of much that was to come—and much, no
doubt, still to come. For by the early 60s there was the worldwide
figure of the "Beatnik," almost as evident on the Spanish Steps,
Rome, and in the coffee houses of the Midlands, England, as in
the beach shacks of Venice West, Los Angeles, and on the streets
of the East Village, New York. The defiantly outcast costumes and
manners and sensibility were continued and enlarged in the mid-
60s with the successor Hippies. By the late 60s there were many
variations, such as the politicized Yippies and the religiocized hip
communes. From post-World War II ex-GI-Bohemians of the
late 40s—their military left-overs set the first styles of dressing
down, of marginal living and of revulsion against authority—
through the Beats, the Beatniks, the Hippies, the Yippies and
others, and seeping into faddish adolescent "teenieboppers" and
fashion-exploiting adult "swingers," we can find a minority sensibility expanding through and beyond the "underground" of Western culture.

155

By the late 60s, cultural symposia and literary moralizers were finally recognizing all of this as a vast though rather amorphous rebellious movement. Often called "the youth culture," though both its youthfulness and artistic culturation were in some doubt, it evidently involved millions with their communal ways and public festivals, with their distinctive communications (underground papers) and entertainment (folk, blues and rock groups), and with their own costuming and commerce, manners and morals. The bizarre personal decoration, ritualistic use of marijuana, and polymorphous sexuality merely provided the more obvious signs of a large para-community of the dissident. Though the evidence is quite clear that all of this has been developing for some decades, the mass media hireling commentators still treat it, as they did the Beats, as a "generational" problem, as a temporary malaise of late-adolescent delinquency. Righteously focusing on the "pot" mystique (developed by marginal groups in the thirties), the preachers of middle-class manners (and the pretenders to "social science") often reduce the movement to "the drug culture." The Beats and their successors have defiantly taken up the metaphor and made drugs into sacrament and magic and pot into poetry and politics. Also, since the under-Bohemians—the Beats and the Hippies—have emphasized their disenchantment with American competitive patterns and disaffiliation from the controlling institutions, they often get labeled the "drop-out culture." At least one hostile commentator condemns the erotic openness of the movement (obscene language and gesture, nudity, homoeroticism, and other mixed libidinal ways as well as rejection of the anxious nuclear family of the suburbs) as the "porno culture." A more disinterested observer would simply grant that it must be a large cultural movement, not to be reduced to a single sick attribute. The denigrations and dismissals by the custodians of the "straight" (formerly called "square") culture largely express the resentment of those identifying with social domination.

On one side, the movement towards a countering culture can hardly be separated from the blues-folk-rock musics, which in the past decade have considerably transformed popular entertainment, and from the increased impetus toward communal and immediate arts (happenings, new modes of decoration, participatory theatre, etc.). On another side, the counter-culture can hardly be separated from dissenting social action, including "civil rights," peace-protest, campus rebellion, utopian communalism, and many other ways of dissent which both adapt and inform the cultural movement. Movement it must be since in three decades it has grown from artistic coteries and deviant grouplets to a collective social and cultural process of large proportions. While the life-styles are quite evident that come out of this, the movement was, and is, characteristically American in being too various, elusive and often vague to be contained in a single artistic or religious or social doctrine. It cannot adequately be defined by its leaders since none of its better known figures seem to have achieved the roles of heroic prophets, nor by its creative works since none of these seem recognizable as masterpieces. Both culture heroes and art works remain secondary to communal styles of responding and living. Since the Bohemian-Beat-Hippy-deviant-underground-dissident movement goes beyond its social dimensions to a popular and protesting tradition of feeling and style, I suggest seeing it as a new populist culture based, like its predecessors, on a revolt against apathetic decorum as well as against social and political legitimacy.

The Beat should now be recognized as but one phase in this development. By way of definition, *beatness* might be analogized as social alienation, vagrant religious beatitude, a mode of humble moral resistance, a confession-spontaneity aesthetic, and the historical under-Bohemianism of the fifties. Possibly, we could include in *beatness* some of the ecstatic-melancholy beat of the blues, enthusiastically admired by most of the Beat litterateurs and then in process of transformation to popular rock music. Additional slang overtones might not be irrelevant: "beat-up" could describe the usual costuming (jeans, work shirts, boots, "war-surplus" jackets, etc.); "beat-out" suggests some of the a-political and a-intellectual disenchantment; and "to-beat-it" points to the mobility, the wandering outsiderness, which marked the movement. All of these carry a conscious revulsion, a wary disaffiliation, from a competitively repressive and blandly dehumanizing mass technological civilization.

Some years ago I wrote at tendentious length in *The Literary Rebel* on the parallels between the Beats and analogous earlier social-cultural rebels, including the Greek Cynics, certain Christian heretics, some figures of the Taoist movement, the Medieval Goliard poets, Bohemian vagrants, Thoreauvian individualists, American hobos, and the moral *enragés* of modernist art. The literary role of the Beat was in good part a recognizable variation on the anti-academic one that runs from Walt Whitman through Henry

Miller. But the movement was a melange which included orientalism and avant-gardist aesthetic experimentation, Western America
populist folk motifs and nostalgic political dissent (a considerable
number of the beat pace-setters were children of Leftists of an
earlier period), and a broad recrudescence of antinomian, utopian
and deviant styles. The Beat movement and its successors belong
to a long minority social, religious and artistic history. Perennially,
something similar blooms in late-urbanized and post-religious civil-
izations marked by counterfeit and exploitative culture, such as
ours, and would seed a revolutionary change in sensibility.

Since these movements would change consciousness and life-
styles, art—at least in the "high culture" senses—usually sub-
ordinates to personal and communal needs. We should hardly
expect, and we rarely get, complexly subtle art from such a movement. Its thrust works against the specialized craftsmanship and
elite-class connoisseurship which provides the conditions of "high
art." For the Beats, "creativity," when not a rather forced religious
euphemism for states of feeling, was a defensive definition of their
unemployed, irregular and outcast state. It bulwarked them
against the pressures of the Protestant work ethic and our religiosity of competitive aggrandizement. Art also served as a recognized rationalization for deviance. This in several senses. The
high proportion of identifiable homosexual writers and of obses-
sional homoerotic motifs in the literary works not only uses art as
a justification but would undermine the compulsive American
"he-man" sensibility. As a British poet-critic recently noted,
minority cultural movements in America tend to flaunt "feminine"
qualities, from long hair through sexual inversion to emotionality
and tenderness, as defiance of the narrow and repressive mascu-
linity held as the standard of character. The working out of
homoerotic problems may have given them an exaggerated place,
though it also points to the therapeutic role that dominated so
much Beat activity as well as, perhaps, new bi-sexual ways.

Since marginal life styles and communities provide a haven
for various deviancies, especially in our highly rejecting society,
the proportions of such people run high, and so do the therapeutic
expectations for art. Thus confessional modes dominate. By need
as well as defiant ideology, subjectivist and narcissistic emphases
encourage an anti-formalist aesthetic. Beat poetry pushed a mystique of loose poetics: anti-iambic ("the breath unit"), refusing
established patterns, heavy on colloquial and obscene and mixed

dictions, depending on progressions by association to the extreme of surrealist disjunctions, and generally insisting on expressive irregularity and openness. The more purely verbal poetic functions —the chant, the curse, the celebratory shout, the prayer—played a major role.

Beat prose was usually autobiographical, with personal awkwardness and fragmentation taken as expression of social reality as well as of individual sincerity. Many of the writers pontificated on not being "literary" and "intellectual" but personal and direct. Social rebelliousness encouraged parody and burlesque of the officially received forms. With wearisome insistence, taboo indicated literary subject—a quickly self-defeating direction of much of post-modernist writing—and so most accounts are of sexual inversion, drug addiction, pathology, and other outcastness. Since initially the movement was quite self-consciously a dissident literary minority, coterie allusion and other personal reference runs heavy. For the same reason, cultish exoticism, in the jargon of addiction and Buddhism (and, to lesser extent, of Amerindian lore, the Beat foreign circuit, nostalgic pop culture, antique Leftism, and the San Francisco Bay Area) received elaborate play. The cultism, of course, got justifications as essential to psychic transformation and enlarged awareness. A major social function of Beat literature was to "witness" to changes of consciousness, or at least of cultural and social allegiances. The assumed audience usually seems to be other dissidents, or potential dissidents, especially the young. In that direction, it had a considerable, if sometimes rather opportunistic, success.

In its largest ambitions, Beat literature presents a personal entree into the process of apocalyptic vision. It prophesies and demonstrates, by idiosyncrasies and hysterias, against a dehumanizing and exploitative technocratic civilization—bomb-ridden, consumer-compulsive, competitively anxious, sensually confused, mass-media warped, institutionally boxed, politically mad—and therefore incapable of simplicity and contemplation and intense experience and tenderness and community and love. And surely doomed!

II. Soft and Hard Confessions

Probably two of the best as well as most influential Beat novels are Louis-Ferdinand Céline's *Journey to the End of the Night* and Henry Miller's *Tropic of Cancer*. Though written in the early

30s, a full generation before the Beat mode became a populist movement, they contain much of what was to come, and remain largely unsuperseded. Miller, rewriting his fragmented and self-glorying Whitmanian autobiography in Paris when he enthusiastically read Céline's *Journey*, adapted some of that hard and rancorous outcast view to his bumptious innocence and surreal expressionism. The mad French doctor's bitter burlesque and nihilistic perceptiveness about his wanderings through twentieth-century war, colonialism, industrial America, Parisian suburbs, alleys and asylums, and other human rottenness, carried far. Allen Ginsberg, Jack Kerouac, William Burroughs, and other Beats, highly praised, and drew from, Céline. Curious, since American genres of sentimental confession and hobo documentary would seem to be more appropriate to what is usually recognized as Beat fictions.

Yet central to Beat writers, though little noticed, is the desperate flight from lower middle class life and its culture of anxiety. The unredeemable horrors of petit bourgeois meanness and restriction combine, as also in Céline's *Death on the Installment Plan*, with dissociated child fantasy, savage forbodings, and strange moments of tenderness. This characterizes most of the Beat confessions. Kerouac's lyrical-ruminative documentaries of his anxious *wanderjahrs—On the Road* (1958), *The Dharma Bums* (1959), the travel sketches not masquerading as fiction such as *The Lonesome Traveller* (1960) and his later imitations of his earlier work (such as *Big Sur*)—depend essentially on the softness of the child in flight from a petty order. This is not only the guilty-ecstatic adolescent romanticism and its poignant muddle (and its artistic correlative of the inability to realize character and scene other than in ragged detail and forced private mood—in the Thomas Wolfe manner) but the yearning for the return to innocence, both of the self and the American order. Identifying his wanderings with the quest for freedom, from that of Zen monks and American hobos through the prophetic outcasts ("Jesus was a strange hobo who walked on water"), hardly modifies the personal pathos.

Kerouac touches at moments on the existential intensity and profundity of the traditional wanderer: the defiant separateness, the sharp moral comment of a life denuded of surplus, the suspension of time by those wedded to motion, and the outcast's brilliant perceptions of most of what passes for humane order and meaning. But childishness usually takes over. On looking at the lights in the night, Kerouac comments: "I wish I was a little child in a crib in a little ranch style sweet house." In similar forlorn need, and incisive prose, he describes "kid dreams," juvenile ideas and adolescent tastes. As he notes of his "gang" of rather over-aged "boys," "We sorta wander around like children." The ideal is to return to "the happy life of childhood again." The style corresponds, with inflated and run-on sentences (perhaps an attempt to give a literally breathless heightening) and cute expletives ("comfy," "heavenly," "raving great," "glady," and the catatonic "Wow!"). The insights show similar quality, it being a great revelation of Kerouac that everybody walks around with a "dirty behind," or that most people are "crazy," or that buddies are "great," or that America is a "nutty" place. Of course there is a rather burbling charm about intensifying the commonplace, such as eating a hot dog or hungering for home. LIFE is unalterably "sad" or "fun," we are regularly told. Recurrent paranoid episodes, the guilty sexual fears, the eager and then disillusioned identifications with more manly or purposive buddies, and a constant anxious inadequacy block any more incisive ordering of experience. Yet intermittently Kerouac's kid-world, as heightened by a series of trips across America in the late 40s and middle 50s, opens into some suggestive responsiveness of a rebel on the road, junior division.

Kerouac's aesthetic, if such we can call a widespread quasi-art ideology of salvational self-expression, claims rebellion against intellectualized literature and thought. This generally comes out as free-associational confession but also, as with Ginsberg, includes efforts to "spiritualize" the flight from American lower middle class sensibility. While the material of *On the Road* mostly consists of some of the history of the coterie which became publicly identified as the Beat Generation, the novel attempts something more. Focusing on a touchingly flamboyant psychopath, Dean Moriarity (the late Neal Cassidy), it presents him as profound wanderer and "HOLY GOOF," the wild pilgrim. To achieve romantic apotheosis in an otherwise blandly repressive society, Kerouac exalts a delinquent intensity, an amoral posture and personality without much specific content. Awe, more adolescent than sacred, covers "the ones who are mad to live, mad to talk, mad to be saved, desirous of everything at the same time, the ones who never yawn or say a commonplace thing, but burn, burn, burn, like fabulous roman candles exploding like spiders across the stars and in the middle you see the blue centerlight pop and everybody goes 'Awww!' "

The fireworks hardly light up the intellectual and social vagueness, any more than do the temporary Buddhist trappings put
on in *Dharma Bums*. There the hero-narrator is the outdoors
American boy turned contemplative, with Japhy (Gary Snyder)
providing Kerouac's pattern for a religious-therapeutic summer in
the mountains and woods. The mystagoguery, and an excess of
reportage on fatuous Bohemianism in the Bay Area, muddle an
interesting larger theme—a call for a style of "rucksack wanderers,"
"Dharma bums," American Don Quixotes of tenderness who refuse
to be imprisoned in a system of pointless work, forced consumption,
and control by the "Master Switch" in a wired-up civilization.
That moving ideal is still with us, still a leading edge of the
"youth culture" in its perceptive disaffiliation and poignant
vagary.

The interest of Kerouac's writings is mostly documentary.
Sometimes they give apt details, hardly ever developed, about the
American scene, when not obscured by "real straight talk about
souls." While the trips start in earnest zest and pursue romantic
intensification, they rest on an elegiac sense of lost dream and
innocence. "Isn't it true that you start your life a sweet child
believing everything under your father's roof? Then comes the
day of the Laodiceans, when you know you are wretched and
miserable and poor and blind and naked." The sense of disin-
heritance of the outcast child—really the American lack of community which encourages both resentment and generosity—leads
to a moral awareness with a sympathy for "the great fellahin
people of the world." Though in Kerouac this sense of suffering
and injustice is mostly sentimental, here is part of the change in
sensibility which resulted in the Civil Rights and New Left Movement of the sixties. In Kerouac's repeated and desperate "wishing
I were a Negro," or a Mexican, or almost anything other than a
"disillusioned" American defeated in responsiveness and wholeness because of "white ambitions," we find fragmented dramatiza-
tion of the Lawrencean revulsion at willful and anxious "white
consciousness." Kerouac's "deliriums" of outcast otherness sound
plaintive cries for holistic feeling and life.

On the Road ends with a frenzied journey in Mexico with
glimpses of what is taken to be a more real and primordial life;
Dharma Bums ends with the trip down Desolation Mountain with
glimpses of what is taken to be a primal therapy and spiritual

transformation. Somewhere on those journeys, the author hopes, he has rediscovered life as it has eternally been, and will be again after the "Apocalypse" willful and arbitrary and mad American civilization is inevitably creating.

In spite of the childishness of much of the writing and thinking, Kerouac's yearning flights show us something about the American scene of the time with its harshly alienating places and lavishly fraudulent order and forlornly dissociated young. The "road is life," we are told with typical sententiousness and repetition of an old American metaphor, but it leads to both a vaguely visionary sense of a different life, "the ragged and ecstatic joy of pure being," and a "senseless nightmare road," in which even an inadequate sensibility recognizes our existential failures and foresees the collapse of the old culture.

In John Clellon Holmes' *Go,* a somewhat more analytical fiction about the same material as *On the Road,* which helped define the movement, the rebel-delinquents group motive is developed as "an inability to believe in anything . . . and the craving for excess which it inspired." However, the "youth culture," from orientalizing Beats through occultizing Hippies, equally shows a frenzied willingness to believe in almost anything so as to escape the existential perplexities. Perhaps the religiosity and the disenchantment, the disaffiliation from mainstream America and the fanciful nostrums which become fads out of the underculture, provide simply variant expressions of the deepest inability to believe in the American culture because it doesn't merit acceptance.

The soft rebellion in sensibility of a Kerouac, the All-American boy as Beat cynosure of the spiritual vagrant, melts away. Jack Kerouac went on in the 60s to mere idiosyncratic legendizing of himself (books about his own ancestry and dreams) and further pathetic withdrawal. The literature, like the figure, seems mostly symptomatic. So, I would also argue, with the more artful and arduous, and genuinely excessive, sensibility of William Burroughs. That demonic father-figure of some in the Beat coteries helped pattern a certain style of hard extremity, of drug experiment and addiction, of marginal living in New York and Mexico and Tangiers, and of paranoid and pastiched excremental vision.

Naked Lunch (first published in Paris in the late 50s), and its continuation in *The Soft Machine* and *Nova Express,* and some related literary experiments of cut-up and fragmented writing, display a peculiarly destructive anti-art which in other forms became fashionable in the sixties. *Naked Lunch,* for example, is the excreta of the drug-addict's consciousness. But the self-hating author, in order to counter the sick compulsions which dominate the work, willfully shatters plot, character, even page sequence, and other usual signs of order. This ambivalently plays with addiction's fragmentation and nausea; the art becomes homeopathic, with verbal disintegration and revulsion to counter that of consciousness. Method and madness conflict. Paranoid fantasies receive a science-fiction cast and claim to prophesy a police state implicit in our society. An ostensible attack on addiction becomes a loving catalogue of its nausea and cultish expertise. Amidst fantasies of sadistic pederasty and naturalistic treatments of addiction and poetic-obscene meditations, the positive impetus seems the most outrageous: the defense of cooperatives and the arguments for reform of cruel laws, the hortatory call for spirituality and passion, and even the simple flashes of human suffering ("Last night I woke up with someone squeezing my hand. It was my other hand."). The hated addiction, and its loving account, confirms Burroughs' major, and libertarian, insight that domination of people can never lead to the good, control *"can never be a means to anything but more control."*

Some of the ingeniously nasty fantasies of scientistic destruction aim at fairly specific satire of doctors, modern technology, cops who are really criminals, and the willful national character: "Americans have a special horror of giving up control, of letting things happen in their own way. . . . They would like to jump down into their stomachs and digest the food and shovel the shit out." But Burroughs' very style depends on just such willfullness, on such delighted shoveling from the gut. So, too, control and destruction fascinate him and take over the art. In spite of claims to exposing himself because he wishes to reveal the underside, his "prophetic mutterings" don't really leave the excrement and control and destructiveness which he excoriates. Following the logic of Celinish revulsion, the victim demands the torturing civilization. The author, too, is one of the "Citizens who want to be utterly humiliated and degraded—so many people do nowadays, hoping to jump the gun." The harsh personal confession claims to be representative of what is happening underneath our civilization, an apocalyptic awareness of the future forming. Burroughs exploits his own dissociations and perversities and pathologies in the attempted downward path to illumination. Thus redemption becomes a metabolic drug problem, anal rending opens up a greater reality, bodily discharges provide ecstatic colorations, until "we see God through our assholes."

Burroughs' best fragments come forth as surreal comic rhetoric ("mail order whorehouse," "osteopaths of the spirit," etc.), as pieces of caricature of junkie and police and technologue types — aren't they really all one type?—and as intermittent burlesque of usual claims to goodness and beauty and sense. But the excremental obsessions, the pedantry about drugs, the forced poeticism with addict analogies (a mystic search for "connections" which contradicts his basically positivistic bent), and the willful fracturing of the material reduce the suggestiveness to the merely artful. This is melodrama, not only an insistence on degradation so to be *the* bottomside moralist but also literary wickedness. For homoerotic and addict flagellation of the flesh are not, in fact, the evil of our time, not the horrendously banal dehumanization and destruction which we must struggle to comprehend. The confessional author indulges in rather than enlarges the personal nausea which provides the dominant tone, and tedium, of *Naked Lunch*. We are force-fed literary excrement in the name of a truthful diet, an interesting effort, but most of it turns out to be a private snack.

The confessions of Kerouac and Burroughs, and a good many imitations of these soft and hard, adolescent and pathological, artistic manners, don't really produce major literary experience. Both writers make righteous claims of going beyond literary "intellectuals" and "entertainers." Indeed they do, but then their proper effort is no longer intelligent literature. They do not succeed, and perhaps one cannot, in having it both ways. Apocalyptic confession has been better done before, by such as hard Celine and soft Miller, who managed to confess more reality with more art. Nor do Kerouac and Burroughs, and the many others, allow us to fully transcend literary judgment; we can hardly see them as saints of the present and therefore prophets of the new culture.

III. The Art of Poetic Saintliness

The Beat movement encouraged, and practiced, public performances of poetry—coffee house readings, poems recited in bars to a jazz beat, group word-fests of those high on pot or wine, as well as more *outré* (and sometimes nude, mystical or belligerent) use of the poetic. Those who did not see these sometimes quite effective performances can recognize from the published remains that the real effort was not towards what we usually consider the literary object but to the half-verbal occasion for ritualism, therapy, curse, exhibition or celebration. Valid activities in their own right, we should not expect them to also produce the precious artifacts, conventionally bound in small volumes or academic anthologies and used for private meditation, that we usually call poems. The words of prayer, rage and festival do not gain from printed permanency. They depend on the physical situation and communal spirit and therapeutic function, far more than on verbal craft and formal order, and so are not "literature" in the academic or modernist senses. The Beats enlarged and spread the uses of the poetic, though the purely literary results tend to be thin and unartful.

No doubt some of the self-identified Beat poets thought, and some of the careerist ones still think, they were being Artists in the "high culture" senses. Mostly they were not. Separated from the group or occasion, the poetry is no more high art than the lyrics of blues or rock separated from the musical performance. Probably the poetic impetus that moved the Beat littérateurs is more generally found now amongst the creative performers at musical festivals. There would seem to be considerable continuity between the poets chanting at The Place in North Beach, San Francisco, in the mid-50s and the composers singing at the massive Peace and Art Festival near Woodstock, New York in 1969. A decade later than the literary Beats, their progeny, the Hippies, more fully recognized the communal focus of their artistry in ritual and celebration. By the late 60s, those in the underculture far less often practiced unconscious parody of the high culture in claiming officious careers as Artists. But in the 50s even many of the most dissident still treated the Man of Letters as culture hero and aspired to Poet or Novelist as justification for marginal life style as well as self-sanctification of sensitivity.

Before noting some other characteristics of the Beat poetic role, we might ask what text we should use. With the one main exception of Allen Ginsberg, it is hard to identify major progenitors of Beat poeticism. As with the New Left political movement developing slightly later, and as with the Hippies of the 60s, there were exceptional persons (frequently not the most celebrated ones) but an essentially egalitarian tone and truly anarchical quality which does not allow us to fully identify one, or several, figures as *the* movement or the sufficient personification of its characteristics. In revolt against hierarchies of values as well as persons, much of the endurance of the underculture depends on its amorphousness—a temper and style fluid, tolerantly various, loosely grouped, anonymously carried by persons more than publications, and unprogrammatic and unstructured. In short, libertarian in social reality as well as in literary imagination. Surely, too, the movement, and its continuation, shift and change in resistance to the co-optation by the mainline cultural institutions which, empty and cannibalistic, desperately seek new material for titillation and profit. Thus an unauthoritarian cultural revolution attempts, with only partial success (the Beats served much in fad and fashion), to evade a hostile and counterfeiting order.

Many of the writings linked to the Beat movement seem more accidentally than essentially so. Even one of the better known figures, Lawrence Ferlinghetti, denies much relation to the Beats, except as publishing friend. His own poetry, as in *A Coney Island of the Mind*, at its best shows an urbanely comic cast hardly in accord with the usual tone of the movement. So, too, with Ferlinghetti's political broadsides. Propinquity also accounts in considerable part for some confusing the Beat writers with the "Black Mountain school" of poets. Though there is some overlap, the latter is a much more restricted, rather cultish, poetic experimentation linked to the charismatic figure of Charles Olson. His fervently idiosyncratic writings (*The Maximus Poems*), and his synthetically narrow and flat verbal aesthetic, considerably contrast with the free surrealism and communal therapeutic common to the Beat movement. Various other writers loosely connected with the Beats relate by time and place and only secondarily by some loosely common sense of dissidence from American social and cultural orthodoxies. Many of these were simply figures present in the 50s as part of long-time Bay Area Bohemia: the mannerist-proletarian Kenneth Rexroth, the religionized Jeffers, Brother Antoninus, and others such as Robert Duncan, Philip Whalen, Jack Spicer, Robin Blazer, etc.—hardly of one style or aesthetic or prophetic role. Perhaps second best known in the 50s as a Beat poet was the nasty-clever gamin Gregory Corso (*Bomb* and *Gasoline*) who came up with cute-Dadaist verbal flourishes, such as "fried shoes." There were quite a number of them. With more moral than literary appropriateness, some social-religious spokesmen also identified themselves as poets with the Beats. Perhaps the best known of these, Gary Snyder (*Riprap* and *Myths and Texts*) had, and has, serious interests in natural living and Buddhism, which, unfortunately, do not much improve his poetic quaintness and flat writing. There are others who may merit discussion as minor poets or prophets, though not especially because of their role in the Beat movement. But there could hardly be a *good* anthology of Beat poetry as such.

Allen Ginsberg, because of his central and continuing role as well as representativeness, merits fuller discussion. I think it should be granted from the start that he is not much of a poet in most usual literary senses, though he may well be an admirable and important practitioner of poetic saintliness. Carefully going again through his three volumes of published poetry covering the 50s (*Howl and Other Poems, Kaddish and Other Poems 1958-60,* and *Reality Sandwiches 1953-60*), I find three pieces that could well bear rereading as poems: 'Howl," "America," and "Death to Van Gogh's Ear!" Other pasages here and there give a curious surreal twist, or are informative of matters mostly Ginsbergian, such as the bitter-bathetic physical description of his mad mother in the elegy-prayer "Kaddish," or maybe of some other non-literary interest. But most of it is poorly realized, pastiches of awkward language which many a poet could rewrite into more consistent style and apprehendable experience. The stuff of it seems more often unmade than crafted, and it is patent that Ginsberg never quite found a literary style of his own. Much of what he published as poems can better be considered pre-poems, fitting his own categories of "notes" and "nightmares" (including the drug "visions") and "musings." He is less writing poems than awkwardly adumbrating a personal and public "spiritual" mission. He adapts poetic methods to "widen the area of consciousness" and, while translating personal therapy as public revelation, hopes that the reader will "taste my mouth in your ear."

Certainly Ginsberg displays considerable ambivalence about his poetic role, but finally degrades the writer to justify the seer. Though posing sometimes as a *naif* who wants a visceral poetry of direct screams and obscenities—a stance partly contradicted by his public as well as private acts of charm and intelligence and charity —he is also highly, probably excessively, literary, full of commemorative allusions to his whole tradition from Blake through Whitman to Apollinaire and his own contemporaries. In the provocative surrealist styled poem, "Death to Van Gogh's Ear!" he uses disparate images of the "mad" visionary poets, such as Mayakovsky and Crane, set against more truly insane public leaders and their order of "Money" and "Owners" and "vanishing Selfhood!" He suggests a government cabinet of mad poets, an anarchic cultural order in place of a repressive political one. With wry aptness, he comments within the poem on what he is doing: "History will make this poem prophetic and its awful silliness a hideous spiritual music."

Not so silly, with its vivacious disjunctures, wit, and (for once) meshing of syntax and sense, it sweepingly extends that most basic theme of modernist art, the culture against the society. This can also be said about the burlesque "America." Though ending with a comic pledge of allegiance ("America I'm putting my queer shoulder to the wheel."), he lashes out at an exploitatively false and insensitively technological civilization. "Your machinery is too much for me./You made me want to be a saint." This conversion, though hardly realized as poetry, runs through all. Apparently central is that night in New York when he had a Blakean vision of eternity: "my eyes were opened for one hour/seeing in dreadful ecstacy/the motionless buildings of New York rotting/under the tides of Heaven." This intensity he desperately seeks to recapture in drugged and mythic and other gropings which don't quite translate into mere words.

The terms, the needs, of the conversion experience may be found in exacerbated awareness of loneliness, cruelty, madness and death. Their scene serves as equally important, the placement in the marginal ugliness of industrial-urban America and the indifferent skidrow human dumps of an aggrandizing society. The homely Jewish invert from the wastelands of New Jersey ("My Sad Self" and the recurrent images of his own ugliness) wants to transcend his unsatisfactory self and world, transform all not only into "one moment of tenderness" but into that which will sustain it: "A MAGIC UNIVERSE." Of course he sees the absurdity of it, the grotesque effort to put "a flower in the ass." But "It's hard to eat shit, without having visions."

To love all, even one's ugly, perverted, inadequate self, requires the largest effort, beyond mere art, beyond the sophisticated whimper, then, to the "Howl." In that poem's run-on of fractured details (Part I) of the cold, junky, mean, loveless misorder forced upon marginal and outcast men, we find the bitter images which demand conversion. The semi-hysterical chant against such a world's false gods (Part II), against "Moloch," whose "mind is pure machinery," and the Molochs of stone and government, of war and oil, of blindness and antennae, of abstractions and money, denounces the loss of human sensitivity and "natural ecstacy" that leave us "lacklove and manless in Moloch!" Therefore one can only choose union (Part III) with the sensitive mad, the lost visionaries, and chant the dirge "I'm with you in Rockland [New York State Mental Hospital]." One ends, one hopes, transformed, endlessly praying ("Footnote to Howl"), in hip fractured variations on Blake's penultimate aphorism of *The Marriage of Heaven and Hell*, "Everything is holy!" Nothing less than the anguished sacramental sense of life will restore us.

"Howl" serves as one of the best known poems of our time, though not in the schoolteacher anthologies and literary racketeering. Or perhaps it would be more accurate to say that its anguished view of contemporary life and yearning for tender poeticization of existence provide the most influential saintly gesture for a generation. Ginsberg's effort to spiritualize the self in a destructive order of commercial and technological domination—quite consciously a social-political as well as literary-religious rebellion—provides essential style for the underculture. It is poetry mostly because the poet is priest of the confession-conversion-protest. For this, it seems, the traditions of modernist poetic culture provide a better discipline than does theology and ritual, or ideology and politics. It is from modernist culture that he finds the delineations of sensibility in revolt against a commercial—technological order and the grounds for a consciousness that can include delight and death, sensitivity and sodomy, far-out drugs and fractured myths, Dadaist disjunctions and libertarian perceptions. Modernism, then, may finally result less in poetry than in saintliness, including a good bit of holy foolishness.

The later Ginsberg, dressed in denims, beard and indulgently ethereal smile, silencing on television the abstract Rightist rant of William Buckley by chanting an erotic imitation of Wordsworth, or the half naked, bead-draped, sutra-chanting Saint Allen leading a circle of dancing kids in the middle of a massive war-protest march, carries on, with proper Surrealist decorum, the poetic saintliness. That is the imagery that we, along with a whole populist culture, should focus on. The society needs it, the culture exists by it, and that is the real art and imagination of Allen Ginsberg.

IV.   The Reverberating Beat

The Beats appear to have had a considerable, perhaps even disproportionate, effect on American sensibility and life styles. Or at least we see them that way because, willy nilly, they provide as well as represent much of the rebellious mode of the time. While their most significant effects belong to a larger social and cultural movement which goes quite beyond them, and the 50s, they also seem to have had considerable literary significance, less individual than as a movement. Beat writings were not the only but were certainly one of the largest and most influential refusals of the academic baroque and "little magazine" neoclassicism which dominated post-World War II serious writing. In both poetry and prose, the Beat impetus gave considerable "freeing," opening up subject matters and loosening forms. In style, the Beats carried the recurrent Romantic return to more direct and intense language. The "obscenity" and colloquial spontaneity and, less positively, the argot (such as that of the addict sub-culture) certainly spread widely from the Beats and related writers. Beat use of surrealist disjunctions and visionary metaphors and Dadaist burlesques and nihilist mockeries gave new life to such imagery even though varied writers, including Henry Miller and Kenneth Patchen and Nathanael West, employed it a generation before. More broadly, the Beats helped regenerate the cultural rebellion and allied social dissidence which the hot-and-cold-war cultural nationalism of the preceding decade and a half had muted in literary and social awareness.

Probably cultural movements, like ideologies, show more import in their climatic effects than in their own ideas and arts. While "fictions" such as those of Kerouac and Burroughs may help us understand the byways of a larger movement of sensibility—of the movement itself they tend to be more signs and symptoms than players and prophets—their art is less interesting than other works only peripherally related to them. For example, Norman Mailer's *Advertisements for Myself* aggrandizingly utilizes the confessional and extremist ways of the Beats (just as Mailer had previously imitated the naturalistic War Novel, the Ideological Melodrama, and the Hollywood Novel). He then took on from the Beat weather the obscenity, the therapeutic and drug postures, the rhetoric of rage, the magic, the glorification of the psychopath ("The White Negro"), and the stance of exacerbated revolt against

American civilization. Some things, such as the adolescent egotism, he already had; others, such as simple living and orientalism and the return to nature, were quite alien to the New York ideologue. Adding tough-guy bluster, and considerable intellectual adroitness, Mailer came out with his own version of Beatness. Mailer, of course, was manipulating, as usual, and passing through to something else, yet another Mailerism. But that sophisticated ambivalence, which makes him a rather exploitative public figure, adds some intriguing and perceptive richness to his writing—more than with the simpler, and no doubt more sincere and honest, Beat literary cynosures. As rebel-pretender and prophetic posturer, Mailer displays the alter-ego of much of what he attacks. But because he is partly a genuine fraud, he is truly responsive to much of what is happening in American culture, as he was with the Beats and his own pose of Hipsterism, and makes up in artful perception for his moral dubiousness. Or almost.

In another direction, the most delightful novel of the 50s may well be J. P. Donleavey's *The Ginger Man*. Apparently a once-only achievement (his later works are coy and sentimental), *The Ginger Man* carries out, at an artful distance, the mocking and tender wanderings and the intense and disenchanted life-hungerings we find in the Beats. This comic and bawdy picaresque of an Irish-American student abroad may have no direct relation to the Beats (though it apparently comes out of some of the same sources), and in amorality belongs outside any movement, yet in longer historical perspective it may reasonably appear as the best artistic ordering of much of the Beat sense of life in that time.

A later exceptional novel, considerably and directly influenced by William Burroughs' *Naked Lunch,* especially by his paranoid metaphors and vision of control by a technological-psychiatric bureaucracy, may most fully realize in fiction the rebellious side of the Beat movement: Ken Kesey's *One Flew Over the Cuckoo's Nest* (1962). Its defiant and wandering rogue-hero becomes the therapeutic-sacramental martyr in modern society's microcosm of a mental hospital—a Western version of "I'm with you in Rockland." *Cuckoo's* McMurphy provides the most persuasive image of the Beat hero, the brilliant psychopath fighting the system unto saintliness. Kesey, of course, also famously carried on outside of literature the rebel-saint role established by the Beats, and, therefore, provides proper completion to our sense of the movement. He gave up mere novel writing to become a psychedelic guru in the Bay Area, far-out holy leader of the drug-and-rock Merry Pranksters, frenzied wanderer across the American landscapes (even with some of the same people who were in earlier Beat pilgrimages), and major founder of redemptive Hippy communalism. The Beat poetic saintliness continues.

Thus the main significance of the Beat movement of the 50s, I believe, was not literary but cultural in a far broader sense. In attempting to change the bland bureaucratic-technological society by transforming sensibility and trying to radically revitalize a false order by creating a different life-style, the movement was toward a cultural revolution. The new populist culture contained considerable malaise: adolescent addiction — and addictive adolescence—but also rather synthetic religiosity, morality replaced by relativistic muddle, a decline in artistic craftsmanship in the name of self-expression, and an often naively ineffective politics of rebelliousness and tenderness. But the movement itself, and our need for it, remains considerably greater than its obvious failings. Whether the final result will be a new religion, a full social revolution, or merely a quaint phase of cultural history, we cannot yet be sure. In the meantime, we can feel with the reverberations of the Beats many more of the deficiencies of our culture and society. Not least, we should more fully recognize that art is not a remote elitist creation of artifacts to be preserved but the often desperate and poignant expression of a way to live and the attempt to re-create human community. That is the beat of it.

The Whole of Harmonium: Poetic Technique in Wallace Stevens

by DONALD SHEEHAN

> . . . Thence come the final chants, the chants
> Of the brooder seeking the acutest end
> Of speech: to pierce the heart's residuum
> And there find music for a single line,
> Equal to memory, one line in which
> The vital music formulates the words.*

*From "Extracts from Addresses to the Academy of Fine Ideas," *The Collected Poems of Wallace Stevens* (New York, 1954), p. 259; further references to this volume will appear in text and with no abbreviated indication of the volume. References to Stevens' *Opus Posthumous* (New York, 1957) will appear in text and the volume will be abbreviated as *OP*. Stevens' collection of essays, *The Necessary Angel* (New York, 1951), will be abbreviated in text as *NA*. Arabic numbers in text will refer to pages of the volumes in which the quoted matter occurs. Finally, in latter part of this essay I borrow certain ideas, as well as some phrasings of them, from a different context in Paul Ricoeur, *The Symbolism of Evil,* trans. E. Buchanan (Boston, 1969). I shall refer to Ricoeur in text and will abbreviate the book as *R.*

In the 50s, finally, the poetry of Wallace Stevens received its long-overdue acclaim: the National Book Award once in 1951 for *The Auroras of Autumn* and again in 1955 for *The Collected Poems*. By decade's end, Stevens' position was sufficiently firm and distinguished as to be undisputed. Some thirty years of critical ambiguity seemed over and, with *The Collected Poems* (1954), Stevens was recognized, along with Eliot and Pound, as one of America's contemporary masters. In accepting the 1955 award, Stevens began, "When a poet comes out of his cavern or wherever it is that he secretes himself, even if it is a law office or a place of business, and suddenly finds himself confronted by a great crowd of people, the last thing in the world that enters his mind is to thank those who are responsible for his being there" (*OP*, 245). The great crowd was, surprisingly but at last, there, and the years in the cavern a thing of the past. The 20s aesthete, the 30s snob, the 40s hermit — all the old labels felt embarrassingly wrong; for what Stevens had all along been doing was steadily and surely creating an *oeuvre* whose magnificence, variety, and power had eluded all those earlier uncomprehending glances. Once out, the truth seemed obvious, and so the final recognition followed fast: books, articles, Ph.D. dissertations, and so more books and articles, about his poetry. By the mid-60s, Stevens attained the grey eminence of the great poet.

The problem of such eminence, of course, is the patina it leaves on the verse. Nothing can dull poetry like a reputation of greatness, and Stevens' art has from the 50s on been subject to a peculiar conspiracy of praise not seen since the days of the Robert Browning Societies: the poems have been read as the musings of an Important Philosopher. Almost without exception, the books and articles on Stevens since the 50s have dealt with his poems as statements of an aesthetic theory that is in itself interesting and significant; moreover, this theory is taken to constitute by itself that *oeuvre* we took so long to perceive. It apparently matters little if one definition of Stevens' aesthetic theory sounds almost nothing like another — that only illustrates the theory's immense variety. And it matters just as little, too, if his poems begin to sound very like one another — that simply proves the theory's vital omnipresence. Now, this ruling view of Stevens' poetry — and so something of his two-decade eminence — has about it the self-sufficient air of the self-fulfilling argument, and its circularity is maddening until one realizes, abruptly, that with this view one sees only "depths" and has almost no perception of surfaces. How, that is, are Stevens' poems put together? What aesthetic and prosodic techniques does he use? What — to use Stevens' own splendid metaphor — is the "vital music" that "formulates the words"? Such questions seem to me ones wholly about the surfaces of Stevens' poems and not about the patina which two decades of eminence have left in the guise of philosophic "depths." For I feel that Stevens is almost everywhere a genuinely great artist and almost nowhere a theoretician of aesthetics or of anything else. It is something of a truism to say that a good poet is first of all a good *poet;* it is quite another thing, in Stevens' case, to feel the truth of it; and something else again to demonstrate it. Yet the fifteen years since *The Collected Poems* have seen so sadly little on the subject that even a failure, at this point, might be worthwhile.

Poetry for Stevens is first of all speech; it is the sound of a single human voice speaking with a certain rhythm in a certain register with a specific timbre:

> It has
> To construct a new stage. It has to be on that stage
> And, like an insatiable actor, slowly and
> With meditation, speak words that in the ear,
> In the delicatest ear of the mind, repeat,
> Exactly, that which it wants to hear, at the sound
> Of which, an invisible audience listens,
> Not to the play, but to itself, expressed
> In an emotion as of two people, as of two
> Emotions becoming one (240).

Stevens' rhythm, register, and timbre are absolutely his own, and no poem of his *sounds* like anyone else's, for only his voice pauses with such rich portent or elaborates with such graceful precision. So unalterably central and significant a fact is Stevens' voice that, when he writes prose, he sounds very much the same:

> The deepening need for words to express our thoughts and feelings which, we are sure, are all the truth that we shall ever experience, having no illusions, makes us listen to words when we hear them, loving them and feeling them, makes us search the sound of them, for a finality, a perfection, an unalterable vibration, which it is only within the power of the acutest poet to give them (*NA*, 32).

The structure of a prose sentence in Stevens is very like that of a verse sentence, and the reason why Stevens' essays so often seem like his poems also provides the basis of his *vers libre*: nothing matters so greatly to him, whether it be poem or essay, as getting the voice to sound exactly as he wishes. As he said: "I am rather inclined to disregard form so long as I am free and can express myself freely" (*OP,* xxxvii). The voice in Stevens *is* the generic form.

This characteristic sound in Stevens' poetry depends to a surprising extent upon a single thing: the capacity for complex syntax. Not since Wordsworth has a poet displayed in English the talent for handling long, difficult, intricate verse sentences whose parts, as we encounter them, are yet somehow simple and immediate — as in this from "Notes Toward a Supreme Fiction":

Perhaps there are times of inherent excellence,

As when the cock crows on the left and all
Is well, incalculable balances,
At which a kind of Swiss perfection comes

And a familiar music of the machine
Sets up its Schwarmerei, not balances
That we achieve but balances that happen,

As a man and woman meet and love forthwith (386).

The points where syntactic expansions occur in Stevens are almost always grammatically and verbally the simplest: *and, or, if, as, like.* Such points provide him his characteristic pauses and the places for his definitions, qualifications, and elaborations. And these expansions give Stevens' poetry a kind of drama of aesthetic surfaces (poetry "has / To construct a new stage") one finds only, if anywhere else, in the later novels of Henry James: as we move into a fresh sentence, we cannot possibly foresee what turns it will take (either as meaning or as structure), and yet we negotiate them all in a way that at the end we are surprised by the particular details and satisfied by the overall design. The phenomenon is a matter of the most exquisite balances, for the parts are at once immediate yet surprising, while the whole is simultaneously complex and satisfying.

This dramatic balance gives Stevens a superb aesthetic instrument, for he can vary its effects almost endlessly by shifting complexity from design to detail and simplicity from detail to design.

When the detail is complex, it is usually either an aphorism or a bizarre image, and the syntactic design is correspondingly simplified; or both detail and design are simplified, or (though rarely) both complex. When, in some poems, the balance is upset or never achieved, both become either too complicated to grasp or to simple to bother about—or, as in Stevens' longest poem, "Owl's Clover," at once too complicated and too simple — which is, I think, what Stevens meant when he omitted the poem from *The Collected Poems* on the ground that it was "rhetorical" (*OP,* xxiii). A characteristic verse sentence from "Owl's Clover" thus reveals the limits of Stevens' drama of aesthetic surfaces at the same time it demonstrates a central fact about it (the "It" of the first line refers to "a sprawling portent" that moves "High up in Heaven") :

> It is the form
> Of a generation that does not know itself,
> Still questioning if to crush the soaring stacks,
> The churches, like dalmatics stooped in prayer,
> And the people suddenly evil, waged, accused,
> Destroyed by a vengeful movement of the arms,
> A mass overtaken by the blackest sky,
> Each one as part of the total wrath, obscure
> In slaughter; or if to match its furious wit
> Against the sleepers to re-create for them,
> Out of their wilderness, a special fane,
> Midmost in its design, the arms grown swift,
> The body bent, like Hercules, to build (68-9).

This passage's failure — and the whole poem's — is, I think, to a great extent due to Stevens' attempt at a sustained narrative. For the balances his technique demands are so elusive and so delicate that they preclude any real possibility for continuous narration. The surface of a good poem thus tends to be a sequence of such balances, only thematically connected, rather than a single whole whose unity derives from narrative cause and effect. Stevens' remark in his notebooks is an expression of his primary technique as well as an admission about its major limitation, "Thought tends to collect in pools" (*OP,* 170). The pools are the points in a poem where the drama of surfaces succeeds; when they are forced to function narratively, as in "Owl's Clover," the thought behind them stagnates.

Stevens' prosody reinforces his primary technique. Since the balances in a poem are sequential rather than causal, and so can only be momentarily achieved, the poem's prosody must not offer the slightest resistance to reaching them. Unlike, say, Auden or Frost or A. D. Hope, Stevens does not depend upon the symmetries of conventional metric for his poems' music, and so he uses an irregular pentameter line that is so unvaryingly simple as to be wholly unassertive. (In fact, Stevens will mock poetry that does use strict metrics — as in the Arabian "With his damned hoobla-hoobla-hoobla-how" [383], which are of course perfect trochees and therefore meaningless noise.) This absence of a metrical ordering gives his poems a curious lack of continuous *inner* resonance, for there is no fixed outward symmetry working in counterpoint to a constant inner asymmetry. Instead, the prosodic resonance is all outward and discontinuous since what there is of it in itself is wholly implicit in the momentary balances between detail and design. Stevens' favorite verse forms — blank verse, the unrhymed couplet, triplet, and four-line stanza — are thus very few, are always employed, and have one common characteristic: they allow the drama of aesthetic surfaces to move unimpeded. The true "unit" of his prosody is precisely the primary element in the drama: the verse sentence; and his prosodic technique therefore merges into his larger aesthetic in a way that raises a crucial question. Given the essential discontinuity of his technique, how does Stevens unify his poems?

The answer is, through a poetic personality. Everything in a Stevens poem tends to pull to the surface — except, in his words, "the thing that is incessantly overlooked: the artist, the presence of the determining personality" (*OP*, xxxix). Since it cannot sustain a narrative and since its prosody has no independent existence, a Stevens poem relies largely upon its speaker to provide it with structural continuity and unity. Stevens' primary aesthetic attention lies in creating within each poem a literary character capable of speaking exactly what is spoken and in precisely the way it is said; and the creation of a capable character is simultaneously the creation of a coherent structure. The axioms of capability are kept as fluid as possible, for what matters to Stevens is that the character and the utterances of a poem should harmonize, since "A change of style is a change of subject" (*OP*, 171). One can sense the vital structural importance of character, and the coalescence of speaker and subject, in the opening stanza of "St. Armorer's Church from the Outside":

St. Armorer's was once an immense success.
It rose loftily and stood massively; and to lie
In its church-yard, in the province of St. Armorer's,
Fixed one for good in geranium-colored day (529).

The phrase "immense success" instantly establishes a complex character, one capable of either mocking or lamenting the present failure of churches, and the adverbs "loftily" and "massively" tip it toward an explicit lament which is then transformed into the explicit satire of "Fixed one for good" in the fourth line. The speaker's complexity is thus firmly established, so that he can dispense with the apparatus of past religion at the same time he can assert his own and so any imaginative man's spiritual and meditative capacities in a way that is not merely negative:

Its chapel rises from Terre Ensevelie,
An ember yes among its cindery noes,
His own: a chapel of breath, an appearance made
For a sign of meaning in the meaningless,

No radiance of dead blaze, but something seen
In a mystic eye, no sign of life but life,
Itself, the presence of the intelligible
In that which is created as its symbol (529).

Four stanzas later he plainly and without argument asserts "the need of each generation to be itself, / The need to be actual and as it is" and says, "St. Armorer's has nothing of this present, / This *vif*, the dizzle-dazzle of being new / And of becoming" (530). The speaker's complexity has thus progressed to the point where, while he affirms his own thinking, he can mock slightly — not St. Armorer's — but his own central idea: "this dizzle-dazzle." He is by now fully capable of such intricacy, and he becomes a complete and unified character only in the poem's final phrases:

The chapel underneath St. Armorer's walls,
Stands in a light, its natural light and day,
The origin and keep of its health and his own.
And there he walks and does as he lives and likes (530).

This resolves into a harmony the complications of satire, lament, and assertion and so creates the poem's unifying personality; and the structure of the poem thus results from the structure of the character who speaks it. The unmistakable voice of Stevens' poetry, is, then, not an abstract essence but an aesthetic presence, and the ideas in his poems are always subordinated to the particular act of utterance that includes them and gives them their dramatic accent. There is thus no "philosophy" in Stevens' poems, in the sense that they employ a system of ideas that is valid and makes demands by itself; instead, the ideas in them are the modalities of each poem's presiding presence, the dramatic expression of its will, mind, and imagination. And this act of utterance, vaster than its own speculative content, imparts structure to the poem and so gives coherence and continuity to the technical discontinuities of the poem's surface (cf. *R*, 52-3).

The "determining personality" in Stevens' poetry recurs in poem after poem, so that it not only structures each one but provides the pattern for a genuine *oeuvre*. There is thus something aesthetically infinite about him, while his acts of utterance are finite; and the *oeuvre* springs from a dialectic between his infinite possibilities for utterance and his finite acts of speech. He is Stevens' "major man," the "hero" who at once propounds and is the "first idea" because he is at once anterior to the particular acts of speech and their invented, fictive source and ground. His relation to the poems is thus essentially vatic, hierophantic, quasi-divine in a way; and this relationship becomes in the *oeuvre* part of a vast, mysterious, elusive analogy between the functions of human imagination in modern existence and the role God used to play in it. Thus, as in the St. Armorer's poem, for example, Stevens' relation to religion cannot become simply quarrelsome, for the underlying analogy keeps the fictive hero of his poetry and the God of the past in separate, mutually exclusive spheres. The analogy serves definitive functions. The semi-divine, orphic nature of the poems' hero accounts for the peculiar *present-tenseness* in Stevens, for it is as if the presiding personality were born whole and complete, with no personal past to disentangle and no private future to cause concern and with only the present moment to respond to and sing about — in short, a being not ourselves but "An accretion from ourselves, intelligent / Beyond intelligence, an artificial man / At a distance . . . *A being of sound*" (311; my italics). He is, in other words, a being created through an analogy to God and is therefore one "whom one does not approach / Through any exaggeration" (*ibid.*) or other faulty acts of poetic utterance: this Orpheus is capable of wrath and will strike you speechless. And since this central, guiding being is infinite, he can never be fully realized and articulated in a finite single poem and so only surfaces in the *oeuvre* randomly, as it were, and mysteriously (see "Chocorua to Its Neighbor," 296-302, which is a sustained meditation on "the motions of the spirit and the sound / Of what is secret"). And since he exists by virtue of an analogy to the older God, his one significant memory and single sense of a past is of Him. The only history in Stevens is the history of religion, his only conclusion from it is that God is now merely "a symbol for something that can as well take other forms, as, for example, the form of high poetry" (*OP*, 167).

The presiding presence in Stevens' poetry is thus at once infinitely whole and infinitely unfinished; and since his nature is not discursive, neither are his utterances: he is in essence not a philosopher or narrator but a singer of songs and a teller of fables and parables:

> On her trip around the world, Nanzia Nunzio
> Confronted Ozymandias. She went
> Alone and like a vestal long-prepared.   (395)

> Rou-cou spoke the dove,
> Like the sooth lord of sorrow,
> Of sooth love and sorrow
> And a hail-bow, hail-bow,
> To this morrow.   (519)

> The dry eucalyptus seeks god in the rainy cloud.
> Professor Eucalyptus of New Haven seeks him
> In New Haven with an eye that does not look
>
> Beyond the object. He sits in his room. . . .   (475)

> It is the natural tower of all the world,
> The point of survey, green's green apogee,
> But a tower more precious than the view beyond,
> A point of survey squatting like a throne,
> Axis of everything. . . .   (373)

Towers that are axes of everything, constant quests for adequate gods, songs that are purposely "about" nothing and so are pure *enactments* of singing, countless parables of the imagination's encounters with reality — all this constitutes not a representation of the Primary World (to use Tolkien's terms) of everyday, empirical reality but the creation of a fully self-sufficient Secondary World. Within it, we can have "Description Without Place" (339), since place is wholly the *ex-nihilo* creation of the central singer's song and so is "an artificial thing that exists,/ In its own seeming, plainly visible,/ Yet" — as in all Secondary Worlds — "not too closely the double of our lives,/ Intenser than any actual life could be" (344). "It is a world of words to the end of it. . . . alive with its own seemings, seeming to be / Like rubies reddened by rubies reddening" (345, 346). And the *chef d'orchestre* of this World, by virtue of the analogy that joins him to the Creator of the Primary World at the same time it separates them because we no longer believe in such a Creator, sings songs and tells tales whose explicit subjects are most often himself and his own actions and purposes. For since he is the first idea that explains all others, the comprehensive and generative "theory of the word" (345) behind every finite utterance, he is his own most significant subject; and yet, again analogically, since "the word is the making of the world" (*ibid.*), his meditations on himself are no more self-expressive than God's creation of the world was an act of egotism. He is not, that is, Stevens' "Jumbo," the "bad-bespoken lacker,/ Ancestor of Narcissus" in whose vain world "There are no rocks / And stones, only this imager" (269). He is the infinitely capable and therefore Supreme Fiction, omniscient and omnipresent, about whom there can necessarily only be "Notes" and momentary revelations and, as Stevens said, without whose "reality no amount of other things matters much" (*OP*, xxxix). He provides, in short, the integrity of Stevens' *oeuvre*, that is, the means of its total aesthetic integration.

What is discontinuous at one level of Stevens' technique thus merges into continuity at another; and the dialectic between infinite possibility for utterance and finite acts of speech can often become, within a poem, an alternation between meditations on its own essential shaping music and perceptions of inessential detail — as in "Variations on a Summer Day":

I

Say of the gulls that they are flying
In light blue air over dark blue sea.

II

A music more than a breath, but less
Than the wind, sub-music like sub-speech,
A repetition of unconscious things,
Letters of rock and water, words
Of the visible element and of ours.

III

The rocks of the cliff are the heads of dogs
That turn into fishes and leap
Into the sea.   (232)

The technique of non-narrative sequences perfectly expresses the
deeper dialectic; and his dialectic, as everywhere Stevens, never
rises to the level of pure speculation or a logic of being; it
remains always a dialectic in imagination and experience (cf. *R,*
68). There is thus a related and equally crucial set of analogical
connections in Stevens' poetry: the operations of poetic technique
at once relate to and reveal the acts of the presiding mind, which
are, in turn, at once relations with and revelations about the endless and changing stream of reality. For the infinite potentialities
of the central mind create endless possibilities in technique; and
these infinities are the modes for apprehending a reality infinitely
in flux. Stevens' Secondary World thus moves always toward the
Primary, and it is thus not only always *in* experience but is at the
same time always in an *interpretation* of experience (cf. *R,* 68).
And, consequently, within his world a bare empirical occurrence
is absolutely irrevocable — it is Reality — while its meaning is
absolutely revocable and so capable of endless interpretations. The
resulting play of revocabilities upon the irrevocable yields Stevens
his favorite, constantly reiterated rubric about Imagination and
Reality. Yet the rubric conceals a host of contradictions and paradoxes that, apparently in despite of Stevens' constant meditation
upon it, remains utterly impermeable to speculation. For the
rubric posits without explanation that Reality is a core "something" *which is there* and that Imagination is a psychic "force"

which is always *finding* it. But Stevens' unsuccess in reflecting upon this impenetrable rubric is self-aware and strategic, for what resists reduction to speculation is the essential *praxis* or action of his poetry: "The poem of *the mind* in *the act of finding*" (239; my italics). In his poetry, there is a constantly specified aesthetic presence engaged in a constantly specified dramatic action, and Stevens will not deny or reduce this presence or this action. Thus, to approach this *praxis* — this dramatic, non-discursive, supra-rational essence — through means of speculation is not to move toward an understanding of Stevens' poetry but to shatter it at its very center.

Any discussion of technique in Stevens is thus limited to the extent it conceives it merely as technical, that is, mechanical. Stevens thought *The Collected Poems* should be entitled *The Whole of Harmonium,* and the suggestion touches our experience of the indivisibility of his *oeuvre*: from beginning to end, we find technique turning into substance, surfaces into depths, in such a way that to isolate one from another is to transform the dramatic *praxis* that constitutes the substance of his poetry's wholeness into the speculative accidents of *dianoi* (theme). The suggestion has further meaning. The whole of Stevens is profoundly musical, in the sense that the set of related analogies which underlie the *oeuvre* create the vast rhythms of its primary action. "Analogies," Stevens said, "are much the larger subject," adding instantly: "And analogies are elusive" (*NA,* 129). Beyond a certain point, one cannot objectify these central analogies or the motions of their music, for it is only because we are in them that we are led by them beyond the point where such matters of technique are objective and explicable. Maurice Blondel said: "Analogies are based less on notional resemblances . . . than on an interior stimulation, on an assimilative solicitation . . ." (quoted in *R,* 15). The genius of Stevens' poetic technique lies in its capacity to move us along the rhythms of its primary analogies with "solicitive" ease and always toward what he terms poetry's transcendence: "It is a transcendence achieved by means of the minor effects of figurations and the major effects of the poet's sense of the world and of the motive music of his poems and it is the imaginative dynamism of all these analogies together" (*NA,* 130). And it is within this consequent "transcendent analogue" that is Stevens' world that we hear his most vital music.

Richard Eberhart:
Romantic Poet and Love Child

by Lois Gordon

Richard Eberhart has been writing poetry since 1930. Throughout these forty or so years, he has continued to write lyric poetry in a Romantic vein, in the traditions of Blake, Wordsworth, and Whitman — a poetry relatively free from the great technical innovations of the twentieth century.

Eberhart's way of writing is also alien to the method of the twentieth century which, in great part, has worked for the spare, hard line. Eberhart writes in inspirational flashes, and often completes a poem at a sitting; and he revises little. "Poetry is dynamic, Protean," he says, and "in the rigors of composition . . . the poet's mind is a filament, informed with the irrational vitality of energy as it was discovered in our time in quantum mechanics. The quanta may shoot off any way. (You breathe in maybe God.)." Such a mode of writing has produced a perhaps inevitable but marked unevenness in quality, and has led some thirty years of critics — amidst great praise — to belabor the poet for his many poems marred by banal abstractions, empty undisciplined rhetoric, naive diction, and forced rhythm.

But "at his peak the poet writes with a whole clarity," adds Eberhart in his "Notes on Poetry," and this well describes Eberhart at his peak. For at his best, he speaks in a simple, direct yet

187

emotionally charged language, which makes his best poems immediately moving and evocative and subsequently thought-provoking. Furthermore, the mystery, which he often talks of in his poetry, ("Mystery is forever the same/Wake to the life of the flame") is never academic. It is clearly the mystery of ultimates.

To place him in a volume on the 50s is in a sense arbitrary — although his *Selected Poems* appeared in 1951 and his *Collected Poems* in 1960 (as well as *Undercliff* in 1953 and *Great Praises* in 1957). Essentially it is an overdue recognition of a steadily accumulating body of significant verse. Although in some sense each of Eberhart's poems has a separate stance and viewpoint, for he is constantly shifting to remain true to the moment of perception, (to capture the essence of an experience though it may contradict another one also deeply felt), persistent themes can be seen in his best poems — death as an end or a transcendent experience, nature as indifferent or immanent, the intellectual life in opposition to the affective or active one, the need for personal love and love of humanity, and the nature and experience of poetry. It is these, or rather it is the poetry, that shall be our subject.

"This Fevers Me" begins the 1951 *Selected Poems*, as it does all of Eberhart's volumes), and it announces the fierce exhilaration that nature provokes within the poet:

> This fevers me, this sun on green,
> On grass glowing, this young spring.
> The secret hallowing is come,
> Regenerate sudden incarnation,
> Mystery made visible
> In growth, yet subtly veiled in all.

The sense of the enormous vitality in nature, its teeming life that stimulates the senses to the peaks of spiritual transcendence, is typically Eberhart. Nature is "lyric" and "lovely," the "earth breathing and the sun," but it is also God incarnate, the "mystery forever the same."

In another poem, ("Necessity"), again utilizing images of impregnation, Eberhart describes how we participate in both an active union with nature and a passive one with a force greater than our own, the ultimate reality:

> We are always about to be used
> And are used by nature, without escape,
> Save that our wills are with hers fused
> And we would impregnate her with our shape
> But in the great moments of being, something
> Beyond our wills, is the prime mover.

Also typically Eberhart is "Now is the Air Made of Chiming Balls," with its lyric exaltation of nature as a healing power. ". . . Fresh air/Blesses the vanished tear; the bunched anguish./The laughing balls their joyful pleasure tear./Renewed is the whole world and the sun/Begins to dress with warmth again every thing."

"We have a wound in our souls," and "poetry heals us," writes Eberhart, and this idea also underlies many of his best poems. In "Go to the Shine that's on a Tree," the poet commends the reader to first look to nature and then to make it an internal experience:

> Go to the shine that's on a tree
> When dawn has laved with liquid light
> With luminous light the nighted tree
> And take that glory without fright.
>
> Go to the song that's in a bird
> When he has seen the glistening tree,
> That glorious tree the bird has heard
> Give praise for its felicity.
>
> Then go to the earth and touch it keen,
> Be tree and bird, be wide aware
> Be wild aware of light unseen,
> And unheard song along the air.

To experience the beauty of nature's light is to gain visionary intimations.

Even in a later poem like "Ospreys in Cry," the poet watches the fierce untamed beauty of the seabirds and feels "a fleshed exultance," the "spirit in the flesh" that he says poetry reveals, and he concludes:

I felt a staggering sense
Of the victor and of the doomed,
Of being one and the other,
Of being both at one time,
I was the seer
And I was revealed.

Nature is both permanence and transience as it is manifested in man; man is the seer when immersed in the beauty of it, and the revealed when a part of its life and death processes.

There is a delightful little octave called "Cover Me Over" which ends: "Green arms about my head,/Green fingers on my hands./Earth has no quieter bed/In all her quiet lands." In a light way, illustrating Eberhart's versatility, the poem encompasses another duality in nature — earth as mother-lover and as resting place in death.

Death occupies Eberhart in many of his poems and here, too, his treatment varies. It is the moment of truth and revelation, in a mystic sense; but it is also "merely death," the end. The latter view is typified by his "I Walked Over the Grave of Henry James," where he writes: "I crushed a knob of earth between my fingers,/ This is a very ordinary experience./A name may be glorious but death is death." This same attitude underlies "Sestina," which he begins: "I die, no matter what I do I die."

But as befits a man of visionary tendencies, his imaginative apprehension of death produces greater poetry. For example, in "Imagining How It Would Be to be Dead," he projects death as the release from bodily imprisonment and as transmutation into the elemental wind:

And this was an embrace most dear,
Final, complete, a flying without wings.
From being bound to one poor skull,
And that surrounded by one earth,
And the earth in one universe forced,
And that chained to some larger gear,
I was the air, I was the air,
And then I pressed on eye and cheek
The sightless hinges of eternity
That make the whole world creak.

Or, in "The Soul Longs to Return Whence It Came," as he thinks
upon his dead mother, he writes:

> ... I thought of the roots;
> They would have pierced her seven years.
> O all peoples! O mighty shadows!
> My eyes opened along the avenue
> Of tombstones, the common land of death.
> Humiliation of all loves lost,
> That might have had full meaning in any
> Plot of ground, come, hear the silence,
> See the quivering light.

But after becoming oppressed with a sense of fear in being alone,
the son experiences a wild and primitive lust, a "worldless
ecstasy/Of mystery," and only then can he say, as the poem ends:

> ... I went away,
> Slowly, tingling, elated, saying, saying
> Mother, Great Being, O Source of Life
> In whom in wisdom we return,
> Accept this humble servant evermore.

Again, the earth and the Woman are equated as the poem moves
from despair to a kind of visionary joy.

In "Rumination," through the unifying image of earth, which
he associates with both dead and growth, Eberhart imagines death
as the very force of life:

> When I can hold a stone within my hand
> And feel time make it sand and soil, and see
> The roots of living things grow in this land,
> Pushing between my fingers flower and tree,
> Then I shall be as wise as death,
> For death has done this and he will
> Do this to me, and blow his breath
> To fire my clay, when I am still.

An interesting poem on death is the famous "The Groundhog,"
beginning, "In June, amid the golden fields,/I saw a groundhog
lying dead." In it Eberhart describes his overwhelming sense of

evanescence as he compulsively searches after the gradually disappearing evidence of the groundhog's existence: "It has been three years, now./There is no sign of the groundhog." Throughout the three-year period, the poet has sojourned to the funeral site, and he has sharply felt man's, as well as the animal's, "naked frailty." Yet his sharp confrontation with death has produced within him "a strange love," a "fever," and a "passion of the blood." He has expressed no hint of the *sic transit gloria* theme; instead, he has prayed for joy in the sight of decay. And even at the end, he evokes the transience of even man's substantial cultural, political, and religious monuments through a peculiarly vivid language — "vigorous," "ferocious," "flame," "passion of the blood." Although he has cried out about the inevitable passing of power, knowledge and the love of God, as well as the fact that death visits even the mighty, there remains a sense of stimulation in the images of "whirling summer" and "wild lament." Death as a stimulus to the poet's imagination can produce through the imaginative vision of the poem an act which can transcend death (as the bones bleaching in the sun are "beautiful as architecture.")

Joy in the sight of decay — the imagination overcoming the terrifying — is the theme of many of Eberhart's later poems, such as "The Cancer Cells," where he takes an aesthetic glee in the various shapes and forms of malignancy. "They looked like art itself, like the artist's mind," he writes, "I think Leonardo would have in his disinterest/Enjoyed them precisely with a sharp pencil." And in "When Golden Flies upon my Carcass Come," this same exaltation in decay returns as the poet foresees in the flies attacking his rotten flesh "some beauty . . . even at the guts of things."

Another recurring dualism in Eberhart concerns his wish to experience all sensation and the fullness of desire. Although these alone will allow him to see "the incomparable light," the poet also knows that somehow life is too complex for such experience, that morality demands that one be faithful to it. This essential ambivalent morality of vision seems to haunt Eberhart as he writes, for example, the famous "If I Could Only Live at the Pitch that is Near Madness." He longs for the possibilities of innocence, ("When everything is as it was in my childhood/Violent, vivid, and of infinite possibility"), and yet he cannot escape the "batallions of the race . . . / . . . demanding a moral answer." Or, in "The Sea-Hawk," again he cries: "How many centuries of sight/In this piercing, inhuman perfection/ . . . to make the mind exult/At the eye of a sea-hawk,/A blaze of grandeur, permanence of the impersonal." Or, finally, in the last two stanzas of "Great Praises":

> I used to hate the summer ardour
> In all my intellectual pride,
> But now I love the very order
>
> That brushed me fast aside,
> And rides upon the air of the world
> With insolent, supernal splendour.

In all of these, the sheer power of sensual stimulation confronts intellectual and moral pride and obligation.

The sense of human endurance in the face of tragedy persists in Eberhart. If the tragedy is personal, (i.e. a malignancy in the mother), and its effects weigh upon the individual (a child in the case of "Orchard"), Eberhart writes, typically:

> And in the evening, among the warm fruit trees
> All of life and all of death were there,
> Of pain unto death, of struggle to endure,
> And the strong right of human love was there.

The same strength persists when the tragedy is the experience of a group of war prisoners ("The Brotherhood of Man," the last poem in his *Selected Poems*):

> And yet I know (a knowledge unspeakable)
> That we were at our peak when in the depths,
> Lived close to life when cuffed by death.
> Had visions of brotherhood when we were broken,
> Learned compassion beyond the cure of passion,
> And never in after years those left to live
> Would treat with truth as in those savage times,
> And sometimes wish that they had died
> As did those many crying in their arms.

Love is the counterbalance to tragedy.

When Eberhart states, in the Foreword to his *Selected Poems 1930-1965*, "Poetry states the case for mankind. . . . It is ultimately a recognition of man's estate and of his fate," it seems as though he balances the Romantic and mystical elements of his poetry with a classic tragic awareness; as he says elsewhere "The poetry of tragedy is never dead." One can imaginatively comprehend death within a mystical system, but at other times, he must confront it, with love and poetry as his weapons.

Other issues also reverberate throughout Eberhart's verse, such as the life of the intellect in opposition to the force of will, action, or feeling, but again the poet is true to the moment of imaginative perception, so that he, as he puts it, often "sits on the fence," first assuming one pose and then its opposite. For example, at times he writes that he will "kill all delight" and allow intellect to "my flesh protect"; nevertheless,

> . . . the hard intellectual light
> That kills all delight
> . . . brings the solemn, inward pain
> Of truth into the heart again.
> ("In a Hard Intellectual Light")

At other times, he accepts the dualities of man's nature, that he is flesh yet spirit, cruel yet magnanimous, rational yet animalistic —on the isthmus emotionally, psychologically, and physically between the primitive and heavenly planes. In "Seals, Terns, Time," for example, he gazes upon the water with its "blurred, kind forms/That rise and peer from elemental water," but he is also driven to watch the birds flying above him whose "aspirations dip in mine." He concludes:

> I am in compulsion hid and thwarted,
> Pulled back in the mammal water,
> Enticed to the release of the sky.

In many of his poems Eberhart sees human love, "concrete, [and] specific," as the primary human experience:

> It is love discoverable here
> Difficult, dangerous, pure, clear,
> The truth of the positive hour
> Composing all of human power.
> ("The Goal of Intellectual Man")

Or, he concludes that love will not allow man the comfort that he seeks:

> Praise to harmony and love.
> They are best, all else is false.
> Yet even in love and harmony
> The human being is a lonely creature.
> ("The Human Being is a Lonely Creature")

Or, he laments the absence of love in either man or the universe. At times, it seems to him that the ultimate reality is man's cruelty in a universe without God. First, he may say:

> There is a somber, imponderable fate.
> Enigma rules, and the heart has no certainty.
> ("Flux")

But there is also the fury of the following:

> Was man made stupid to see his own stupidity?
> Is God by definition indifferent, beyond us all?
> Is the eternal truth man's fighting soul
> Wherein the Beast ravens in its own avidity?
> ("The Fury of Aerial Bombardment")

The weight of Eberhart's verse extols love beyond both the absolute of death and the solipsism of either contemplation or participation in any consuming vision:

> Who talks with the Absolute salutes a Shadow,
> Who seeks himself shall lose himself;
> And the golden pheasants are no help
> And action must be learned from love of man.
> ("I Walked Out to the Graveyard to See the Dead")

Eberhart writes somewhere that he would like to be the completely contemplative man, the poet at all times, but, he also says, "the next generation howls for food." And, to provide, after his schooling at Dartmouth and Cambridge and until World War II, he taught at St. Mark's, a prep school; then after a period as a Naval gunnery instructor and officer, he worked for the Butcher

Wax Company, succeeding to an executive level. His non-aesthetic publications during this time include "Helpful Hints for Home-makers" and the Navy's "Free Gunnery Handbook" ("If you have to hit an enemy in the gas tank, direct your fire to the gas vapor and the ship will blow up."). In recent years he has been a poet-in-residence at various universities and is now at Dartmouth. Along the way, he married and had two children.

Eberhart was born in Minnesota into a family of means, but he knew early personal tragedy in adolescence, when his mother died of cancer and his father's business fortunes declined. (The birth-life-earth-mother symbolism in his poetry may be related to his mother's catastrophic illness — to his horror about the suffering involved in dying and perhaps to his unconscious longings for reunion with her. Eberhart makes additional connections between death and the writing of poetry in his "Notes on Poetry": "Divisive man can know unity only at death [or so he can speculate], and he cannot know what kind of unity that is. He lives in continuous struggle with his imperfection and the imperfection of life. If one were only conscious of harmony, there would be no need to write.")

The most overtly romantic adventure in his life — besides his poetry — appears to have been his trip around the world on a tramp steamer and his one-year sojourn as tutor to the son of King Prajadhipok of Siam. It is interesting to me, and I think interesting to note in a volume on the 50s, that like the Beat poets, and their successors, the Flower Children, Eberhart took the journey to the East, but unlike them he did not use it as a prelude to bogus religious pretensions, madness, or bad poetry. I think it may be, in part, inherent talent that enabled him to make of his experiences good poetry, but I suspect that character and training had just as much to do with it. The poet may breathe in God, but he writes down words. And he must be prepared for his task — possibly educationally but certainly through a personality capable of integrating as well as regressing to the pitch that is near madness.

I do, however, find Eberhart very close in spirit to what the Beats and the Flower Children have sought after. He has never been political in a programmatic sense, and he survived, as Kenneth Rexroth has noted, his own generation of 30s poets who surely were. In addition, Eberhart has never been academically allusive in his poetry, although he is a learned man. Also, he has been, as the Beats and Flower Children are, in search of "sacred" values, the revealing light, and yet despite occasional poems which use Christian imagery, his verse subscribes to no conventional religious philosophy. As the Beats have hit the road and the flower children convened in communities at Big Sur, Eberhart has looked to nature for revivification of the sense and of the spirit. The wish for madness, the madness which reveals, which brings one "into things" and close to absolutes by shedding the skin of convention, could almost represent a credo for a generation on acid. The cry for love, human love, against "the fury of aerial bombardment" is really the message of the Love Children.

One always suspects of the Love Children who come, by and large, from middle-class families, as did Eberhart, that they will someday either return to Westchester, Evanston, or Atherton, just as rigid and system-oriented as their fathers, or that they will find their homes in mental hospitals. One cannot live at the pitch that is near madness for too long, and besides, a moral answer is demanded, as well as material sustenance. One hopes, however, that Eberhart's work will find an audience in the Children of the Now Generation, as it seems to have in each of the past four decades, for perhaps it can help them to return to society and yet retain the values of their trip into vision, as the poet himself seems to have done.

Theodore Roethke:
"In a Slow Up-Sway"

by DAN JAFFE

There's nothing like a favorable literary synopsis. It may even decorate the jacket cover of the writer's next book. Such synopses may occasionally spear truths; more often, like their TV equivalents, they distort by oversimplifying or hide by substituting a ringing adjective or a clever metaphor for an observation of substance. Images besiege us, and too often they are not the images of the poems we are reading but those projected over-simplifications encouraged by critics and publishers or poets playing the game of you pat my image and I'll pat yours. So, for too many readers, despite the enormous weight of evidence to the contrary, Robert Frost remains a Vermont cigar-store Indian with attractively chiseled features and an unforked tongue. For such readers Theodore Roethke is undoubtedly an obsessed adolescent groveling in a pile of damp autumn leaves. This is the kind of image encouraged by Stephen Spender, among others. It's possible to understand the reasons for such a view without accepting it. It strikes me as having about as much truth as the photograph of a political candidate, a photograph taken purposefully from the worst angle at the precise moment the subject had his mouth open and his tonsils showing.

During his lifetime Roethke encouraged all sorts of rumors about himself. A number of his friends were nearly convinced that he was the literary ambassador to the Mafiosa. At the same time his objectives and achievements often became haze in the corner of the continent. So to many he was an obscurantist, even while he published lyrics in the *Ladies Home Journal,* of all places. Others thought him a hyper-sophisticate, even as he penned poems about serpents that sang and sloths that swayed. Probably no American poet since Whitman has wanted the wide audience as much as Theodore Roethke. And probably none who sought it so assiduously remained so anonymous for so long. Roethke's name and a few facts about him seeped slowly into sight. The poets knew him, the *aficionados,* but few others. There are certainly some profound reasons for this, but it may be merely that "Roethke" is difficult to spell and ambiguous to pronounce. A producer might well have instructed him to change his name if he wanted stardom. Names like "Frost," "Stevens," 'Williams," "Pound" — they are ideal for a marquee.

During the 50s Roethke's poems won him the Pulitzer prize (1953) and the National Book Award (1958). Nevertheless his was not a name one would have expected the average freshman-English instructor to recognize. Other poets of the 40s and 50s — Wilbur, Shapiro, and Jarrell, poets of integrity, talent, and achievement — were better known. John Ciardi missed the prizes but soared into public prominence after his devastating review of Anne Morrow Lindbergh. Allen Ginsberg and Lawrence Ferlinghetti penetrated the national consciousness despite widespread academic and establishment disapproval. But who knew or cared that Theodore Roethke was a member of the National Institute of Arts and Letters?

The mist about Roethke was so thick that the Indiana University Press was still advertising him as a "young poet" on the cover of the paperback edition of *Words for the Wind,* the last of his books published while he lived.

Why did it take so long for any word to get around?

It is easy to blame the philistinism of the time, to note aristocratically that few in the mob care about any poetry, let alone modern poetry, or to conclude sardonically that a nation that would elect Dwight David Eisenhower to two terms could hardly be sensitive enough to language to respond to poetry or to care about poets. But it takes more than two half-truths to make a whole truth.

It was at the very beginning of the decade that two Hunter

College graduates, Marianne Mantell and Barbara Holdridge, cashed in on of all things, modern poetry. They built a company on the voice of Dylan Thomas. His reading, the first record on their label, Caedmon Records, sold over 200,000 within the first eighteen months, far better than almost any classical disc. The audience for modern poetry might not be massive, but it was substantial. Sadly and ironically, however, while Americans opened to the great Welsh poet they remained generally unaware of an American poet who shared many of Thomas's strengths, yet remained distinctly himself. Still, Roethke's anonymity was clearly not the consequence of their being too small an audience capable of responding to poetry of consequence.

Saul Bellow has suggested that those who believe America is dull, those who think its key symbol is Levitttown, who find, as Matthew Arnold did so many years ago, only a dreary uninformed sameness wherever they go, have not really looked at all. Bellow believes that many people fail to note the unique or to register the different, because they cannot grasp the enormous complexity and variety that is America. It may well be that Ted Roethke's specialness, his very existence gets lost in the rush of the 50s, an era in which excellent poets, whole schools of poets in fact, vie with each other with such intensity and regularity and perform new and extraordinary tricks so dexterously that it is easy to overlook the single voice not married to a magazine, publishing house, or other public relations institution engaged professionally in grabbing attention. Maybe somebody could have sold Ted Roethke, but no one did. A certain amount of errant absurdity and political nicety may also be involved. The marketplace was glutted and the anthologists were pushing their own boys. Not until recently have Roethke poems appeared regularly in college texts. While one can argue unremittingly with editors about their choices, I need only point out that a volume self-importantly entitled *Chief Modern Poets of England and America,* edited by Gerald DeWitt Sanders, John Herbert Nelson, and M. L. Rosenthal, includes Carl Sandburg, Edna St. Vincent Millay, and Howard Nemerov, but fails even to mention Ted Roethke, not even by a fourth printing in 1964.

John Ciardi's anthology, "Mid-Century American Poets" (1950), presented a group noted for solid craftsmanship and sound liberalism. Richard Wilbur, Robert Lowell, Elizabeth Bishop, John Frederick Nims, Randall Jarrell, Karl Shapiro, Winfield Townley

Scott, Richard Eberhart and Delmore Schwartz are among Roethke's companions in the volume. This imposing array of professionals would produce a steady stream of more than worthwhile books for the next ten years.

Nor was this all the competition. One needs to remember that Eliot, Pound, Stevens, Marianne Moore, W. H. Auden, E. E. Cummings, Robinson Jeffers, H. D., Conrad Aiken, and others who had established big reputations earlier were publishing important new books. Pound's poems from Confucius and Eliot's *Confidential Clerk,* no matter what their real merits, attracted considerable attention that might easily have been focused as fruitfully elsewhere.

At the beginning of the decade William Carlos Williams completed the fourth book of his epic, "Paterson." Book V came later in the 50s, after a number of other Williams' books. John Berryman's *Homage to Mistress Bradstreet,* another poem of magnitude, punctuates the middle of the decade.

And what of those other poets of merit, Leonie Adams, Louise Bogan, Muriel Rukeyser, Kenneth Rexroth, and Reed Whittemore, to name just a few who produced work worth study and attention. Meanwhile craftsmen like Robert Fitzgerald, Dudley Fitts, and John Ciardi produced translations many readers and critics considered as fresh and significant as the range of new offerings.

On the surface, to the uninitiated the decade may have appeared "placid," all the hard workers making honey in their cells. But it was anything but. A revolution was underway. Karl Shapiro would by the end of the decade denounce most of his own early work, damn most of the masters who seemed beyond criticism, and search for a new way of going, a new basis for poetry. Allen Ginsberg, Lawrence Ferlinghetti, Gregory Corso and other Beats had challenged the controls with unexpected energy. By 1958 the battle lines were forming, the anthologists girding themselves for selection.

This is a flimsy summary; its purpose not to be fair but to give some sense of the dimensions of activity, some notion of the great difficulty of picking out a new figure of real dimension, whose poems do not call attention to themselves because of epic proportions, political daring, contemporary relevance, or a programmatic aesthetic that could easily be turned into a photographic essay for the picture magazines.

It has become a cliché of the modern poetry class to point out how divided critical and anthological opinion had become by the end of the 50s. The so-called academic anthologies excluded the Beat poets; the Beat collections excluded the academics. Roethke might well have been included in either kind of collection, it seems to me. Perhaps that's one reason why he was not sufficiently appreciated. Both camps probably found him suspect. During the 50s Roethke had three books: *Praise to the End* (1951), *The Waking, Poems 1933-1953* (1953), and *Words for the Wind* (1958), the last, a collection of new and earlier work. Poems like "The Shape of the Fire," "Praise to the End," "I Cry, Love! Love!" "O, Thou Opening, O" follow from "The Lost Son," Roethke's 1948 breakthrough. This group of poems is probably the most startling. Each of these poems contains many of the same ingredients in different proportions. The poet's tactics are similar in each. They are highly imagistic, contain only minimum explanation of feeling or idea. Thematically, they generally move from terror toward hope, from fearful questioning toward tentative affirmation. Although single lines may fall into easily scanned metrical patterns, the line lengths are highly irregular and no metrical norms are established. These are poems of creatures, plants, stones, bits of flesh, childhood touches and gestures; only rarely do the objects or the apparatus of our technological civilization get into the poems. Time and again the poems turn back to close approximations of nursery rhythms and rhymes. Repeatedly there are references to the elemental, to Mother and Father, to earth and water, to growth. They shift from the literal to the figurative unexpectedly, often without warning.

But such generalizations, even if they are accurately descriptive fail to provide a sense of the poems. One feels like saying, "The hell with prosody!" The experience is the consequence of the poet's virtuosity; the poems are linguistic performances. Who can deny it? But these are poems beyond admiration, beyond even the "new" criticism, fine tool that it may be. They reach directly for experience. Somehow the smaller the area between art and the world, the less room there is for the critic to move around in and justify himself. Roethke doesn't leave much room. Are his images symbols or psychic actualities? Do they represent ideas or are they the direct embodiment of feelings? The professor of poetry ordinarily selects the first of these alternatives. Even the poet talking about his own work discusses what he means to symbolize. But the discussion of symbols immediately introduces an intellectualization alien to the spirit of these poems. They take one down below the mind or out beyond it.

More important than any technical or thematic observations are the drench of feelings, the corporeal itch, the agony, in the colloquial and classic sense of that word. This is a poetry of stretch rather than repression. It accomplishes what the Beats maintain they mean to accomplish. It is flying or diving rather than an instruction pamphlet or a superbly fashioned machine. Here one is more aware of the pitch of feelings than the skill of achievement. What one wonders about is how he managed himself while making it, rather than how he made it, how he faced such dares of feeling and still functioned artistically. Each of these poems seems to be a return to a tightrope stretched in a heavy wind across an enormous abyss. The old notion of aesthetic distance breaks down. We become the poet, the dramatic voice, the renewed self, amazed by suffering and survival.

These poems do not provide us touchstones of correctness; they do not call attention to the erudition or prowess of the poet. By being most himself he becomes one with basic forces the American at mid-century may easily forget. His poems somehow seem a corrective for the time in which they were written. They reply to the strangulation of the spirit threatened by Senator Joseph McCarthy and the computer collective. These are not poems of quiet, good taste. They refuse to be prim. They don't even hide in the acceptable realms of intellectual achievement, though they are without a doubt justification for philosophizing and theological discussion. Roethke has craft; he has intellectual scope. But that comes later; the first thrust is the thrust of unleashed feeling, of the insides opened out, the wiggle, push, threat of living forms rather than the safety of a shaped fortress. The poems cry, "Risk," in a time devoted to security. And so in an indirect way they have social significance, although they point outward toward what Roethke calls "the kingdom of bang and blam" at only rare moments. I don't even want to quote, not even to prove my points. A few lines out of context will probably seem more epigrammatic than intended, more brilliant tidbits than part of a rush of psychic development, more proof than bite.

> Mother me out of here. What more will the bones allow:
> Will the sea give the wind suck? A toad falls into a stone.
> These flowers are all fangs. Comfort me, fury.

Wake me, witch, we'll do the dance of rotten sticks.
from "The Shape of the Fire"

A cursory look at "The Shape of the Fire," however, may provide a sense of some of the tensions Roethke brings us to. In the opening section, from which the above lines are taken, the dramatic voice cries out. His is a cry of confusion, compensation, terror; he seeks nourishment amid the elemental forces that tremble around him and make him tremble. In section two, the dramatic voice reasseses the sources of fear: the self is a "varicose horror," "A two-legged dog hunting a new horizon of howls." The images are primitive, animalistic; underneath the human clothes are swamp instincts. He is trapped by his own flesh, but is that all? Section three answers symbolically with affirmations of glisten and rose-sway. It is a kind of epiphany: a promise of progress in "the journey from flesh." Section four is faintly reminiscent of shining passages of Dylan Thomas, whom Roethke admired. Light, birds, flowers — they sing life. Section five is a joyful recapitulation of the rising of the rose, the snail, the man, toward the sources of sustenance. Even such a simplistic summary ought to make clear that these poems are essentially psychic narratives drawing a great deal of force from the archetypal metaphor of the journey. But beware of phrases like "archetypal metaphor." They have the text book ring.

What matters most here is the movement from dream to dream. And these are real dreams, couched in fact. They leave sweat and sperm on the sheets. In our culture what could be more forbidding and embarrassing? Imagine our politicos owning up to their dreams, Mr. Nixon or Mr. Agnew disclosing to the nation something of their inner lives. This is akin to Allen Ginsberg stripping at Columbia. What could be more scandalous than such revelations? Ted Roethke threatens the self-assurance of the culture; he makes the men of cool, practiced efficiency look at themselves and their circumstances: Wrenched and fleshy feelings in an unpinned universe.

But Roethke was not a single minded poet who wrote a single kind of poem. *Words for the Wind* illustrates the fallacy of thinking of Roethke as simply a greenhouse poet of slugs and soil. There are those who would dump all modern poetry into one basket. It's not possible to do that with even a single poet of caliber. And certainly not with one of exceptional stature.

Set against the narrative-dramatic poems of the inner life that identify Roethke as a poet of energy and exuberance are poems of clasical grace, poems like "I Knew a Woman," whose form is summed up in the line, "The shapes a bright container can contain!" Roethke can soothe with a gentle villanelle like "The Waking." Here the substance of the wilder poems is gentled within the confines of the strict iambic line, "The lowly worm climbs up a winding stair." In poems like the "Four for Sir John Davies" Roethke illustrates how well he can step to familiar cadences:

> Things loll and loiter. Who condones the lost?
> This joy outleaps the dog. Who cares? Who cares?
> I gave her kisses back, and woke a ghost.
> O what lewd music crept into our ears!
> The body of the soul know how to play
> In that dark world where gods have lost their way.

It's enough to melt the heart of any old academic to note the heavy rhyme, assonance, and alliteration. One can almost bring this safely into the classroom in order to discuss traditional poetic techniques.

Here the great energy has harnessed itself to shape, transformed itself into the most expressive kind of poise, the poise of performance and the poise of potential. These poems give us control, the matter caught; they also give us, to use Roethke's metaphor, a bird singing at the center of a tree, stir and ripple choreographed by a master.

So, "All the Earth, All the Air" might be a text book for those concerned with the glide of vowels and the shift of consonants. Poem after poem is a virtuoso performance without being a cheap tour-de-force. The skill is the kind that doesn't obtrude. Roethke juggles only to mean, but that does not diminish our admiration for his dexterity.

The poet tries to make form a liberator; uniqueness a habit. The Beats tried to break out of the straight jacket they felt the dictates of T. S. Eliot and Ezra Pound had imposed; the academic poets sought to preserve the virtues of craft. Ted Roethke managed the balance between energy and control; that is the measure of greatness.

He is a poet of wider resources and tactics than has been appreciated. He reaches from torment to joy, from absolute fear to mystical affirmation. He can provide the touch of the brute world and a sense of the indefinable. He can be witty and passionate at once. One moment he is on his nubs in the loam, the next soaring in meditation. He can be elliptical and conversational, and he seems to have constantly polished and reassessed his equipment so that while he developed new ways of going he never lost the techniques of the earlier poems. There is a lyrical, a dramatic, a discursive, and an epigrammatic Roethke. Many of his poems come clear on at least one level immediately. Others may baffle readers for long periods. His work can be viewed as a modern Divine Comedy: he moves from the Inferno to Paradise. One can read the poems as theological and philosophical examinations, forays into the nature of the human condition, the function of suffering, the sources of evil, even the generation gap. One can consider them psychological dramatizations.

Most importantly Roethke transforms language into actualization; the poems bombard us, stroke us, shake us. No American poet has approached the subject of physical love with such love, the body with such foreboding. Children, lady editors, lovers — he has poems for them all.

Critics, anthologists, and professors who ignore Roethke do so at the risk of offending posterity. The 50s gave us a major poet whose reputation is already moving "in a slow up-sway," the appropriate motion of Roethke's poems. The new generation of readers has already found Roethke provides what it needs: a sense of self; a willingness to report on the personal, emotional life, in order to share rather than to confess; a willingness to be different, even strange. And, at the same time, a kind of connective tissue that links us all.

Virtues in Style,
Defect in Content:
The Poetry of Richard Wilbur

by KENNETH JOHNSON

Partially because the free-verse styles used by Walt Whitman and William Carlos Williams became the dominant influence in the world of poetry during the 50s and 60s, Richard Wilbur's poetry, despite receiving many accolades, has not been given the critical attention it deserves. If the form and subject matter of Wilbur's poems and of contemporary free verse are compared, significant — and unjust — reasons why Wilbur's work has been relatively neglected become clear. Such a comparison also discloses certain advantages in Wilbur's stylistic practices. However, there is one major aspect of Wilbur's poetry — namely, the overall content — that is seriously defective. After first comparing Wilbur's poetry and modern free verse, I want to focus on the pattern of beliefs and attitudes contained in his poetry.

With regard to form and subject matter, a comparison of Wilbur's poems and contemporary free verse reveals several interesting facts. The latter can be described as a poetry of assemblage or, in other instances, a poetry of assertion; the poems either assemble a montage of images that imply some statement — a statement that must be relatively simple if it is to be discerned amid the welter of evocative descriptive details — or they fervently acclaim or denounce (but rarely scrutinize) some viewpoint that is presumed to be correct or incorrect. In contrast, Wilbur's poetry is usually a poetry of analysis. After first presenting a scene or situation, Wilbur weighs possible responses or interpretations. That Wilbur's type of poetry has been relatively neglected is, then, an interesting comment on readers of poetry. Apparently, most readers exclusively prefer a poetry that features a dramatic immediacy and that contains simple statements or that only intensifies their prejudices; they do not want a poetry that stimulates their intellect as well as their emotions. Surely readers — and critics — should be more willing to respond to a variety of poetic techniques.

A second point of comparison centers on Wilbur's belief that each poem should be a separate entity in which the particular form a poem takes evolves as the total poem evolves. In contrast, free verse writers, scorning all other forms as "too limiting," are often unaware that, in using only the free verse form, they have in fact limited themselves much more than Wilbur has. They also refuse to see that the traditional forms Wilbur frequently uses have dealt with our most complex experiences just as successfully as free verse forms have.

Finally, concerning subject matter, Wilbur's work contains more variety than most free verse poetry. The latter focuses obsessively on the poets' personal lives, on abstract concepts, and on the esoteric. Wilbur, on the other hand, takes his subjects not only from these areas but also from quotidian reality. Indeed, Wilbur is almost a poet-revolutionary in his inclusion of the diversified daily world — (even the suburban daily world!) — in his poetry. Yet Wilbur's use of such material, when noticed at all, has gained him only scorn, not praise. Here, again, I think the root of the problem is the now widely held — and narrow-minded — belief that the poetry must attempt solely to provide the reader with the same kind of intense emotional jag offered by the noisiest jazz festival. Spurred by this belief, the reader (and critic) prizes only those poems that feature a highly unusual and emotionally-charged subject matter; and regards poems about quotidian reality with contempt. Yet this reality is what the reader is most commonly confronted with in his lifetime; and so, if he is going to live an emotionally rich life, it is this reality that he must learn to recognize as containing more than a dulling drabness. And this is precisely what Wilbur's poetry tries to help the reader to do.

But it is the overall content of Wilbur's poetry that I want to concentrate on. As part of the process of enriching the reader's sensibilities, every poet's works form a pattern of beliefs and attitudes. As readers, we trace that pattern, then evaluate it. Thus, before we can evaluate Wilbur's content, we must first pinpoint his basic concerns.

One major concern is tangible reality, a reality seen — in "Driftwood" for instance — as composed of enduring elements. The assurance that such elements do endure offers Wilbur — living in a world filled with uncertainty and destruction — a much-needed solace. Scenic beauty also offers this solace, the point implied in "First Snow in Alsace." However, Wilbur believes that man is helplessly cut off from that reality. A key poem that delineates his views here is "The Beacon," a poem in some ways quite similar to Wallace Stevens' "The Idea of Order at Key West." The beacon, representing man's mind, not only reveals the sea but creates an order — "searoads" — out of it. But once the beacon's light is turned away, we have only the chaotic "sea-in-itself," a reality that is beyond our knowledge. We may sometimes sense hidden layers of reality (Wilbur's theme in "A Hole in the Floor"); but, as stated in "The Lilacs," all that nature clearly reveals is "death's kingdom."

This view of reality triggers one primary emotional response in Wilbur: fear — the emotion depicted in "The Pardon." It also causes Wilbur to turn his attention to man's imaginative powers and to a separate ideal realm. Concerning the former, Donald Hill, in his excellent book *Richard Wilbur,* observes that, for Wilbur, art can create a reality that is in some respects superior to the tangible world, the theme of "A Song" and "L'Etoile." So, too, in "Junk," Wilbur's imagination leads him to envision the enduring, but battered objects as being remade by Hephaestus. Wilbur directly celebrates man's imaginative powers in "For the New Railway Station in Rome," which praises our ability "to imagine excellence, and try to make it." Concerning the ideal realm, "Grasse: The Olive Trees" reports Wilbur's yearning for the "far away." And "Clearness" describes a vision of that ideal realm. But the vision is later judged to be only subjective, and, so, worthless.

Mindful, then, of the many pitfalls that exist in both the actual world and the path to the ideal world, Wilbur ultimately strives to maintain a sense of balance between both worlds, a balance that will also enable him to better observe human experience. In "Love Calls Us to the Things of This World," Wilbur admires the nuns who manage to "keep their difficult balance" between those two worlds. However, the struggle for balance is a formidable one because Wilbur has an intense longing for the ideal world. This problem is defined again and again in such poems as "In the Elegy Season," "Castles and Distances," and " 'A World Without Objects Is a Sensible Emptiness.' "

Wilbur himself, in *Poets On Poetry,* guides us to the core of his concern when he states that the poems of his which he has quoted in his article "all have to do with the proper relation between the tangible world and the intuitions of the spirit" and stress his inclination "to favor a spirituality which is not abstracted, not dissociated and world-renouncing." So, too, Hill points out Wilbur's wish not to surrender "the Earth in despair to science" and Wilbur's belief that instead of seeking "supernatural realms, the imagination . . . should establish itself on earth and become a refuge for all natural things." For the power of external reality — as Wilbur, in his lecture on Emily Dickinson, emphasizes — "depends on our state of mind"; the soul can "select a superior order and scope of consciousnes which will render it finally invulnerable."

Wilbur's powerful individual poems on various aspects of these themes constitute the major reason why he must be ranked as one of our finest living poets. Wilbur is a master of descriptive writing, of rhythm and sound-patterns, and, especially, of rime. And his best poems, replete with his almost peerless craftsmanship, present vivid definitive studies of contemporary problems, choices, and reactions. Nonetheless, the overall position that his poems formulate is, I think, seriously flawed. First of all, for someone who wants to focus primarily on the tangible world, Wilbur too often fails to do so. One is, in fact, prompted to ask: if Wilbur so highly values and is enamored by this tangible world, why is he so often — and so easily and gladly — lured away from it? and, secondly, why — as in "Love Calls Us to the Things of This World" — does he feel so regretfully duty-bound, even "bitter," about returning to the tangible world?

So, too, the tangible world seems to be something that Wilbur celebrates only when it is immediately attractive. When the scene or situation is unattractive, Wilbur almost always quickly retreats from it in one way or another. For instance, in "Junk" he gains an all-too-quick comfort from the fact that a pile of junk can, in the hands of a "Hephaestus," be re-used — (why can't he accept junk as junk?). Similarly, in "Stop" he quickly likens the color of a truck parked at a drab railroad station to "the phosphorus of Lethe/Or Queen Persephone's gaze." He does not really enhance these scenes by introducing mythological elements into them; rather, he uses mythology only to soften these scenes' drabness, to "prettify" them. This is not so much a way of coping with reality as it is a way of evading it. At other times, as in "First Snow in Alsace," he enjoys a pretty snowfall only in order to escape from other grim segments of reality — a natural but not very positive reaction. And rarely does he confront — or even allude to — the existence of evil in the world. Thus, we are dubious about Wilbur's celebration of the tangible world.

It also seems that Wilbur does surrender "the Earth to Science." Actually, he is a product of the scientific point of view; for, despite his desire (stated in "Poplar, Sycamore") to "never know the dry disease/Of thinking things no more than what he sees," Wilbur finds precious little in tangible reality other than "what he sees." What more he does find he usually decides is chaotic — and terrifying. Most often, however, he finds nothing at all.

As a result, the imagination, for Wilbur, does become a "refuge" — not an expedition moving toward the hidden treasure of richer levels of reality, but a citadel where one can find protection from reality. This explains why he stresses Dickinson's discovery of a consciousness which is "invulnerable." So, too, though Wilbur wants a spirituality that is not "world-renouncing," he describes no experience that instigates any deep lasting spiritual rapport with the tangible world. He seems to do so in "October Maples, Portland." But, although he declares that the light makes a lasting spiritual impression on him, in point of fact his later poems indicate no decrease in his basic spiritual uncertainty. Thus, the "lasting" spiritual experience is really only momentary — only the result of one of a variety of temporary happen-chance moods. As "Clearness" more typically indicates, his spiritual visions are ultimately judged to be totally subjective, invalid. The world is always something irrevocably "outside" of him. This also holds true concerning other people; even in his love poems, the lovers do not "fuse" — they only "counter" one another.

Wilbur's yearnings for an ideal world are interesting in this connection too, for they remind one of the poets of the Romantic

Period. But there are useful distinctions to be made between the viewpoints of, say, Keats and Wilbur. Keats firmly believed in two distinct worlds, the tangible and the ideal, and that the tangible world contained "messengers" from or symbols of the ideal world. The nightingale was, of course, such a symbol and, as such, greatly prized by Keats. Wilbur almost never sees objects in the tangible world as valid messengers of the ideal world. Consequently, in this respect, Keats valued the tangible world much more highly than Wilbur does — even though Wilbur wants to focus on this world, while Keats saw it only as a flawed replica of a better world and wanted more than anything else to transcend this world. Wilbur, in truth, does not feel at all certain about that ideal realm. In "Grasse: The Olive Trees," that realm, symbolized by the olive trees, "dims and dries"; in "La Rose des Vents," it "dissolves." "For the New Railway Station in Rome" indicates that heaven might well be, after all, only man-made — a wistful daydream. Unlike Keats, then, Wilbur does not really want to go to that ideal realm — or, more precisely, he often *wants* to go there but never wants to *attempt* to go there. Consequently, his insistence on not renouncing this world turns out to be not an affirmation of this world, but only the result of his uncertainty about the existence of any other world.

What does such a man have left? His mind, his imagination— a subject that particularly interests Wilbur, as it did another poet I wish to compare to Wilbur — Wallace Stevens. Stevens, denied the traditional Absolutes, wanted us to view the tangible world via a mind shaped by his theory of poetry. This desire led him to study the nature of reality and, more, the means by which man gained knowledge of reality — that is, the workings of the mind itself. As a result, Stevens' poetry presents us with an almost innumerable number of detailed findings concerning this fundamental area of human experience. Wilbur's poetry, in comparison, suffers. From Wilbur we learn that the imagination can enrich reality (and so, too, our lives) and that, at other times, it can trick us into false dreams or idle mental constructions. Because this subject most excites Wilbur, the majority of his most exciting poems are on this topic. But he tends only to repeat the same observations in poem after poem; he does not give us nearly the variety of valuable, vibrant insights that Stevens does.

Another difference between these two poets is that Stevens *committed* himself, while Wilbur, perhaps too aware of the possible dangers a firm commitment can contain, just won't do this. He insists on remaining detached in order to better judge particular experiences as they occur. Here, then, we have a stance that is admirable in some contexts but flawed in others. For while such a stance enables Wilbur to perceive aspects of human experience that others, enmeshed (because of their commitments) in those experiences, cannot see, by the same token this stance denies Wilbur the knowledge that can only be learned by a person who is enmeshed in those experiences.

With regard to this desire to remain an observer, Wilbur is more like Robert Frost than Stevens. Like Frost, Wilbur is willing to lean toward heaven; but wants to dip back toward earth — and, so, to wholly abide in neither world. Like Frost, Wilbur will admit that the woods of complex reality are lovely, dark, and deep; but won't go into those woods. Unfortunately, although this role offers one the chance never to be wrong, it does not offer one the chance to be ever dynamically right. Also, such freedom becomes increasingly sterile; for freedom is, finally, only as valuable as the worth of what you give it up for. Nor will this kind of freedom give sustenance. When pressured by reality, Frost in fact did not attempt to remain uncommitted. Rather, as Yvor Winters pointed out in "Robert Frost, Or the Spiritual Drifter as Poet," Frost, when harrassed, fell back on an unexamined Emersonian belief that life was, after all, basically good. Wilbur is too honest and too thoroughly analytical to allow himself this bland escape-hatch belief. However, instead, he offers us nothing.

Does this mean that Wilbur's poetry contains little of serious value? Not at all. Earlier, I cited several praise-worthy qualities present in Wilbur's work — his skill at descriptive writing, his mastery of rhythm, sound-patterns, and rime, and, most of all, his ability to vividly capture the particular scenes and situations, thoughts and feelings that he does use as his subject matter. Still earlier, I suggested other achievements of his concerning form and subject matter. I would now, in conclusion, stress still other values. First, there is Wilbur's continuous, brilliantly formulated questionings, questionings which make him more valuable than the vast majority of poets. For I would assume it is clear that merely for a poet to offer us an emphatic affirmative belief — however unexamined, sentimental, and illogical — does not, by any means, automatically make his work more valuable than Wilbur's.

Finally, although the lack of a vibrant commitment denies

Wilbur's poetry the momentum, density, and power that the works of our greatest poets provide, his readers are offered an incisive portrait of a man caught in the dilemma of the modern world, a man who has been pressured into denying himself any lasting assurance either in the existence of any metaphysical realm or in his ability to comprehend the physical world. My final point, then, is that Wilbur's poetry should be read from quite a different approach than that which reading an anthology-selection of his pieces might suggest. That is, what we will find in Wilbur's collected poetry is not the portrait of a poet who will offer us a confident, exuberant affirmation of life, but a poet who is entangled in all the same fundamental problems that we must confront and must work through — as Wilbur might yet do.

From Protest to Paradox: The Black Writer at Mid Century

by C. W. E. Bigsby

I

In 1950 *Phylon,* the Atlanta-based magazine of "race and culture," devoted an entire issue to analysing the state of Negro literature. The mood of most essays was summed up by the title of one article which saw the Negro writer as being "On the Threshold of Maturity." Virtually all were agreed that his record thus far was not overly impressive, although there was an understandable tendency to exaggerate the achievement of those who had scored moderate public success. Thus, Nick Aaron Ford, while declaring forthrightly that "no Negro author before Richard Wright's *Native Son* (1940) had deserved a listing among first-rate American novelists," tempers his severity by remarking that "Frank Yerby and Willard Motley have earned such a place since." This rather bizarre judgment serves at the same time to highlight the almost universal praise accorded to those who chose to turn away from the supposed 'limitations' of a purely racial theme. One critic even went so far as to declare that the "preponderating use of racial subject matter has handicapped the Negro writer . . . it has retarded his philosophical perspective to the extent that he has made only meagre contributions to national and world ideologies . . . it has

217

usually limited his literary range to the moods and substance of race in the United States . . . it has helped certain critics and publishers to lure him into the deadly trap of cultural segregation." If this particular critic's admiration for Frank Yerby were not sufficient evidence of the consequence of such dogmatism, the emergence, during the 50s, of writers like Baldwin, Ellison and Hansberry served to underline the naivete of this attitude. For the weakness of Negro novelists stemmed not from their use of racial subject matter but from a simple failure of craft. Like the proletarian novelists of the 30s they were too easily convinced of the intrinsic merit of significant subject matter.

If the temptations of propaganda remained equally strong in the 50s, especially with the accelerating interest in civil rights and the sad melodrama of Little Rock, the Negro novelist did now begin to transcend those assumptions formed originally by the exotic self-indulgence of the twenties and the fierce commitment of the thirties. The confident aggressivenes of James Baldwin and the sophisticated control of Ralph Ellison showed just how wide the gulf was between the extravagant claims of those early decades and the genuine achievement which came at mid-century.

The 50s, which opened with the award of the Pulitzer Prize to Gwendolyn Brooks (the first such award to a Negro) and closed with Lorraine Hansberry's New York Drama Critics Circle Award, proved profoundly important both socially and culturally. The explosion of literary talent served to articulate the fears and frustrations of a generation which had only now begun to take its own fate securely into its own hands. While the country demonstrably failed to move "with all deliberate speed" towards the establishment of racial justice the black community began to recognise its own power to act. At the same time the black writer began to challenge those stereotypes which had satisfied a former generation and to speak with a distinctive and authoritative voice.

For all the success of Gwendolyn Brooks and Lorraine Hansberry, however, the decade really belonged to the novelists: to Baldwin and Ellison and to the lesser lights — Killens, Motley, Smith and Demby. It is their efforts and their achievements which made the fifties as significant for the development of Negro writing as for the growth of the protest movement which in part it reflects.

Those who accuse the Negro of a fondness for protest fiction long after that had become passé are ignoring the social realities of the time. Commitment was considered passé by the white critic not because its deficiencies had suddenly become apparent but because its social justification had disappeared. The protest literature which marked the thirties grew naturally out of the social and political realities of that decade. Eventually, however, the war boom removed the immediate cause of this protest while the bitterness which followed the Hitler/Stalin pact seemed to destroy the integrity of those radical solutions which had appeared so attractive a few years before. For the Negro, economic recovery was slower and anyway mostly irrelevant. The battle was clearly still to come. The tentative and largely unreal alliance between Negroes and poor whites, which had been momentarily forged and exaggerated out of all proportion by committed propagandists, was now seen for what it was: a marriage of convenience which stopped far short of fighting for racial justice.

Thus, although Robert Bone, in his study of the American Negro writer, sees the minimal gains in civil rights up to 1954 as leading to a revolt against the protest novel and "in some instances, a conscious abandonment of the materials of Negro life," the best known Negro writers of the forties and fifties remain those whose work is rooted in the black experience or the protest tradition of the thirties (Himes, Killens, Motley, Smith, Demby, Mayfield, Baldwin, Ellison). Even those novels which Bone somewhat casually characterises as 'raceless' are often intended as oblique comments on the race situation, while Killens' *Youngblood* and Motley's *Knock on Any Door*, though written at mid-century, are actually set in the Depression (as, less relevantly, is Baldwin's *Go Tell it on the Mountain*).

Yet there was a clear and constant desire on the part of virtually all these novelists to escape at least some of the constructions of color and one by one they followed Richard Wright into self-imposed exile. James Baldwin, William Gardner Smith and, later, William Melvin Kelley and Carlene Polite retreated to France, Willard Motley to Mexico, Chester Himes to France and Spain, and William Demby to Italy. To a degree this flight from America is reflected in a move towards that sense of racial anonymity so admired by the *Phylon* critics. Yet as we shall see even those novels which seem most clearly to desert the immediacies of the color problem (such as Smith's *Anger at Innocence* or Baldwin's *Giovanni's Room*) have finally a persuasive relevance to the plight of an embittered and oppressed minority.

II

John O. Killens' first novel, *Youngblood*, was published in 1954 when the author himself was 38. The fact that he had grown up during the Depression working for the National Labour Relations Board goes some way towards explaining what is in effect a proletarian novel in which the role of the Party has been taken over by the NAACP.

The protagonist of the novel, Joe Youngblood, is proud of his strength and independent spirit but is gradually cowed and broken by the power of the white world. Despite his bitter hatred for his oppressors his desperate conviction that "my day's coming" seems little more than an ironical comment on his impotence in the face of injustice and inhumanity. Yet the whole movement of the book is devoted to instilling some reality into this otherwise pathetic threat, and discovering a means to solve an apparently intractable problem.

His own son, Robbie, understands the futility of isolated acts of bravado and recognizes the need for some kind of corporate action. Accordingly he helps to organize a union and a local chapter of the NAACP. While the Negro leaders temporize he places his faith firmly in inter-racialism. Yet the liberal whites are equally equivocal, slipping easily into the cant of racism as the problem comes nearer home. The only white person who shows a genuine humanity and who is presented in any detail is a man with the significant and ambiguous name of Oscar Jefferson (Jefferson himself being famous for his public rejection and private practice of slavery). Whether his sincere concern is sufficient to justify our faith in an inter-racial solution is extremely doubtful and this points to one of the book's central contradictions.

The injustices of the South are spelt out in great detail but the mood is nonetheless one of confident expectation: the union is established, the NAACP branch formed. Coalition with the whites is presented as offering a viable and realistic hope. Yet there seems little justification for this hope in terms of the book's white characters. As in so many of the novels which had come out of the 30s the resonant confidence of the author fails to carry any real conviction as he is unable to demonstrate in action the substance of his optimism. The whites, with one exception, are vicious, hypocritical and depraved while the Negroes, Uncle Toms excepted, are gallantly heroic and human. Thus we are left with what is surely an unconscious ambiguity as a preacher pledges his faith in inter-racialism while adding, somewhat ominously, that "We going to make them pay one day soon. . . . There's going to be a reckoning here in Georgia." Despite the book's contrary emphasis it is this last apocalyptic warning by the Georgia-born author which seems to represent Killens' feelings most directly — a fact which is perhaps supported by his second novel, published in 1963, which has as its climax a war between black and white American soldiers. Intellectually and politically optimistic, Killens is emotionally attracted by the satisfaction to be derived from a bitter confrontation. The book thus resolves itself into a confused and unsubtle protest in which the demands of art are too readily sacrificed to the imperatives of the cause.

Like Killens, Willard Motley is rooted in the protest tradition and is essentially a hangover from a previous decade. He is an unabashed naturalist and in his final novel, *Let Noon Be Fair*, published as late as 1963, he offered a defence of naturalistic protest fiction which would not have been out of place thirty years before. "The writer," he insists, "is involved in life. The artist, the realistic writer, is involved with life as it is, involved with poverty, ugliness, corruption, evil, and in his involvement tries to alleviate the cause, tries to change, or at least to point out. He explores the ugly, the miserable, the humble, to show the beauty and humanity in it. He is involved with wanting man to stand erect. He repeats and repeats, 'Here is life. Here is its ugliness. It need not be so.' " Motley's novels, which Robert Bone characterizes as raceless, are so only in the most superficial sense. His protagonists are almost invariably hyphenated Americans whose experiences make them close kin to the Negro. In *Knock On Any Door* and *Let No Man Write My Epitaph* the plight of the Italian-American protagonist scarcely differs from that of Bigger Thomas; indeed the similarity is painfully close at times. The hero's poverty, his social unacceptability, his helpless situation all serve to underline the relevance of his experiences to the black community. In fact the parallel is pushed still further in a sub-plot.

A similar point can be made with regard to Motley's third novel, *We Fished All Night*. This chaotic book, which lumps together the impact of the war and the problems of the second and third generation immigrant provides yet another image of the Negro in American society. Moreover, the situation of a Polish Catholic, Chet Kosinski, who tries to pass as a WASP under the name of Don

Lockwood, has obvious relevance to the plight of a Negro author himself making a bid to be accepted as an "American" rather than a Negro writer. When another character, a young Jewish boy called Aaron, looks forward to a time when "the Jews are accepted by all people as just people, part of all humanity" and expresses the hope that "the Jews will stop being clannish and will become assimilated," it is no wonder that Motley was so popular with the *Phylon* critics of the early 50s and so little regarded by the more miltant writers of the 60s. What he took to be a legitimate means of universalizing his personal sense of the racial dilemma seems in the last resort litle more than an evasive strategy. This evasiveness, indeed, is mirrored in his style which is a curious mixture (common to a certain school of American writers) of brutal realism and turgid sentimentality — an amalgam of Wright and Steinbeck. It is as though he were afraid to follow his naturalistic vision to its logical conclusion. His ultimate retreat to Mexico in the final years of his life is thus in many ways an appropriate image of his desire to pursue a sense of personal commitment while apparently avoiding an exclusively racial approach.

Much the same could be said of William Gardner Smith, who after writing a first novel centered on the race situation, retreated to Paris. Smith published his first novel at the age of twenty. *Last of the Conquerors,* like Killens' second book, is a bitter exposé of white American bigotry as revealed in the ranks of the U. S. army. Like many others, Smith was struck by the irony of a racist army fighting fascism. At one stage his protagonist, obviously reflecting the author's own resolve, announces that on his return he will "write a book and tell how the Germans listen attentively to speeches on democracy and then look around at the segregated camps and race riots over white women and the slurs on Negro soldiers on the streets." Instead of allowing the implicit irony of this situation to speak for itself, however, he feels obligated to spell out his thesis in embarrassingly direct terms. Thus a young German who has been in an American P.O.W. camp makes the obvious remark that "in America they do almost the same thing with your people — the black Americans — as the Nazis did here to the Jews." This dubious observation is repeated again and again while Smith details both the reality of slum conditions in America and the squalid prejudices of American army life, which include not only a vigorously enforced color bar but also a rabid anti-Semitism.

Last of the Conquerors was an impressive piece of work for a man only twenty years old but it was overpraised. Although it transcends some of the obvious limitations of the protest tradition, its characters are never fully realized and tend to be merely functional elements in Smith's rather facile argument. The sense of commitment expressed in his first novel, however, was an accurate enough reflection of his personal involvement in the civil rights struggle. When he wrote it he headed the NAACP's youth movement in Pennsylvania and was a member of CORE. Nevertheless, like so many black writers, he began to feel overwhelmed by the racial situation and in 1951 he moved to Paris, married a French wife and took up permanent residence, announcing that he "couldn't take the small facts of life back there any longer." This expatriation was ostensibly matched by a corresponding withdrawal from the immediate problems of race and discrimination in his second and less successful book.

Largely in the mode of Carson McCullers, *Anger at Innocence* concerns a tragic love affair between a middle-aged nightwatchman-come-poet and a young girl pickpocket whose mother has convinced her of her innate evil. These two "grotesques" enact an agonized affair which is doomed by the girl's conviction of disaster and the deserted wife's cunning manipuation of her husband's sensibilities. Convinced by a Mexican friend that her romance can only succeed if her lover becomes as evil as herself she precipitates the process which ends in his death at her hands.

Anger at Innocence is a poor novel. The central plot seems hopelessly contrived, while the strange logic which seems to dominate the characters is never fully established. Paradoxically, the main interest of the book centers on a sub-plot which does have racial implications and which alone gives some degree of conviction to the sense of determinism which Smith is at pains to establish. Like Motley before him he consciously avoids using Negro characters to make his social point, choosing rather to simulate a degree of detachment by ascribing the role of outcast to a Mexican. Both writers are presenting an oblique comment on racial injustice in such a way as to emphasize its more general implications. Yet neither Motley nor Smith makes any attempt to draw on the culture of the national group which they choose and the apparent objectivity is largely specious. If one simply substituted the word 'Negro' for 'Italian' or 'Mexican' the point would remain the same. Indeed, the setting of Smith's novel, described with all the relish of the protest writer, plays no functional role at all.

Juan, the Mexican, experiences all the difficulties of a Negro. He can only command the most menial of jobs and actually works as a short-order cook. When he tries to date one of the waitresses he is told to "get yourself one of your own kind, boy." His brothers and father "had Mexican kinds of jobs and wore Mexican kinds of clothes and lived in a Mexican kind of tenement house with dirty wall paper and soiled sheets and loud profanities." As a result, like Bigger Thomas, "he hated all who reminded him who he was. So he had hated all those who were treated as inferiors: the Jews and Negroes as well as the Mexicans." There can be little doubt that this is a sublimated account of the plight of the Negro, and as such it constantly threatens to dominate the book. The novel thus suffers from a structural fault which is an explanation of much of its weakness and perhaps an indication that Smith's real strength as a writer lies in precisely that Negro experience which, paradoxically, he seemed so anxious to transcend.

By way of contrast William Demby, by rooting his novel in the Negro experience, achieves just that sense of universality at which Motley had so consciously aimed. Demby is a southern novelist and his work falls easily into that group formed by Carson McCullers, Flannery O'Connor and Tennessee Williams. His concern is with the desperate search by lonely and disillusioned individuals for a love which can temper the harshness of their existence. Like Williams he seems to feel that "we are all sentenced to solitary confinement inside our own skins for life." But where Williams only rarely establishes a direct connection between this desperate solitude and the racial imperatives of the South, Demby is at pains to tie the two together.

Beetlecreek is a small town in which the black and white communities are themselves separated from one another — a reminder of the social dimension of human isolation. The principal characters in the novel are all desperately lonely people, uncertain of their own identity and afraid to reach out to those who might be able to offer them some reason for hope. While avoiding the melodramatic approach to racial antipathy which had characterised the work of writers like Wright, Motley and Killens, Demby demonstrates the extent to which this antipathy serves to exacerbate the plight of those already overwhelmed by a sense of anomie.

Bill Trapp is a white man who has settled on a farm symbolically situated midway between the Negro part of town and the white business section. His own life has been a solitary one. Orphaned when young his relationship with his sister was destroyed by a society which had instilled her with a desire for respectability but which had failed to teach her the need for simple humanity. After her death he was left totally alone. As he stood beside Niagara Falls, "the roar of the water blasted away his identity" for "never before in his life had he been without someone who could confirm his own existence." Following a one-sided and brief relationship with an Italian circus performer he had retreated to Beetlecreek and became trapped like the tin cans and refuse in the reeds of the creek itself. Yet after the death of the Italian, whose own solace had been derived from an old and repulsive dog, "he came close to understanding why it was that he had never lived, why it was that his life had been incomplete, only half tasted; he understood (though vaguely, without the thoughts taking the form of words or ideas) the necessity of giving himself the right and power to reach out and touch people, to love." It is not until a young Negro boy trespasses on his land, however, that he feels the companionship he had needed. He realizes that the Negroes "were the same breed as he"; outcasts who "were always dodging something . . . ashamed of something."

He gains from his relationship with the young boy, Johnnie Johnson, and his uncle, David Johnson, but they also gain from him. He plays an important part in the boy's tentative moves towards manhood, teaching him the need for a common humanity. To the uncle he brings companionship and understanding. But to those who are dominated by racial prejudices this relationship is difficult to understand and the bigotry and suspicion of black and white alike eventually destroys their mutual compassion.

Unjustly accused of molesting a young girl he becomes a scapegoat for the community's fears. He is persecuted and his new-found companionship destroyed. But David Johnson, though unable to sustain his friendship with Bill Trapp in the face of society's condemnation, has at least learned his lesson and leaves town with a girl who has herself known the solitariness of being an orphan. His nephew, on the other hand, is infected by the prejudice of society at large and in order to demonstrate his orthodoxy sets fire to Trapp's house, striking the old man in panic as his treachery is discovered.

Thus Demby attacks racial antipathies not on the basis of

justice or political rights but because prejudice intensifies the solitariness of the human situation in a way that, as David points out, "had nothing to do with not having opportunities or 'civil rights'" but which was rather "a strange feeling, very difficult to explain to himself, which had to do with feeling death, feeling frozen, suffocated, unable to breathe, knowing there was little to be done about it." This last note perhaps explains Demby's personal retreat to Italy, as he moved away from a situation which seemed to admit of little solution. But the real nature of this problem, as his own novel indicates, goes far deeper than racial antipathy.

If Motley has written apparently raceless novels which are in fact about the race situation then Demby has written a book which while ostensibly concerned with the plight of the Negro is in effect an enquiry into the plight of man in the modern world. If for Motley it is a naturalistic detail; for Demby, it is an image. *Beetlecreek* demonstrates the degree to which Demby did accept Richard Wright's contention that "the Negro is America's metaphor."

III

For Wright himself the decade opened with the publication of *The God that Failed*, a book in which six writers explain the nature of their relationship with the Communist Party. In many ways this occurrence is curiously apt for his ambiguous relationship with the Party was responsible not only for the vigour of his early stories but also for the didactic tone of work produced long after he had turned in his Party card.

The strength and vigour of *Native Son* derived precisely from Wright's ambiguous response to communism. Theoretically still involved with the Party but spiritually alienated he produced a document of greater subtlety than is usually admitted. Beneath the bland statement of political philosophy was another work of insight and sensitivity, for the stereotypes of *Native Son* were in many ways the living reality of ghetto consciousness and the sad monotony of Communist analysis an accurate image of the genuine product which distorted Negro existence until it matched a Marxist essence. For a dialectic which at base had no place for self-definition outside of a strict social and economic rationalism was bound finally to seem irrelevant to the real Black man living in a real ghetto. Our discontent with the Marxist diatribe in *Native Son* thus mirrors the discontent nestling in Wright's own soul. Perhaps far from being the novel's chief weakness, this outpouring should be seen as an honest confession of the author's own disaffection.

The existential implications of the novel stem from his growing concern for the individual in the face of the blandishments of a party which could only acknowledge that individual as a symbol of political abstractions and a society which resolutely refused to recognize his individuality or to ascribe him a significant role.

The weakness of *Native Son* does not so much lie in the potentially deadly slabs of ideology or the brutal stereotypes which so shocked James Baldwin but in Wright's failure to create characters who can bear the weight of his social and moral philosophy. As Ralph Ellison has pointed out, "Here lies the source of the basic ambiguity of *Native Son,* wherein in order to translate Bigger's complicated feelings into universal ideas, Wright has to force into Bigger's consciousness concepts and ideas which his intellect could not formulate." This applies with equal force to all of Wright's novels. His social and philosophical theories are carelessly grafted on to characters who lack the intellectual capacity to understand or verbalize them. Thus he is forced, as in *The Long Dream,* to fall back on disastrously feeble strategies, remarking on one occasion that his character "did not understand all this well enough to explain it" and on another that he "felt rather than thought this; it came to him in a flash of intuition."

Native Son demonstrated that at heart Richard Wright was something of a schizophrenic. Committed to the inclusion of Party dogma he nevertheless placed his main emphasis on the plight of the individual. Yet fourteen years later he could demand of an African leader that he win the masses to his side and report with disapprobation his reply that "I don't like this thing of masses. There are only individuals for me." Wright was intellectually a Marxist and subsequently an existentialist but emotionally he was a humanist. Accordingly he could combine the most cynical posturing with a sensitive compassion. His exile in France, however, in divorcing him from his fellow Negroes separated him also from the source of his compassionate humanity. What was left was an insensitive admiration for dogma and theory untempered by that commitment to his fellow man which had animated his early work. Thus in *Black Power,* published in 1953, he urges an

African leader to identify himself with the cause of Dr. Nkrumah against his better judgment with the advice that "It's not a matter of believing, it's politics." One looks in vain for conscious irony. The same is true of the novels. Those written in the fifties seem to reveal only one side of his complex personality.

The Outsider in particular demonstrates that for Wright ideas had become more important than people. The Negro protagonist is a cultured and conscious Bigger Thomas fully alive to his existential possibilities but totally lacking in that tentative humanity which had marked his predecessor. The text is sprinkled with existentialist jargon, with references to 'dread' and 'contingency', together with repeated assurances that "a man creates himself." At one stage in the book, indeed, the hero is permitted a protracted explication of his philosophy while a group of Communists sit mutely listening to his alien theories. But if the book itself is a disastrous failure it does offer what is surely a direct insight into Wright's own state of mind. Speaking of his protagonist, but with obvious relevance to his own situation, he says of him that

> The insistent claims of his own inner life had made him too concerned with himself to cast his lot wholeheartedly with Negroes in terms of racial struggle. Practically he was with them, but emotionally he was not of them. He felt keenly their sufferings and would have batted desperately for any Negro trapped in a racial conflict, but his character had been so shaped that his decisive life struggle was a personal fight for the realization of himself.

This is not to imply that Wright did not feel himself to be involved in the fight for racial justice but that he was emotionally removed from the immediate reality of discrimination and left to wage a more personal battle. This surely goes a long way towards explaining the gulf between the Richard Wright of *Native Son* and the author of his later novel of racial protest, *The Long Dream*. The former novel was written before his long sojourn in France, an exile in which Wright sought desperately to come to terms with his own situation. Married to a white woman but compulsively seeking some kind of heritage in his experience of America's black ghettoes (*Black Boy*) and his atavistic attraction for Africa (*Black Power*), by degrees he began to identify more and more closely with those Europeans who had shown him such respect and treated him with such cordiality. Understandably he no longer felt the injustices of Negro life so acutely, and the Negro began to become a convenient image of more general metaphysical truths. As he remarks of Cross Damon, the protagonist of *The Outsider*, "dimly he realized that his dilemma, though personal, bore the mark of the general." The metaphysical implications of *Native Son* had grown directly out of Bigger Thomas' anguished humanity; those of his later novels are the product of inelegant manipulation.

Unfortunately for Wright the decline of craftsmanship in his work during the 50s, whether it be the phony symbolism of *The Long Dream*, in which a Negro called Chris undergoes a "cruel crucifixion," or the undigested and naïve existentialism of *The Outsider*, was underlined by the contrasting achievement of James Baldwin and Ralph Ellison. The Richard Wright who had started his career by announcing that "I AM A RED SLOGAN . . . I flaunt my messages from a million banners" ended his career with the same commitment to didacticism. Placed beside Baldwin's lucidity and Ellison's subtle metaphysics his own efforts seemed more crude than they might otherwise have done, but it does Wright no service to pretend that his later work was anything but inferior. To admit as much does nothing to diminish the very real achievement of books such as *Uncle Tom's Children* and *Native Son* which at one blow freed the Negro writer from the turgid tracts of former years and cleared the way for writers of the calibre of Ralph Ellison and James Baldwin.

IV

The publication of Ralph Ellison's *Invisible Man* in 1952 was an event of major importance. It was a novel which not merely escaped the naturalistic protest tradition, which had by now become synonymous with Negro literature, but, in the use of race as a powerful and animating image, added a new dimension to the modern American novel.

The plot traces the experiences of a young Negro as he moves from the South to the North and is gradually exposed to the prejudices of American society. Starting as a passive assimilationist he subsequently flirts with political authoritarianism (in the guise of "The Brotherhood") and witnesses the excesses of the Black nationalists. In the process of detailing this progress

Ellison adapts his style to the protagonist's changing state of mind and the society which he encounters. As he explains, "In the South, where he was trying to fit into a traditional pattern and where his sense of certainty had not been challenged, I felt a more naturalistic treatment was adequate . . . . As the hero passes from the South to the North, from the relatively stable to the swiftly changing, his sense of certainty is lost and the style becomes expressionistic. Later on during his fall from grace in the Brotherhood it becomes surrealistic." The boy who started life as an acquiescent creation of White power ends up in the cellar of a northern building having formulated his own response to White society.

In his movement from South to North, from rural to industrial America and from the passivity of Booker T. Washington to the more active stance of the Communists, the young boy re-enacts the movement of America's Negroes as a whole, the novel is thus in a sense very much a direct comment on the racial situation. But this is merely one aspect of what remains today a complex and powerful work.

Both Ralph Ellison and James Baldwin were actively encouraged by Richard Wright. Ellison was commissioned to produce a review for Wright's *New Challenge*, while Baldwin was awarded a literary fellowship as a result of Wright's sponsorship. But neither men responded to Wright's particular vision.

Wright was both a Marxist and an existentialist, but, lacking Sartre's dialectic dexterity, he was never able to resolve the implicit contradiction. While renouncing the Party, rebelling finally against its cynicism, he retained a fundamental determinism. Although Ellison also began his career under the influence of the Communist Party, producing articles and stories for the *New Masses*, his sense of alienation grew from the Party's ideological inadequacy rather than from a sense of personal betrayal. The Party simply failed to account for the complexity of life as he saw it, as did the Manichean simplicities of the Black nationalists. Ellison could never generate Wright's ideological fervor, or approximate the narrow commitment of a Garvey. As he himself explained, "I think I felt more complexity in life and my background made me aware of a larger area of possibility . . . . Also, I think I was less interested in an ideological interpretation of Negro experience." This did not mean that Ellison wanted to desert that Negro experience but merely that he saw it as an image of something broader, the bewildering multiplicity of American experience and the individual's desperate attempt to define and confront reality. While modest in his assessment of his own achievement he saw himself as returning to the tradition of nineteenth-century writing rather than following Negro writers such as Motley, McKay and Wright. Indeed his interpretation of the nature of that tradition goes a long way towards explaining the intention of his own novel, *Invisible Man*:

> I came to believe that the writers of that period took a much greater responsibility for the condition of democracy and, indeed, their works were imaginative projections of the conflicts within the human heart which arose when the sacred principles of the Constitution or the Bill of Rights clashed with the practical exigencies of human greed and fear, hate and love. Naturally I was attracted to these writers as a Negro. Whatever they thought of my people per se, in their imaginative economy the Negro symbolized both the man lowest down and the mysterious, underground aspect of human personality. In a sense the Negro was the gauge of the human condition as it waxed and waned in our democracy.

Thus when the protagonist of *Invisible Man* retreats into a basement "shut off and forgotten during the nineteenth century," Ellison is suggesting that he sees the novel as being in the tradition of Melville and Whitman — an attempt to determine the true nature of reality and assess the relationship between the individual and society while accepting the Negro as "the gauge of the human condition."

The book opens with two epigraphs, one from Eliot's *The Family Reunion* and the other from Melville's "Benito Cereno." Both serve to underline Ellison's fundamental concern with the substance of reality. But the quotation from Melville has a further significance. For it is Captain Delano's inability to concede the humanity of the Negro in that work, which lies at the very heart of his failure to apprehend reality. Coming upon a Spanish ship whose captain is held hostage by his rebellious cargo of black slaves, Delano is unable to see the situation for what it is for he can no more credit the Blacks with sufficient intelligence to conduct such an operation than he can grant the existence of disorder and chaos in a universe which he has always regarded as carefully regulated and patterned. When the deluded Delano asks Benito Cereno to tell him "what has cast such a shadow" over him, the answer, not quoted by Ellison, is "The Negro." Delano's comforting patterns are shattered and he is forced, like the terrified Cereno, to face a threatening chaos. Ellison's Negro hero plays a similar role. It is his experience which offers a key to society's malaise. He too finds that reality can be terrifying (in his case it is a fantasy castration) but unlike Captain Delano he can exult that "at a price I can now see that which I couldn't see." He is able to recognize the absurd.

The alienated individual recurs in American literature almost as a gesture of defiance against the democratic urge towards conformity. If Hawthorne's man of adamant is patriotically put to death for isolating himself from his fellow man, Cooper's Deerslayer retains a noble solitude, while Melville shows a strange fascination for the heroic alienation of Bartleby the scrivener. In terms of the twentieth century the *isolato* has become the 'outsider'; man made aware of absurdity. "The absurd," Camus has said, "is the confrontation of the non-rational world by that desperate desire for clarity which is one of man's deepest needs." To the American writer the absurd is a concept which it seems can only be acknowledged if it is susceptible of transcendence and the history of modern American literature is in many respects a catalogue of attempts to come to terms with the absurd on this basis. From Hemingway's obsession with the ordered violence of the bullfight in contrast to the anarchy of war to Bellow's attempts to reconcile his protagonists with the empty frenzy of the urban environment or Ellison's to bring his "invisible" hero to terms with irrational prejudice and the sheer flux of life, the American writer has sought to establish a context within which native optimism could operate as something more than a recurring irony. It is one thing, however, for Bellow to denounce those "comfortable people playing at crises, alienation, apocalypse and desperation" and for Ellison to call for an end to that "unrelieved despair which marks so much of our current fiction" and pledge himself to presenting "images of hope, human fraternity and individual self-realization" but quite another to find in life itself the justification for hope. Neither Bellow nor Ellison deny the fact of chaos and irrationality but they refuse to capitulate in the face of it. Thus the paradox which is the absurd is not sustained but is finally resolved by emphasizing the need to confront reality and recognize the value of human relationships — a shift of emphasis which parallels the progression which Camus himself had noted from absurdity to love and which reconciles Bellow's and Ellison's protagonists to their fellow men. As Ellison has explained, "The way home we seek is that condition of man's being at home in the world, which is called love, and which we term democracy. Our task then is always to challenge the apparent forms of reality — that is, the fixed manners and values of the few, and to struggle with it until it reveals its mad, vari-implicated chaos." So, too, his persecuted hero insists that "I *have* to love. I sell you no phony forgiveness . . . too much of your life will be lost, its meaning lost, unless you approach it as much through love as through hate."

Like Saul Bellow, Ellison sets himself the task of reconciling the individual to the chaotic reality of contemporary life without resorting to despair and without succumbing to a false optimism. His hero battles through experience in order to gain a true perception of reality and a genuine sense of himself. Like Augie March or — in terms of the nineteenth-century tradition which he so admired — Huckleberry Finn, Ellison's protagonist has to discard his reliance on other people's versions of truth and morality before he can come to terms with his situation.

For both Twain and Ellison a physical journey through America functions as a symbol of the hero's growing insight and experience. The white boy moves southwards and the black boy northwards but both learn something about the failure to realize the potential of the Great Experiment. In formulating an individual code owing nothing to the formal attitudes sanctioned by society each of them comes not only to a knowledge of himself but also to a full understanding of social reality and human failings. Both recoil from their new perception; Huck lighting out for the territory and Ellison's protagonist taking refuge in a coal cellar. Yet both are merely delaying an inevitable and necessary confrontation. If the nineteenth-century writer was forever picturing his heroes as heading for the freedom and simplicity of the frontier, whether it was Cooper's forest and plain, Melville's sea or Thoreau's Walden, he knew that a confrontation with society was inevitable. Cooper's natty Bumppo moves inexorably toward his clash with Judge Temple as Melville's Billy Budd meets the inflexible social conscience of Captain Vere. Meanwhile Thoreau treads the path to Concord jail and public commitment. This is a fact recognized clearly enough by Ellison's protagonist as, sitting in his underground shelter, he comes to realize that he "must come out . . . emerge," admitting that "perhaps that's my greatest social crime, I've overstayed my hibernation, since there's a possibility that even an invisible man has a socially responsible role to play" and anyway "hibernation is a covert preparation for a more overt action."

With this new insight the individual can no longer be painlessly absorbed by society. He is now an active rather than passive agent and responds to his new vision of reality by accepting that his world has become "one of infinite possibilities." At last he comes to understand that "life is to be lived, not controlled; and humanity is won by continuing to play in the face of certain defeat." The implicit existentialism of Ellison's novel thus stands in marked contrast to the literary constructs of Wright's, while his recognition of the Negro's mythical value as well as social utility is an indication of his artistic insight. Like Melville and Twain before him he uses the Negro as "the gauge of human condition as it waxed and waned" in America, but because of his privileged position is able to endow his Negro characters with a human reality often lacking from the work of his nineteenth-century forbears.

Despite his failure to produce a second novel in either the 50s or 60s Ellison's achievement in *Invisible Man* has assured him a permanent place in American literature, a place, moreover, which he has won without embracing the spurious advice of the *Phylon* critics to abandon racial subject matter.

V

When James Baldwin fled the United States for the apparent peace and security of Paris in 1948 he was impelled by a number of connected reasons. His father's hatred of Whites had invested him with a complex reaction to his racial identity. He felt alienated from his fellow Negroes and from the country of his birth and this not only for racial reasons for, after all, "If Buchenwald was wrong what, then, *really* made Hiroshima right?" Personally he felt the victim of a "wild process . . . of failure, elimination and rejection," uncertain not only of his racial identity but also his sexual integrity. The single most important reason for his flight from America, however, was the death of his best friend, Eugene Worth, a suicide in which he felt implicated. Baldwin felt and to some extent still feels that his own cynicism contributed to the despair which eventually caused his friend to jump to his death from the George Washington Bridge in 1946. When Worth, despite all the bigotry and prejudice which surrounded him, had pledged his faith in the ultimate goodness of human nature and the power of love Baldwin had replied, "Love! You'd better forget about that, my friend. That train has *gone.*" The flight to Paris was thus an escape not only from the physical oppressiveness of discrimination or, as he later explained, from the plight of being regarded as "merely a Negro writer." It was an attempt to come to terms with his own identity, to conquer the rage which he recognised as self-destructive and to formulate a response to his situation which skirted both naivete and cynicism.

Given his sense of guilt with regard to Eugene Worth it is perhaps scarcely surprising that in his first novel and throughout his work this response proves to be just that faith in the power and efficacy of love which his friend had embraced before his death. As he was to say in a television interview, "I believe in love — that sounds very corny, you know . . . I believe we can save each other." All too aware of the disingenuous sound to this he added, somewhat unconvincingly, "I don't mean anything passive . . . I mean something active, something more like a fire . . . I mean a passionate belief, a pasionate knowledge of what a human being can do to change the world in which he finds himself." Despite the obvious social and political implications of this and similar statements Baldwin has consistently avoided drawing such conclusions in his work. Moreover, his constant faith in the power of love, often, as in his later *Blues for Mr. Charlie,* with no apparent justification in terms of character or action, constantly verges on mere sentimentality. Baldwin, in fact, is a sentimentalist in the same sense as Dickens. While recognising and publicly announcing the need for economic and social action his fundamental faith rests on the innate goodness of humanity. Lacking Dickens' Cheeryble cheeriness and sense of untainted innocence he nonetheless places his faith squarely on the pure in heart — those at peace with themselves and thus able to come to terms with their fellow men. These people, described in his first novel, *Go Tell it on the Mountain,* as "the despised and rejected, the wretched and the spat upon, the earth's offscouring" are close kin not only to Dickens' endearing castouts but also to Steinbeck's similarly sentimental outsiders.

Go Tell it on the Mountain is concerned with the initiation of John Grimes, a fourteen year-old Negro boy. He is exposed to the bitter realities of ghetto life and sees at first hand the consequences of the resulting tensions in terms of individual lives. In the course of the book he undergoes what is apparently a profound religious conversion — a conversion which seems to reconcile him with his situation.

To John's father religion is simply a way of striking back at a white world which he hates and fears; to his mother it is an avenue to middle-class respectability. But his conversion does not represent an acknowledgment of religious truth or an acceptance of his father's bitterness or his mother's passivity. It is a desperate expression of his own need for love and his desire for a sense of identity and common brotherhood. Yet his own mixed motives create a difficulty for the reader which is reflected throughout Baldwin's work. The central ambiguity of the book arises from the confusion between Eros and Agape. John's conversion is not the result of spiritual revelation but of a homosexual attraction which he feels for Elisha, a young Negro convert. "In his heart there was a sudden yearning tenderness for Holy Elisha; desire, sharp and awful as a reflecting knife, to usurp the body of Elisha, and lie where Elisha lay." While setting out to establish the desirability and viability of compassion, Baldwin can only visualize this love in terms of sexual alliances, more particularly in terms of homosexual relationships. The physical is made to stand for the metaphysical but the intensity of the sexual relationship subverts its symbolic effectiveness. Throughout his work it is the homosexual, virtually alone, who can offer a selfless and genuine love because he alone has a real sense of himself, having accepted his own nature. Yet while Baldwin is clearly suggesting that the acknowledgment of one's true identity is the key to a constructive life his overly sentimental approach to the homosexual relationship destroys its utility as an image.

The real core of the book is the struggle between hatred and love which Baldwin sees as the major battle to be fought by Black and White alike. The fight in essence is that between the Old and New Testaments; between retribution and love, the father and the son, servitude and freedom. Old Testament intolerance is now superseded by compassion, a gospel of love embodied in the person of John (the Baptist?).

The most bitter characters, Gabriel, his son Roy and Elizabeth's lover, Richard, are all destroyed by hatred, as are similar characters throughout his work. Salvation it seems lies only through suffering and compassion and Elizabeth's prayer that her son "might be carried, past wrath unspeakable, into a state of grace" is essentially Baldwin's wish for himself and humanity in general.

The basic necessity, as Baldwin sees it, is "to say yes to life" while placing oneself in implacable opposition to those who would diminish the quality of that life. This is the essence of the apparent paradox which he had outlined at the beginning of his career in his first book of essays: "It began to seem that one would have to hold in the mind forever two ideas which seemed to be in opposition. The first idea was acceptance, the acceptance, totally without rancour, of life as it is and men as they are; in the light of this idea, it goes without saying that injustice is a commonplace. But this does not mean that one could be complacent, for the second idea was of equal power: that one must never in one's life accept these injustices as commonplace but must fight them with all one's strength." The division is essentially between Baldwin's personal and metaphysical concerns and his social and political objectives. He has to accept not only his racial and sexual nature but also the fundamental determinism which governs his life and which he had expressed when saying that "the fact that you're born in 1924 in a certain country, a certain color . . . dictates a certain course." But at the same time, as one who is opposed to a social system which sanctions prejudice and retreats in the face of reality, he has to believe in the immediate and continuing possibility of change.

Baldwin's central theme is the need to accept reality as a necessary foundation for individual identity and thus a logical prerequisite for the kind of saving love in which he places his whole faith. For some this reality is one's racial or sexual nature, for others it is the ineluctable fact of death. Like Edward Albee, Baldwin sees this simple progression as an urgent formula not only for the redemption of individual men but for the survival of mankind. In this at least black and white are as one and the Negro's much-vaunted search for identity can be seen as part and parcel of the American's long-standing need for self-definition. It is a theme which runs through Baldwin's work but nowhere is it stated more directly than in the much misunderstood *Giovanni's Room*.

Baldwin has said that "a writer who is bi-sexual is probably but not surely going to identify himself with other minorities," and in many ways this gives us some clue as to his intention in his second novel. *Giovanni's Room* is ostensibly about a homosexual relationship and yet we have Baldwin's somewhat baffling assurance that the novel is "not about homosexuality." The book is concerned with the protagonist's refusal to confront his own bi-sexuality. Having had a brief affair with a young Italian boy, David, an expatriate American, tries to return to the 'normality' of a relationship with his fiancée. In the name of some intangible standard of respectability and in retreat from that element of his nature which seems to make him the victim of his own irrational desires and the equally irrational contempt of others, he callously sacrifices a genuine relationship to one which has the sanction of society. In evading the truth he succeeds only in destroying himself and those he loves. The relevance of this to Baldwin's racial as well as sexual predicament hardly needs underlining. Both were aspects of a personal reality which he had struggled to avoid, but which he had finally come to accept as the substance of his own identity. Thus the predicament of the homosexual, on the fringe of society, regarded with suspicion and prejudice by others, becomes in Baldwin's mind, an appropriate image of those similarly estranged. Therefore, when Baldwin says of homosexuality in America that "if people were not so *frightened* of it . . . it really would cease in effect . . . to exist. I mean in the same way the Negro problem would disappear," it is no accident that the two ideas should appear so closely related. Similarly, when the protagonist of the novel remarks that "I had decided to allow no room in the universe for something which shamed and frightened me" and admits that he has "succeeded very well — by not looking at the universe, by not looking at myself, by remaining, in effect, in constant motion" we are reminded of the author who fled to Paris in order to escape his racial identity and the consequences of that identity.

Baldwin's personal reconciliation with the fact of his Negroness and the reality of his bi-sexuality was a result of just such a process as is described in *Giovanni's Room*. For Baldwin, like David, had travelled to Europe only to discover the need to accept precisely those things he thought he had left behind. Yet particularly in the following decade there were those who doubted the genuineness of that racial identity.

In his essays he tends to adopt a persona, on occasions speaking

as a white American and even embracing a European rather than
an African past, "It is the past lived on the American continent,
as against that other past, irrecoverable now on the shores of
Europe, which must sustain us in the present." This is a rhetorical
device but at the same time it reveals something of the paradox
that is Baldwin. In the 60s he became the target of abuse for
many militant black writers and leaders. His protestations of love
for America, the pledge of faith with which he had closed his first
book of essays, and, in a sense, even his determined literacy made
him the subject of suspicion and contempt. LeRoi Jones, Eldridge
Cleaver and Harold Cruse all attacked him as an assimilationist
who desired nothing more than invisibility — the license to indulge
his sensibility free from the tiresome restrictions and distractions
of the color problem. The fact that his second novel centered on
the relationship of two white homosexuals seemed proof, if such
were needed, of his desire for non-involvement. In part, of course,
they were right. It was not until his return to America and his
first visit to the Southern states that he became finally and in his
own mind irrevocably committed to acting as spokesman. His
repeated demands to be considered as simply a writer rather than
a Negro writer were sufficiently ambiguous to the imagination of
the revolutionaries to damn him as a putative white man. Baldwin's sensitivity to this kind of attack is well known and his later
work tends to reflect the somewhat shrill note which began to
characterize his public statements. Yet even his most forthright
comments, such as are contained in his polemical essay, *The Fire
Next Time,* remained suffused with what seemed a sentimental
faith in the power of love and were anyway soon outpaced by the
rapid developments within the civil rights movement. Even his
protest play, *Blues for Mr. Charlie,* was ambiguously balanced between hate and love, the gun and the Bible. If there were whites
who looked on him as an incendiary after *The Fire Next Time,*
on the principle that the prophet who foretells disaster must have
a vested interest in the fulfilment of his prophecies, the arrival of
far more militant and vocal spokesmen soon muted this kind of
criticism and left him prey to the abuse of those who saw him as
little more than a rather superior and articulate Uncle Tom.

Baldwin's is an uneven talent. For all the measured articulate-
ness of the essays his rhetoric can get hopelessly out of control in
the novels. In *Giovanni's Room,* for example, Hella's sexual
arousal is described in terms which are laughably blasphemous:

"I felt her moving, rushing to open the gates of her strong, walled city and let the king of glory come in." But in spite of this and his unconquerable sentimentality he remains a writer of considerable power and surely one of the most significant American writers to emerge during the 50s.

VI

The success of Lorraine Hansberry's *A Raisin in the Sun* in 1959 came as a fitting climax to a decade in which the Negro writer had steadily worked to liberate himself from some of the more restrictive legacies of the twenties and thirties. Though the demands of social protest continued to exercise a potent influence, men like Demby, Baldwin and Ellison were beginning to detect in the racial situation a powerful image of alienation, absurdity and anomie which spoke to a wider audience than that commanded by either the self-confident exoticism of the Negro Renaissance or the simplistic commitment of the Depression era. No longer content with the mere demonstration of literacy or with pledging a proper allegiance to 'the cause' they forged their work out of the substance of their own experience while avoiding the casual racial clichés which for too long had satisfied both the Negro writer and his white counterpart. It is fitting that in looking back at the 50s the names of Baldwin and Ellison at least should feature so prominently.

Camino Real

by JORDAN Y. MILLER

(Certain of the ideas expressed in this article are taken from the author's essay on *Camino Real* appearing in *American Dramatic Literature* (McGraw-Hill, 1961),.

The night I caught *Camino Real* during its short (60 performance) Broadway run was not a particularly appropriate moment to do so in view of the following day's ordeal: my doctor's orals. The great jumble of miscellaneous information accumulated over months of review seemed, by then, of absolutely no use to anybody whatever, and a thoroughly befuddled mind was in no condition to make reasonable sense out of what I was seeing. But there was one very good thing about watching that performance of *Camino Real*. It appeared so utterly baffling that I was thoroughly confident that whatever I offered to my judges the following day would, by comparison, be brilliantly lucid. In contrast to Tennessee Williams, I, at least, would have some cogent idea of what I was saying.

My orals, it turned out, were a success. *Camino Real* was not.

During the two months when New York supported the play in early 1953 too many people, one suspects, felt much as I had. Hence, faced with unenthusiastic public support and what must have been astronomical costs of financing the huge cast and the highly complex setting, the producers simply could not make a go of it. *Camino Real* demands a rather substantial amount of audience effort to achieve even minimal comprehension, and Broadway has never been known to maintain prolonged enthusiasm

241

for such expenditures of energy. And, appearing considerably ahead of *Waiting for Godot, Rhinoceros,* or other popular "absurd" pieces, *Camino Real* never developed a reputation as the "in" play to see; the numbers necessary to fill the Martin Beck Theatre failed to materialize. Of course, the faults were shared by playwright and critics alike in some respects. While Williams' world view in *Camino Real* is displayed in lively techniques, the picture is not infrequently muddled, and the critical reaction, which could not or would not see what Williams was attempting, was not the kind to help build popular support. For all that, given an audience ready and willing to accept what Williams tried to do, the superb individual performances and the constantly varied technical effects of this highly entertaining *tour de force* might have succeeded. As it turned out, however, nothing could prevent *Camino Real* from becoming Tennessee Williams' most monumental commercial failure.

But *Camino Real* has refused to remain a failure. A sometime paradox, this play of overt theatricality, designed more than most others of its time as a thing to be seen and heard, although meeting with almost no success on the stage itself, is now receiving increased recognition as a significant play of the early 50s as it continues to appear on the printed pages of a number of prestigious anthologies and texts. In fact, it is rapidly becoming the artistic, if not the popular equal of Williams' two best "conventional" plays, forming with *The Glass Menagerie* and *A Streetcar Named Desire* three of the most important contributions to contemporary American drama. Yet, one cannot study *Camino Real* as simply a piece of dramatic writing; it must still be regarded as capable of best appreciation only in performance. Only a few passages display Williams' writing style at its best, as in some of the exchanges between Casanova and "Camille." The dialogue throughout does have excellent pace, and there is fine humor in the characterization of Kilroy. Most of the text, however, is designed to assist the fast-paced theatricality, and it is because *Camino Real* is *all* theatre, and because in character, theme, and technique it makes use of a theatrical style from the past, that we are attracted to the study of the play as a singularly important work. For *Camino Real* is a revival of *expressionism,* an altered but recognizable reincarnation of that stylized theatricality of the 1920s and 1930s which, by the 1950s, seemed long dead and buried. Indeed, so passé was the term, so anachronistic its style, that when the play first opened not a single major reviewer mentioned it in describing what he had witnessed. Descriptions of all kinds were proffered — surrealism, fantasy, exoticism — but nobody seemed to realize that expressionism was the word that fit. Moreover, *Camino Real* is an able use of the style in articulating a specific outlook on man and the world he has created for himself, modified to fit the 50s, but adhering to the basic stylistic tenets of expressionism with considerable skill.

If, then, one faces *Camino Real* with honesty, willing to go some distance in meeting it halfway, it is far from the dismaying jumble it would seem at first to be. It cannot be watched, or, for that matter, read with any thought of "solving" it or arriving at some sort of literal "translation." Total understanding of an expressionistic play is not the point; overall comprehension is. The effort necessary to switch from scene to scene, or to plow through the frequent and cluttering nonsense in order to let the play's distinctive impression grow, is worthwhile in the end. Though flawed, *Camino Real* is a brilliant adventure into highly stylized theatrical experimentation.

In the use of both stage mechanics and subject matter, August Strindberg was, of course, an early, if not the first, true expressionist in his nightmare explorations of human relations in *A Dream Play* and *The Ghost Sonata*. But as the German playwrights before and after the First World War, and others writing elsewhere in the 1920s and 1930s, adopted and adapted the style, expressionism became more and more associated with an artistically subjective identification with the individual's loss of identity and integrity in the midst of a frightening and ever-increasingly mechanistic society which demanded conformity and machine-like responses. Unlike the absurdists of the 50s, who were to see the ridiculous, *i.e.* absurd human plight as a condition of existence itself, the expressionists witnessed a society that was a product of man's own genius, a gift which enabled him to create the wondrous gear-driven monsters that, in the end, would destroy him. In many ways, this became a drama of despair, peopled by lost souls incapable of avoiding annihilation but, at the same time, possessing a certain amount of hope in the awareness that the doom descending, be it through obliteration by the gas that kills, the ascendency of robots, or a Great Depression, was man's own fault. By the end of the 1930s and into the 1940s, however, particularly as another war took over and the end of the world seemed to be not so much a matter of succumbing to machines and robots as to the total inability of one man to get along with another, expressionism as a theatrical style had pretty well burned itself out. Its legacies of more fluid stage design and dramatic composition remained permanent parts of contemporary theatrical techniques, but the term "expressionism" itself no longer seemed functional. Not until 1953 with *Camino Real* (an extension of the 1940 shorter version called *Ten Blocks on the Camino Real*) did the theatre find itself right back in the midst of fully conceived expressionism. Though well encompassing the tenor of the early 50s, Williams had originated his play more than a decade earlier, and the forms of expressionism were obviously well established in his mind.

Mechanically it is very easy to defend *Camino Real* as expressionism. Note the pattern. From balcony to orchestra to boxes and pit the entire theatre combines with the stage to become the acting area. Time and space are without meaning, and individual characters appear and disappear with no relation to probability. Upon occasion, these characters become obvious symbols, while at others they remain frustratingly obscure. With every possibility of electronic control in light and sound employed to the maximum, scene follows scene without pause, bawdy farce intrudes upon horror, meaningless nonsense upon serious thought. Hysteria and frenzy permeate the whole, while decor, costume, makeup, and stage movement are grotesque, exaggerated and distorted.

But all this alone does not make good expressionism, for the expressionist is not producing a mere circus. The totally scabrous Ritz Men Only, the darkly brilliant and erotic Siete Mares, and the dry, dusty square in between are exceptionally graphic displays of Williams' world. It is not the mechanistic, robot world of the pre-war expressionists, for its atmosphere is that of the immediate post-war disillusion of the late 40s and early 50s, a world very much of man's own making. Its desolation is particularly agonizing, for it is one lacking in love and compassion, where the word "brother" may be spoken only on pain of death. The overripe degraded existence on Gutman's side is balanced by the horrors of A. Ratt's little white ships, and both are the creations of men and their inability to rise above the most sensual levels. Those inhabiting the Camino Real are lost souls, prisoners within an enervating universe from which escape is possible only to a very privileged few. There is no more freedom and personal dignity than was the lot of any of the automotons created in the expressionistic plays of Toller, Kaiser, or Rice. Williams creates in *Camino Real* a world of great human despair in some ways even more depressing in its display of man's nature than that expounded at the end of the first great conflict. Now, in the 50s, with further millions dead, a good portion of the globe still in ruins, Berlin blockades, Korean Wars, and stagnating United Nations, man's intransigence seems more and more permanent. Williams shows all this in a vivid expressionistic picture, while sounding a clear warning of the need to escape before it is too late in almost the same urgent tones of his expressionistic predecessors. The scenery has been changed since the 1930s, and the theme is somewhat altered, but the type of man appearing on the stage, and the playwright's attitude toward him, have not really changed at all.

Though the hapless Mr. Zero in *The Adding Machine* is returned to earth in even more degraded form than he left it, and civilization in *Gas* is obliterated, Rice, Kaiser, and other more or less "routine" expressionists of the 1930s constantly reiterated their belief that men, being responsible for the invention of human-replacing machinery and gas that annihilates, still contain within themselves the only hope for survival and escape from the hideous world they have created. Williams' departure from this attitude lies mainly in his initial premise, wherein he does not see the degraded world of the Camino Real as man's creation so much as he regards it as a product of man's being what he is: grasping, sensual, exploitive, selfish. Being all of these things, man is, on the other hand, says Williams, capable of being kind, generous and understanding, though in degree considerably less. Herein lies the hope that Williams provides for ultimate escape. As the earlier expressionists had assigned man himself the capability of avoiding the ultimate destruction he insisted on bringing upon himself, Williams recognizes the same possibility and places that hope for survival within, as well as escape from, the Camino Real in the same human spirit that has created the hideous spot in the first place. Permanent escape is reserved for only a few, but survival can be accomplished and life can be endured by those remaining behind if a certain amount of recognition of the true nature of oneself is admitted.

Considering the persons to whom Williams assigns the capacity of fleeing the Camino Real, it is not difficult to regard his release as a particular form of "escapism," though the term in its usual sense may not be wholly accurate in this instance. Nonetheless, those who do succeed are all dreamers of a sort, and at least two of them seem to be awakening from a particularly bad nightmare, reminiscent of the means by which young Neil awakes from his wild misadventures in Kaufman's *Beggar on Horseback*. Lord Byron, first of those to walk out of the Camino Real and successfully face the Terra Incognita, may not exactly have been dreaming, but the Byronesque outlook is that of another world, and the escape he manages is that of the pure romantic. Himself a practicing sensualist, among other sins, Byron is able to remain aware of what surrounds him in the Camino Real, but he can transcend its horrors and still be capable of the necessary "escapist" attitude which will remove him safely from its premises. Approval or condemnation of Byron's attitudes and his method of escape is not the question; the point is that he is fully able to do so, and is the first to succeed.

The other two are, indeed, the dreamers and, in their ways, the idealists, completely detached from the forces holding all others in the Camino Real. Don Quixote can escape, of course, because he, as only a few others, has remained untouched, uncontaminated; he has been able all the while to "dream" the play, *i.e.*, life, and to proceed onward unaffected by the terrors on either side of the wall. Last, of course, is Kilroy, all naive innocence and purity of heart, but dead. Escape is possible for the Kilroys of the world, far removed from the complexities of a Byron or the utter simplicities of a Don Quixote, although all the physical prowess he may possess becomes useless and he must die and be reborn in a kind of "total" dreaming and awakening, no longer subject to the sensual appeals of the gypsy's daughter nor the materialistic lures of the Loan Shark's den. He surrenders his commercially valuable but personally useless golden heart and follows the other "dreamers" over the wall.

There is no other way. One cannot otherwise flee directly. Against the rest the winds are too strong, the desert too forbidding, and the *Fugitivo* crashes in Elizabeth, New Jersey. Direct assault on the controlling forces is impossible, for the Gutmans and Generalissimos are in control. The live Kilroys become patsies, the Casanovas become cuckolds, and the Lord Mulligans are carted off by the street-cleaners, while the desperate Camilles find their money valueless either for an airline ticket or the affections of the pickup at the local dive.

Conventional faith, witnessed in the constant presence of La

Madrecita, can offer succor to all on the Camino Real, but she is blind and can only cradle the Survivor until he dies, or momentarily protect the collapsed body of the dying Kilroy. The one ironically called The Dreamer, her son, turns out to be the exact opposite in strength and ability of those more "practical" dreamers who do escape, for this one so named is frail, capable only of song, unable to act meaningfully. Williams offers limited relief to some, as for instance, Casanova and Marguerite Gauthier, eternally trapped by what they are, who can achieve some sort of calm through recognition of their own natures and their need to "escape" into each other. The Gypsy's daughter, perpetually corrupted and ravished by the machinations of her exploiting parent, but recognizing what Kilroy's presence in the Camino Real represents, screams her encouragement during his attempted flight and subsequently chooses him as Hero of the Fiesta. But then, once Kilroy satisfies her needs, she returns prattling like an infant to her bed, no longer interested in what her lover's golden heart can bring her. Finally, the fountain flows again and the square seems able to support some kind of decent "life," but it has taken a very special kind of act to bring it about. The Byrons, the Quixotes, and the Kilroys in particular have had to suffer and depart forever in order to accomplish it.

The Camino Real is, then, in the end, a place wherein one can live if he so wishes, provided he can make some of the necessary compromises with himself, and it is one from which permanent escape is possible. To judge the world that Williams thus expresses as totally without hope is wrong, but at the same time it is depressing to realize how very few can make it out, and that under certain circumstances the only real hope is death. Is it real, or figurative death? Has Kilroy "died," or has he merely shed the trappings of the oversimplified world into which he was originally born? Kilroy, Williams' Everyman, must alter materially before escape is possible, and real or symbolic death seems the only feasible method. Williams does insist on change, save for the exceptional ones who may walk away unchanged in the manner of a Byron or a Quixote.

Personally, I have always refused to go along with Williams' world, so often expressed in this and other of his plays as a dichotomy of two evils, set in the midst of an Eliotesque Wasteland. In *Camino Real* Williams has provided only desolate neutral ground inhabited by whores, beggars, and the inevitable street-cleaners of death between the two evil poles of decay in lush and decadent elegance on one side and caveman subsistence on the other, both totally debilitating to mind and body. I would deny that escape is possible only in the psychoses of an Amanda of Laura Wingfield, the ultimate insanity of Blanche Dubois, or in the romanticism and "death" of a Kilroy. I would further deny that the most likely survivors are to be those who reflect Stanley Kowalski or even the played-out Casanova. And yet, who can disagree with what not only Williams but others such as Arthur Miller and Eugene O'Neill have said about the survival of the human spirit which constantly refuses to accept the reality which surrounds it, ever dependent upon pipe dreams, illusions and certain brute instincts. If Williams in the end sets his dry fountain running again and permits the flowers in the mountains to break the rocks, he is not entirely alone. Reality can never be the total structure of existence; somewhere along the line the romantic ideal must enter to provide a modicum of sanity. *Camino Real* recognizes this necessity very well indeed.

If the promise of the post-war 40s, which introduced to the American drama the names not only of Williams but of Miller, Inge, and the posthumous O'Neill, was not entirely borne out in the 50s, there were significant plays nonetheless, among them the exciting, exhausting, infuriating, and baffling encounter with this important, if flawed portrayal of existence in *Camino Real*. Although Williams himself has been writing the same basic theme ever since *Streetcar*, nowhere does he articulate his world view as graphically as in this brash and daring dive into an extremely difficult style. *Camino Real* will, certainly, remain one of the more attractive dramatic pieces of the decade, and it must be praised if for no more than the playwright's willingness to try something so artistically as well as commercially dangerous. Confusing and incoherent as it may be, it remains stimulating and often hilarious entertainment.

The comprehension of what Williams is saying can ultimately be gained, even if a number of pieces of his huge jigsaw puzzle remain unfitted. Here are strong personal feelings, expressed in vivid style, never capable of complete understanding, but always strongly enunciated. The world portrayed may be hideous, and it may not be exactly everybody's idea of what it looks like, but no one can deny Williams' right to see it so, and demonstrate it with vigorous originality.

The Games God Plays with Man: A Discussion of JB

by SY KAHN

When I directed a college production of Archibald MacLeish's *JB* in 1966, I followed my usual pattern of intensely studying the play in order to arrive at a firm notion of its central, controlling ideas from which to shape and structure the production. I also read *Job* and considerable commentary on the Biblical poem, as well as various critical responses to *JB* — but in the end, a director must come to terms with the text before him and translate it into living, dramatic terms.

The play raises questions that have challenged and tormented men for centuries: why do we suffer, and, especially, why do we suffer without seeming cause, unjustly? We leap from these questions to other persistent ones: what sort of God permits the victimization of innocent children, that permits the wicked to flourish? Is there some ultimate and supreme lesson to be learned from horror and injustice? Are God's reasons, if He exists at all, and has reasons, to be understood by men? Why does God permit iniquity, permit those who believe in His watchfulness and benevolence to be victims? One set of contemporary responses speculates that God is hidden, is in eclipse, has forgotten man or withdrawn from him — that He is dead. Or is it, as Faulkner has observed, that man engenders more than he can bear? If this is so, and man is God's creature, why should God have created so driven a creature? Why may he have, as Hawthorne speculated, "natural depravity" in his heart? Melville looked into the shark's mouth and found in the inwardly curved, murderous rows of teeth a sign of God's temper, and Stephen Crane found the heavens empty, nature indifferent, and at the center of the cathedral-woods of *The Red Badge of Courage,* a dead victim of war. Literature has invented numerous images of man's travail, passion, alienation and suffering; it is rich with the red cries of his outrage and horror.

In the 50s writers reverberated to the impact of the events of World War II and especially to the accumulating evidence of Nazi persecution and extermination programs, and these events sharpened the points of the old, excruciating questions. *JB*, the Pulitzer Prize Play of 1959, gives us one literary response to these questions by a playwright and poet who for decades has been sensitive to contemporary social and political life. As MacLeish has said about *JB*, he "constructed a modern play inside the ancient majesty of the Book of Job," because "when you are dealing with questions too large for you which, nevertheless, will not leave you alone, you are obliged to house them somewhere — and an old wall helps." Both Job and JB are targets for catastrophe, and even if one argues that both needed chastisement to correct their complacency, their illusion of invulnerability, one cannot justify the severity of their punishment. They are men more sinned against than sinning.

As I studied the play, two lines emerged more sharply, piercingly, than others: one is Biblical, and the other MacLeish's. The first is Job's wife's malediction, "Curse God and die!" Given Job's and JB's torment, men who have lost fortune, status, children and health, good and pious men about whom the worst that can be said is that they did not see deeply enough into the agony of man on earth, JB's wife Sarah's rebellious cry seems not unreasonable. Anguished, stripped and stricken, JB might well raise a defiant fist before the bland and blank eyes of God. And why not commit suicide, as Nickles (the "Old Nick") persistently urges JB at the end of the play? After such experience as JB has suffered, afflicted by disease, scorned by man, abandoned by his wife, his children destroyed by wars, accident, rape and murder, and finally advised by God's voice in the whirlwind of his puniness and presumption in questioning God and seeking reasons and justification for his immense suffering, JB might well follow Nickles' advice and "take a rope's end." Man can choose to die; he can exercise that final, free act; he can in the concentration camp run upon the electrified barbed wire. "Curse God and die!" is one of the most powerful and awesome lines a man's mouth can shape; it gathers together his outrage, bitterness, defiance and agony and hurls them back at God who has played a vicious game with man — or permitted man to be game for man's viciousness. Man can tell Him off, and end the game. Maybe God loses, if the stake God means to win is that man should love his fellowman and love God.

The other powerful line in the play is JB's, rendered after he has heard the voice of God. Having now assessed God's nature, JB tells Sarah, "He does not love. He Is." With this assertion, JB can now stoically face his life, and we can assume JB, like Job, will make some kind of recovery from his disasters and be rewarded for his trouble. Nickles is defeated. Not able to urge JB to suicide, he walks out of the game disgusted. As for Zuss (Zeus and God), JB has dismissed Him in his line to Sarah, and even forgiven Him for His blind omnipotence. At the end of the play, we have man and woman in rags, almost naked, a damaged Adam and Eve, willing to take their chances, go through the cycle of rise and fall, happiness and disaster, sustained by the fact that man can love, and that is his triumph. MacLeish made these intentions clear when he wrote in the "Foreward" to the acting script, "JB accepts to live his life again in spite of all he knows of life, in spite of all he knows of himself, because he loves life still in spite of life — *can* love it still." Later in the essay MacLeish admits that love conquers nothing, neither death nor chance; it does affirm the worth of life and the wonder and beauty of the human creature; it answers life with life. He concludes, "JB, like Job, covers his mouth with his hand; acquiesces in the vast indifference of the universe as all men must who truly face it; takes back his life again. In love. To live." Clearly, these intentions are realized in the play, in the several endings MacLeish wrote, searching, I presume, for dramatic precision for these conclusions.

The conclusions are right for MacLeish, and they are right for the mood of the 50s; the play updates the old myth of Job, and turns the ancient tale, meant to teach man forbearance and unshakable faith in adversity, into a twentieth century existentialist fable. JB does not deny God's existence — He is — but he violently shifts his notion of God and now stands firmly on his own existential feet, supported by Sarah to be sure. JB will live and love again because he can.

In arriving at this image of man, MacLeish has focused several forces working in him and on him. As we can see in a poem he wrote that antedates *JB* by more than three decades, MacLeish looked into the sky after World War I and found it empty. In his sonnet "The End of the World" (1926) he employs a circus tent for a setting as he does in *JB,* and after giving us in the octet quick images of circus freaks and tricks, metaphors for our bizarre world, he ends the section with the line, "Quite unexpectedly the top blew off." The sextet concludes:

And there, there overhead, there, there, hung over
Those thousands of white faces, those dazed eyes,
There in the starless dark the poise, the hover,
There with vast wings across the cancelled skies,
There in the sudden blackness the black pall
Of nothing, nothing, nothing — nothing at all.

When we know that MacLeish was a young officer of field artillery in World War I, lived in France for five years during the 1920s, we are not surprised that he should share with his compatriot and powerful contemporary Ernest Hemingway a sense of *nada,* of having found, as did F. Scott Fitzgerald's hero of *This Side of Paradise* (1920), "all Gods dead." The ironies of war and the post-war mood of the American expatriate writers in France were enough to have inspired MacLeish's poem. Its point of view could only be reinforced by World War II and, by this time, forced upon multitudes. In turn, the French existentialist writers of the post-World-War-II period further consecrated the death of God and encouraged man to believe in the absurdity of his life and death and keenly to feel his alienation from both man and society. He was urged to rebel against natural chaos, his own death, and against rules and systems that might hamper his experience and limit his vision of himself, human life, and the nature of the universe. JB is, I think, created by these intellectual forces, but not by these alone. The humanitarian concerns of earlier writers who invented stoic and romantic heroes also find their expression in JB. We have only to recall how Stephen Crane, Joseph Conrad and Matthew Arnold created heroes who could respond with answerable courage to the dilemmas of their times: the ebb-tide of Faith, the crush of the industrial revolution and urbanization, the Darwinian and Spencerian images of struggle and survival, and the sense of the accelerating drumbeat of war. When ignorant armies clash by night, when God is distant or dead, when the Yeatsian blood-dimmed tide is loosed, men and women say, "Ah, love, let us be true to one another!" This secular covenant substitutes for the failed one between man and God. Thus JB and Sarah — once again; thus, too, the Beats and the Hippies of the 50s and 60s saying, "It's love baby, love — that's all there is!"

Certainly MacLeish is inventive in the construction of the play, leaning in part against the "old wall" as it were. There are roles for actors that provide opportunities for emotional range, and short, well-wrought scenes that unfold with cinematic rapidity and theatrical power; there are passages of excellent poetry with a texture of short lines and tough diction appropriate to the moods of despair and bitterness, and an imagery as poignant and piercing as the disillusionment and rebellion that impel it. "Curse God and die" is a cue for the dominant rhythms and sounds of the play. There is pleasure, too, in the way MacLeish translates Job's three old comforters into their modern dress and attitudes. Whereas the prototypes attempted to convince Job that he was guilty, their contemporary equivalents tell JB that he is not. Created as spokesmen for psychological (Freudian), economic (Marxian), and religious (Calvinistic, Puritan) views, Eliphaz, Bildad and Zophar account for JB's misery by making him the plaything of powerful deterministic forces, thus removing any possibility that he is responsible for his condition and his guilt. MacLeish has said of the three, "Our comforters are, if anything, less comfortable than Job's for they drive from us the last refuge in which our minds can hide from the enormous silence. If we cannot even be guilty then there are no reasons." MacLeish makes it clear that he has no sympathy for the doctrines of the new trinity; the three spokesmen assail JB for his stupidity and blindness, for his ignorance of the causes of his condition. Theirs is the coldest comfort of all since it removes any meaning his suffering may have, his meaning as a man, and reduces him to a reflex. "Can we be men," cries JB, "and make an irresponsible ignorance responsible for everything? I will not listen to you!"

Since JB cannot know that he is caught in a game between God and Satan (Zuss and Nickles), his desperate response to his catastrophies and Sarah's oath is that God grants and God takes away, and He must have reasons. However, the reasons for his suffering remain unexplained in the play; there is only, as MacLeish says in his "Foreward," the "same unanswering answer." The fact that Zuss and Nickles are two vendors selling peanuts and balloons suggests that MacLeish would have us believe that the whole argument of God and Satan is ultimately unreal sideshow stuff anyway, and as cheaply sold and bought as peanuts and balloons at a circus. There is only the heartfelt, heartbeat response of life and love, the blind faith belief in the renewal of life, as mindless, repetitive and natural as spring. Even the forsythia, newly sprung, Sarah tells us, keeps her from a suicidal leap and returns her to JB, flowers in her hands — symbols of her own future fecundity, we might suppose, or life's. JB wants reasons and justice, and in his cry MacLeish believes we hear our own voices. He has observed, "Our age is an age haunted and driven by the need to know," but as he concludes later in his introduction to the play, there are no answers beyond that of the wonder of life to persist — without God.

The most powerful and attractive spokesman in the play for the agony of man is Nickles, not JB. The old circus vendor, having donned the mask of Satan, sees the world with experienced, jaded eyes; and the ancient knowledge of the repetitive travail of man, or the panorama of his passion, impel his rip-saw diction and imagery. *JB*, like Milton's *Paradise Lost*, suggests that authors may more easily write from the point of view of rebellious angels than of uncorrupted creatures. Man can understand the temptations, frustrations and bitterness of the former but only guess at the minds of the latter. From walking up and down in the earth, man knows what it means to burn, turn in the fire of his own torment, and what he sees and feels sharpens his tongue to sardonic statement — once he masters his outrage sufficiently to stop screaming. Nickles is man with intelligence, a sense of history, and the bitter taste of the poetry of despair in his mouth — a great nay-sayer. Eternal, Nickles as Satan is more than man; being without hope, he is less. Man can answer life with life, unreasonably and without illusion, but Satan can never move beyond the limits of despair. These he knows from constant exploration. Nickles hates Zuss, Satan hates God, because God always wins — the game is set up that way — and Nickles despairs of man because he continues to play and to lose, repetitively, endlessly, and he refuses to withdraw from the game. In the old poem of Job, after God and Satan make their bargain to tempt and to try Job, we hear from Satan no more. In *JB*, however, he is a leading character, if not, dramatically speaking, the leading character. He is the full-blown extension, the elaborate poem of Sarah's cry, "Curse God and die!" He defends man against God's quixotic omnipotence, but he is defeated by the same forces in JB and Sarah that forgive, dismiss and outrage God: the blind will and strength to persist, to live and to love.

JB is MacLeish's modern man, balanced between life and suicide, and the freedom to choose either. He must resist Satan's dangerous arguments and sympathy and persist in spite of God's indifference to his suffering, a God in whose churches the candles are out, in whose sky the light has faded. The "coal of the heart" must now be quickened by human breath. Man stands alone, unquenchable love in his heart, and destiny in his hands.

As I have said, it is a play right for MacLeish, right for a post-war and war-fearing world, right for America in mid-century. For the thoughtful and *au courant,* it provided an image of Job updated to existential man; for the unwary and pious, it was somehow religious and comforting, except where audiences found the language offensive. I liked bringing it alive in production; I liked how it probed the minds and prodded the talents of my young cast; I liked the fact that lyrical drama could find and move a contemporary audience. However, I have never been totally satisfied with the play, despite its literary and theatrical virtues.

I think the trouble is that the old and vexing questions that MacLeish raises in *JB* outreach the answers that the work provides, that the "unanswerable answer" is too easy. Simply, it is not enough to conclude that "God Is," and that man is ultimately thrown upon his own resilent forces, his ability to bear suffering, to love and to live, even with the knowledge that catastrophe, defeat and meaningless death lurk around every corner of his life. Grant that love is fragile, life frangible; grant that the spirit in man is answerable to all his adversities until death undoes him; grant that God is indifferent, remote. Then we have man as stoic, humanistic and romantic — a spoiled romantic, to be sure, but romantic nevertheless. As a character, JB makes no essential advance beyond his type. Is there a great distance between Henry Fleming (*The Red Badge of Courage,* 1895), Frederick Henry (*A Farewell to Arms,* 1929), and JB in their final positions? They seem to me variations on a basic image. Perhaps the American writers of these works, despite expatriate years in the lives of all three, could come only to this image because of their American heritage and characteristic American points of view. There is a pattern: in the hands of our gifted writers during these last seventy-five years, the American hero quickly loses the Puritan-inspired dream of Paradise, a city set upon a hill as a beacon, reflecting the light of God. He learns that America is also on this side of Paradise — a long and impossible distance from the eye and mind of God. Sarah and JB are in this pattern of discovery, but somehow it is not enough to have Sarah return from the brink of suicide, a bough of petals and leaves in her hands, returning from troubled waters like Noah's dove, to bring the message of love and renewal; it is not enough for JB to straighten the furniture, assert that they are alone, and for both of them to look to the dawn together, warmed by the banked fires of their hearts. Perhaps the face of God remains too enigmatic, given the evidence of His nature in the play. "Curse God and die!" comes closer to man's temper, perhaps, than "He does not love. He Is."

Various stories of the Old Testament, including the Book of Job, suggest that God is a playmaker of extraordinary irony, that the games He plays with man are beyond man's reason and endurance. We have plenty of evidence that the game is unplayable for many. Suicide takes many subtle forms; there are too few clean, well-lighted places in the world of *nada*. MacLeish was right not to show JB rewarded as was Job who recovered his family and lived to be one hundred and forty — never mind that ten previous children died — and doubled his wealth. We would have laughed at that. We may be moved by what we do have of JB and Sarah, but we are not convinced. They are not true enough. Nickles, defeated as it were, walks off the stage with a heavier burden of truth, one suspects.

What God is it that so sorely tempts Adam and Eve, torments Cain, so tests Abraham and Isaac, as well as Job? The Jewish novelist Elie Wiesel, survivor of Auschwitz and Buchenwald, is a living Job who speaks with a more rueful tongue and blacker language than MacLeish's JB or Nickles, a writer who probes deep into the void between man and God. In Wiesel's first work *Night* (1958), the narrator, scarcely in his teens, finds himself celebrating Rosh Hashana (the Jewish New Year) along with thousands of Jewish prisoners in the Nazi death camp of Auschwitz. He speculates, "What are you, my God . . . compared to this afflicted crowd, proclaiming to you their faith, their anger, their revolt? What does your greatness mean, Lord of the Universe, in the face of all this weakness, this decomposition, and this decay? Why do You still trouble their sick minds, their crippled bodies?" With the prayers of Rosh Hashana in his ears — "All the earth and Universe are God's — All creation bears witness to the Greatness of God" — and the smoke of the crematoriums in his nostrils, the boy reaches a further conclusion:

> Yes, man is very strong, greater than God. When You
> were deceived by Adam and Eve, You drove them out of
> Paradise. When Noah's generation displeased You, You
> brought down the Flood. When Sodom no longer
> found favor in your eyes, You made the sky rain down
> fire and sulphur. But these men here, whom You have
> betrayed, whom You have allowed to be tortured,
> butchered, gassed, burned, what do they do? They pray
> before You! They praise Your name!

Then came that moment of transformation, that moment when new steel is tempered in his soul.

> This day I ceased to plead. I was no longer capable
> of lamentation. On the contrary, I felt very strong.
> I was the accuser, God the accused. My eyes were open
> and I was alone — terribly alone in a world without God
> and without man. Without love or mercy. I had ceased
> to be anything but ashes, yet I felt myself to be
> stronger than the Almighty, to him my life had been tied
> for so long. I stood amid that praying congregation,
> observing it like a stranger.

JB knew terrible affliction, more than any good man might be expected to bear, but Elie Wiesel's boy, watching his mother and little sister marched off to the ovens of Auschwitz, speaks with a more anguished and fierce voice than JB's, a voice that impels our belief.

> Never shall I forget that night, the first night in
> camp, which has turned my life into one long night,
> seven times cursed and seven times sealed. Never
> shall I forget that smoke. Never shall I forget
> the little faces of the children, whose bodies I saw

turned into wreaths of smoke beneath a silent blue
sky. Never shall I forget those flames which consumed
my Faith forever. Never shall I forget the nocturnal
silence which deprived me, for all eternity, of the
desire to live. Never shall I forget those moments
which murdered my God and my soul and turned my dreams
to dust. Never shall I forget these things, even if I
am condenmed to live as long as God Himself. Never.

The silence and distance of God is more terrible and awesome
than the voice that came out of the whirlwind to Job and JB,
with its great poetry, and its irrelevance to their condition and
questions. For Wiesel it is not enough to forgive God and to dismiss Him; man is now born a rebel against God's old games, against
His silence, against death and all those men and forces that con-
demn him to die. This evolution and tempering of the human
spirit began, it might seem, with ancient Job who did not argue
with God's answers, but covered his mouth with his hand. Why?
Was Job embarrassed because of God's inadequate answers to his
condition, at God's bragging rehearsal of His power in laying the
foundations of the earth, and creating life? Was He too distant
from and too unknowing of human suffering? The creature, man,
sitting on his dunghill, can also choose to be silent and distant
from God; he can cover his mouth and stop his questions, his cries
for justice and mercy, and his prayers; he can dismiss the God of
thunderous power and extraordinary poetry. He can, in time,
refuse the gambit of Heaven and the games God plays with man.
He can die, not a suicide, but a rebel for causes born and borne
out of his own agony. In this way he is still God's creature, but
in a fashion and with a force that JB never seems to understand.

Perhaps this is the difference: JB speaks with the voice of a
toughened and disillusioned New Englander who has learned that
God does not have all the arguments or all the answers. JB and
Sarah, like members of the Anthropus family in Thornton Wilder's
The Skin of Our Teeth, survive human and natural catastrophies
because they are shored up by domestic necessities and routines and
find themselves resilent because of love and the will to live. But
Eli Wiesel is a living Job, the spiritual descendant of the old Job,
embarrassed for and angry at God. Wiesel's characters are God's
rebels, turned hard in the fires of death camps. Both MacLeish
and Wiesel are voices of the 50s, but Wiesel's characters respond

more convincingly to human suffering and the rape of the spirit. They are more finely tuned to their agony and anger than the characters in *JB*, and they play a more dangerous game with God, and for higher stakes.

"*Hell is Other People*": Long Day's Journey Into Night

by JACKSON R. BRYER

> In a tragedy, nothing is in doubt and everyone's
> destiny is known. That makes for tranquility. There
> is a sort of fellow-feeling among characters in a
> tragedy: he who kills is as innocent as he who gets
> killed: it's all a matter of what part you are playing.
> Tragedy is restful; and the reason is that hope, that
> foul, deceitful thing, has no part in it. There isn't
> any hope. You're trapped. The whole sky has fallen
> on you, and all you can do about it is to shout.
> —Jean Anouilh, *Antigone*

One of the many ironies in the career of Eugene O'Neill is
that, in 1931, when he deliberately tried to write a modern play
which would approximate the Greek ideal of tragic drama, he
produced *Mourning Becomes Electra*. This thirteen-act monstrosity is one of the great white elephants of our theater history.
Not only does it lack the great dialogue of tragedy but it also
fails because of its over-simplified view of characters entirely
motivated by Freudian complexes which O'Neill substituted for
the Greek idea of Fate. A decade later, however, when he simply

sat down and wrote out the story which had been torturing him for years — that of his own family — O'Neill produced, in *Long Day's Journey Into Night*, one of the very few modern plays which we can see as tragic.

To talk about any modern play as a tragedy is immediately to enter what are at best muddy waters. For decades critics have quarreled over what constitutes a "modern" tragedy. A few distinctions are clear, however. One is that the strictures which Aristotle supplied in classical times no longer apply. The assumption of the Greeks that theirs was a universe controlled by the gods has never been less warranted than today, when the very existence of any deity is questioned. And there is little or no agreement as to the nature and omnipotence of a God even when His existence is acknowledged. But to remove Fate as the major cause in tragedy is not to suggest that, in the modern theater, we have been unwilling to substitute other forces for this Greek idea. Not surprisingly, we seem to have supplied causes which result from universally held notions of our day, as the idea of Fate deriving from the gods was held by the Greeks. Because we live in a highly scientific age — and because the beginnings of modern drama parallel the dawn of that age — our causes, principally heredity and environment, are major determinants in the lives of individuals and, hence, we accept them as irreversible and uncontrollable forces in the lives of dramatic characters. Thus, Ibsen in *Ghosts* and Chekhov in *The Cherry Orchard* represent the two germinal strands of the modern theater, each writing plays of tragic proportions based primarily on heredity and environment, respectively.

But I would carry this one step further and suggest that for a modern play to be truly tragic we must have more than these uncontrollable forces operating on an individual. His demise must also be partially his own fault before a true ambivalence can exist. Again, the reason can be found in the assumptions of our society as opposed to the Greeks. We live in an essentially humanistic age. Because of this, while we accept the influence of heredity and environment, we do not see them as totally determining our lives. The Greeks, on the other hand, did see the gods in this way. We have a more sophisticated and complicated view of the causes for our actions and for the directions our lives take. To be convincingly tragic a modern play must reflect this more complex perspective. There are relatively few examples of American drama that meet this challenge; but where it is met we can see the attributes noted above. In Tennessee Williams' two great classics, *The Glass Menagerie* and *A Streetcar Named Desire,* and in Arthur Miller's *Death of a Salesman* and *The Crucible,* we see characters who are victims both of their backgrounds and environments and of characteristics within themselves.

Finally, it is possible to make some further observations about the nature of these characteristics which are partially responsible for the figurative or literal downfall of the tragic protagonist. In many cases, the character's flaw — to borrow from Aristotle — is often the quality which in another sense makes him exceptional. Laura's flaw in *The Glass Menagerie* is, at least to some extent, that she cannot exist in the real world (this is, in fact, the flaw of all three Wingfields); but is it not also her strength, the basis of her uniqueness? Similarly, in *The Crucible,* it is John Proctor's integrity and honesty which set him apart; but it is these very qualities which make him choose death instead of a false confession. Even in *Oedipus Rex,* if we discount for a moment the overall causative factor of Fate, Oedipus' outstanding quality is his inquiring mind which has enabled him to solve the riddle of the Sphinx; but it is the same spirit of inquiry which makes him continue to question Tiresias and thus bring about his tragedy. This, then, seems to be one of the paradoxes inherent in tragedy — that a man's weakness is also his strength and that this very quality which sets him apart from other men may cause his destruction — or at least be responsible for his unhappiness.

Long Day's Journey Into Night exhibits most of these characteristics of modern tragedy; and it goes beyond other plays of the modern American theater in two major respects: first, it involves four tragic characters whose lives are inextricably bound but who are nonetheless decided individuals, complexly and completely depicted and explored; and second, rather than offering only heredity and environment as the partial — and uncontrollable — elements in the destinies of these figures, O'Neill offers a far more profound and abstract additional factor — love. Love binds together the four Tyrones; but love is also at the basis of their tragedy. Were there not love between the members of the family, Jamie and Edmund could leave, James could detach himself from his wife's illness and his sons' problems, and Mary could, in a sense, return to the safety of her girlhood. But, as in Sartre's *No Exit,* hell for the Tyrones is other people, each other.

All of them in the course of the play express, either explicitly or implicitly or both, a yearning for an isolated existence. The most overt examples of this are Edmund's speeches at the beginning of Act IV in which he admits that all he wants is "to be alone with myself in another world where truth is untrue and life can hide from itself." For him, the sea is the epitome of this condition and in his long reminiscence about his experiences at sea he expresses total satisfaction with an existence in which he was alone with nature, with "none of the crew in sight," a time when he belonged "to a fulfillment beyond men's lousy, pitiful, greedy fears and hopes and dreams."

Jamie's continual state of drunkenness is an expression of *his* longing for isolation; just as Mary's drug addiction implies the same sort of desire to escape the real world and envelop herself in a protective fog. James' escapes are more subtle. In one respect, his refuge is *The Count of Monte Cristo*, the "big money-maker" on which he has squandered his talents. It has enabled him to stop living creatively. His pose as a patrician land-owner also provides him with an escape from his true heritage as a shanty Irishman and makes it possible for him often to dissociate himself from his contemporaries.

But at the same time that the Tyrones seek escape, they see that it is impossible; they realize that they are hopelessly tied to one another for life. This realization, combined with the desire to escape, produces what is perhaps the major tension in the play, a tension which is expressed primarily in a continual series of expressions of love and hatred on the part of each character. Throughout the play, each Tyrone says and does many things deliberately to hurt another. They strike out at each other like the caged animals that they are; but, in virtually the next breath, they profess deep and genuine affection. This ambivalence provides *Long Day's Journey* with one of its most complex elements.

In Act IV, Jamie drunkenly admits to Edmund that he deliberately introduced him to the dissolute existence that he, Jamie, relishes because he "never wanted you to succeed and look even worse by comparison." He then blames Edmund's birth for Mary's dope addiction and, while he admits that it is not Edmund's fault, he declares, "God damn you, I can't help hating your guts —!" But, almost immediately, he adds, "But don't get the wrong idea, Kid. I love you more than I hate you." Similarly, in Act I, when all three Tyrones are concerned about the possible return of Mary's habit, it is Jamie, whose love for his mother is the cause of his hatred of Edmund, who deliberately lets slip the fact that Edmund's illness is more than a cold, a disclosure which he knows is likely to help drive her back to morphine. Later in the same act, Edmund, who is even closer to Mary than Jamie is, unnecessarily tells her that he heard her go into the spare room the night before, a sure indication that she is back on the drug.

Mary and James accuse one another continually, Mary blaming her husband for not providing a home for his family and for being a miser, James bitterly blaming her for ruining their happiness. Yet, at the end of their most heated exchange, early in Act II, Scene 2, Mary exclaims, "James! We've loved each other! We always will!" And, in Act II, Mary reminds Jamie that he should have more respect for his father: "You ought to be proud you're his son!" Both Mary and James also reminisce often about how happy they were with one another once; and they do so in terms that make it very clear that they still love each other a great deal.

Both sons lash out at their father throughout the play. Mary even at one point tells Edmund, "I never knew what rheumatism was before you were born!" Yet, despite all this rancor, there is abundant evidence of abiding affection. This is ironically and appropriately symbolized at the very end of the play when Mary, completely under the influence of morphine, drifts in dragging her wedding gown and wanders about the room reminiscing about her girlhood. The reverie concludes with her memory of senior year when she decided to be a nun; but then, she recalls, "in the spring something happened to me. . . . I fell in love with James Tyrone and was so happy for a time." This brief passage sums up all of one aspect of the tragedy. Mary's love for James, and all the Tyrones' love for each other, is both their great strength and the cause of their torture. If they did not love each other so much, they could not strike out so cruelly, they could not hate. Edmund's remark about Mary — "It's as if, in spite of loving us, she hated us!" — might well be changed to read because she loves us, she hates us, and then applied equally to all the relationships in this family. And, finally, each character's desire to escape the others, to find an isolation away from the complications of other people, is really no more nor less than a wish to evade one of the major responsibilities of the human condition, contact with other human beings and all the conflicting emotions and attitudes that these contacts produce. As Edmund says in Act IV — and as many an O'Neill protagonist could and does echo — "It was a great mistake, my being born a man. I would have been much more successful as a sea gull or a fish."

But there are other tragic aspects to *Long Day's Journey*. An important one is suggested by my earlier remarks about the forces operating on an individual in modern tragic drama. In O'Neill's play, each of the Tyrones is both responsible and not responsible for the part he is playing. The best example of this is James. The three members of his family accuse him of being miserly and there is ample confirmation of this charge, most especially in his efforts to send Edmund to an inexpensive sanitorium. But, in Act IV, James admits to Edmund that perhaps he is a "stinking old miser" and goes on to explain this trait by describing his childhood when he "learned the value of a dollar" working twelve hours a day in a machine shop, a "dirty barn of a place where rain dripped through the roof," for fifty cents a week. With this disclosure it becomes clear that James is not entirely to blame for his penurious ways. It is not his fault that he was brought up in a penniless and fatherless family. This background understandably has made him overly sensitive to the evils of the poorhouse. And yet we cannot totally excuse this quality in James because we feel that, once he became financially successful, he should have developed more generous instincts in accordance with normal familial devotion. Clearly, however, the responsibility for James' weakness is divided between forces in his background over which he had no control and present factors which he should be able to alter.

The same sort of divided responsibility can be seen in the three other characters. Jamie's drunken and dissolute ways are certainly his own fault to an extent, but they can also be traced to the family situation. His father introduced him to drink and brought him up in an atmosphere where he could meet the cheap tarts and low types with whom he now associates. Jamie's failures in life can also be linked partially to his father's refusal to allow him to be a success. This is perhaps because James realizes that he has sold his own talents for a sure financial return and he must therefore keep his son from being any more successful than he is. Jamie's problems are also further compounded by his relationships with his mother and his brother. He feels, with considerable justification, that Mary dotes on Edmund and ignores him. He also is, as he admits to Edmund in Act IV, extremely jealous of

his brother and of the possibility that he will succeed and make
him look worse by comparison.

Mary also is both victim and causative factor. She is guilty of
forcing her family into an almost death-like inaction by her drug
addiction; but when we look at her background and the cause of
her illness, we find ample extenuating circumstances. She is, in
many ways, still the shy convent girl who, as O'Neill stresses in his
long stage direction introducing her, "has never lost" her "innate
unworldly innocence." Because of this she is totally unable to cope
with the cruel realities of the world around her. In this she shares
more than a literal kinship with Edmund, who also cannot face
the world because of a sensitive poetic nature. Both Mary and
Edmund feel a tremendous lack of belonging, a loneliness. It is
difficult to decide whether Mary's addiction, like Laura's limp in
The Glass Menagerie, causes her isolation or whether the addiction
is merely an overt manifestation of the isolation which is already
there. Mary has not been at peace since she left her father's
house to marry James. While it is true that James has never given
her the house she so desperately wants, she would undoubtedly
have been unable to cope with one had she been asked to do so.
Mary's retreat into the past through drugs is her way of going
back to what was for her an ideal world, an escape from a real
world which she cannot handle. Her addiction is probably no more
than a means towards an end which she would have reached — or
tried to reach — through another method had morphine not been
available. Thus, we cannot totally blame her problems on James
and the "cheap quack doctor" who attended her at Edmund's
birth. Nor can we blame Edmund's present illness for her rever-
sion to dope. Mary's difficulties are far more deep-seated than this.
Her protected childhood has made her constitutionally and emotionally unable to deal with life. On the other hand, Mary *is*
guilty of refusing to face her problem. Unlike James, she will not
admit either to herself or to her family that she cannot exist in
the real world and hence she is torturing her husband and her
sons. James can look objectively at his background and see it as
a major influence upon his present personality; but Mary, while she
can realize that the "past is the present" and "the future too,"
cannot act on that understanding.

As I've already said, Edmund is much like his mother — and
this probably accounts for the fact that he understands her more
fully than anyone else. He is the typical O'Neill protagonist who,

he himself realizes, "never feels at home, who does not really want and is not really wanted, who can never belong, who must always be a little in love with death." Unlike his mother and like his father, Edmund does try to face up to his inadequacies and attempts to understand why he does not belong. Mary totally rejects life because she cannot understand it and does not want to try; Edmund accepts life, understanding that he can never really be a part of it. In his long soliloquy midway through Act IV, after he describes the ecstasy of life at sea, he tells how, after that moment, "the hand lets the veil fall and you are alone, lost in the fog again, and you stumble on toward nowhere, for no good reason." But Edmund too is both the victim and the originator of his troubles. His sensitive nature makes him unable to deal with most of the world around him, just as so many O'Neill characters from the Mayo brothers in *Beyond the Horizon* and Yank in *The Hairy Ape* down to the denizens of Harry Hope's bar in *The Iceman Cometh* cannot belong in the real world with which they are faced. But he is also a victim of that world which is so insensitive to him and to his special needs. He is a poet in a world which rejects its poets. And his understanding of this fact is revealed in Act IV, just as Jamie's and James' awareness are disclosed during this final explosive section of the play.

In fact, this last act serves to complicate our responses to these characters enormously in that their capacity to understand and articulate their own weaknesses makes them fit objects of our respect as well as our pity. Up to this point, we are quite ready to accept James as a miser who has repressed his family disastrously, Jamie as a wastrel who has been the major disappointmnt of his father's life, and Edmund as a foolish dreamer; for these are the pictures we get of them from the three other characters. But when, in Act IV, we hear their side of the story, we can no longer be content simply to dismiss them this easily. What we end up with is the sense of divided responsibility which I defined at the beginning of this essay. It is expressed overtly in *Long Day's Journey* through two brief passages. The first, appropriately enough spoken by Mary, expresses the forces over which she and her family have no control: "None of us can help the things life has done to us. They're done before you realize it, and once they're done they make you do other things until at last everything comes between you and what you'd like to be, and you've lost your true self forever." The second occurs when Edmund remarks to his father that life is "so damned crazy" and James corrects him: "There's nothing wrong with life. It's we who — *He quotes.* 'The fault, dear Brutus, is not in our stars, but in ourselves that we are underlings.' "

The consequence of this divided responsibility is that, as in any tragic play of the modern era, it is impossible to assign blame. Both controllable and uncontrollable forces operate on the lives of the Tyrones, with the added complication that the very family situation they live in is both a contributor to and a result of the tragic situation. Not only could each of these characters by himself be the subject of a tragic drama — as he could — but also a major share of the tragic element is attributable to their inter-relationships. Unlike the Greeks who tended to center their tragedies on one flawed protagonist, O'Neill in *Long Day's Journey* (and, to a certain extent, other modern playwrights like Chekhov, Ibsen, and Williams), seem to see groups of individuals — most often families — caught in webs partially of their own devising but woven by outside forces as well.

The degree of struggle possible within these webs varies from play to play. In *Long Day's Journey* there seems to be very little. In the terms of the passage from *Antigone* quoted as the epigram to this essay, there is definitely a "tranquility" here, a "fellow-feeling" among the four Tyrones, who are, in numerous ways, one character. They are certainly all subject to many of the same tensions and ambivalences. There is, as I've stressed, no easily assigned guilt or innocence; we certainly can find no villain or hero in this play. While there may be some hope for Edmund, it is primarily medically-based or founded quite irrelevantly on the assumption that he is Eugene O'Neill who, after all, did become a successful playwright. Far more germane is the obvious fact that Edmund will never "belong" in the real world any more than his mother will; he will always be "the stranger" that he realizes he is now. Without hope, as Anouilh notes, a tragic play like *Long Day's Journey* is "restful." The characters are "trapped," as the single set for the play and the fog continually rolling in explicitly indicate. There is a good deal of shouting in the play, but most of it is the ultimately ineffectual beating at the bars of four caged animals who have no other means of voicing their frustrations.

Just as in a later American play with which it shares many common elements, *Who's Afraid of Virginia Woolf?* nothing really happens in *Long Day's Journey*. There is very little action, in the conventional dramatic sense of the term; and none of the characters change at all. The reason for this is simple: nothing can happen to four figures in this situation. All we can do is contemplate them in their web and endeavor to understand them with the assistance of the skill of the playwright who unfolds their lives to us. Because no American playwright has depicted more complex and complete characters with more compassion and sheer dramatic power than Eugene O'Neill in *Long Day's Journey*, it deserves a place among the great plays written in any age in any language. It is a further measure of its magnitude that it is also one of the few American plays which meet most of the measures of modern tragedy. That it does so within the framework of a generally conventional realistic four-character domestic drama, rather than through a consciously super-imposed classical mold, merely makes O'Neill's achievement that much more remarkable.

Plays Written on the Air: Television Theatre in the 50s

by Patrick D. Hazard

Television as our most egalitarian medium has a caricaturizing style; it overaccentuates certain salient traits in American culture. It has, for example, nearly apotheosized the amnesiac quality in our national life: America was promises, history is bunk. The future is the dominant tense of American literature as British scholar Marcus Cunliffe sees it. At best there have been only feeble PR-motivated efforts (largely as a reflex to the image-debilitating shock-waves of the Van Doren quiz scandals) to set up well-financed archives to facilitate research in television production and programming. The 54-program retrospective of the years from 1948 to 1961 held at the prestigious Museum of Modern Art between February and May, 1963 can hardly be accepted as adequate corporate paying of dues. As Jac Venza, who directed the project, wrote in the catalog for *Television USA: 13 Seasons*:

> It is estimated that the three networks broadcast 20,000 programs a year (exclusive of local programs). No one could have seen or reviewed every television program ever presented during this period. Yet, clearly, in the consensus there were significant programs and significant forms: this was the major consideration in the selection of these 54

programs. 1948 was chosen as the first year because the kinescoping process was improved to the point where programs could be recorded in 16mm. film.

Venza and his staff winnowed what was available (sad for Clio to learn, there was no necessary correlation between high quality and easy accessibility — network executives have very different thresholds of co-operation on culture projects) by putting this question to some 34 producers and directors in all major facets of TV: "Which of your programs do you remember as the most significant in the evolution of television?" 237 replies included many repeats which four committees pared down to the Museum's screenings. Thirteen of these choices were theatre and deserve a simple chronological listing as evidence of what the creators of the so-called Golden Age of TV Drama recalled as significant:

1. Studio One: "The Storm" 1948 or 1949.
2. Danger Theater: "The Paper Box Kid" 1952
3. Philco Playhouse: "The Rich Boy" 1952
4. You Are There: "The Death of Socrates" 1953
5. Goodyear Playhouse: "Marty" 1953
6. Philco Playhouse: "A Man Is Ten Feet Tall" 1955
7. Studio One Summer Theater: "Mr. Arcularis" 1956
8. Kraft Theater: "A Night to Remember" 1956
9. Playhouse 90: "Requiem for a Heavyweight" 1956
10. Playhouse 90: "The Miracle Worker" 1957
11. Hallmark Hall Of Fame: "Little Moon of Alban" 1958
12. Camera 3: "Actors Choice No. 7" 1960
13. Play of the Week: "The Iceman Cometh" 1960

The best of these (5, 6, 9, 10) have been made into adequate movies, whose signals as often replayed. "Late, Late Movies" all but obliterate any memory of the esthetic uniqueness of their TV originals. Thus ironically, one is able to study very carefully indeed the sociologically revealing series like Jackie Gleason's "The Honeymooners" or Jack Webb's "Dragnet" from the 1950s because such large blocks of syndicated celluloid are vendible while single plays for which each negotiated talent is a legal problem are not — unless the topicality and social consciousness value of plays like "Who Do I Kill?" (on a Harlem rat-bite infanticide) or "No Hiding Place" (on the collapse of a racial liberal in a Long Island integration incident) cause a special-interest film distributor like Carrousel Films, which has access to a socially-conscious producer like David Susskind, with a series-continuity star, George C. Scott, equally committed to a drama of contentiousness in "East Side/West Side," to make them available.

Never has the historian of an art form been so at the mercy of caprice. Suddenly in the summer of 1969, searching *TV Guide* for a movie that could be assigned in an Afro-American literature course, I rediscovered Reginald Rose's fine triptych of perspectives on a school-integration crisis, "Black Monday," on the schedule of a marginal UHF station in Philadelphia. My investigation revealed that the hard-pressed production firm, National Telefilm Associates (which ultimately had to sell its Newark studio to educational station WDNT) was still syndicating what had been one of the first videotaped series of weekly TV dramas. What makes one leery about relying on one's memory (or even one's notes) is what effect the passing of a decade may have had on the treatment of an integration crisis. Although Pat Hinkle's performance as a handicapped ex-G.I.-shopkeeper caught in a crossfire between his business and his ideals remains one of the most moving embodiments of character in TV drama during the 50s, the young punks' beating up the school-janitor-grandfather of the first Negro child scheduled to enter the school seems gratuitous, in spite of the intervening *Bonnie and Clyde* of TV-director-emeritus Arthur Penn and the sheriff's posse of Philadelphia, Mississippi. And so does the retired one-term liberal Senator, whose intimidated son suddenly turns racist demagogue.

Memory's insufficiency is not even adequately compensated for by examining a spectrum of critical responses (overlaying, say, the *New York Times'* Gould, the *Washington Post's* Lawrence Laurent, the *Philadelphia Inquirer's* Harry Harris, and a trade critic in *Variety*). One may approach a convergence, but formal explication remains impossible until there are replay facilities — the videotape equivalent of a movieola for scanning a play with the care now given to the formal aesthetic analysis of motion pictures. Until the industry takes its art and a conservation of its heritage as seriously as it does its parody of the search for standards in the Emmy awards, we can only hope for the establishment of a foundation-funded center for the study of the art of television. There are beginning to be really helpful collections, such as the University of Wisconsin's Center for Mass Communications History, whose Paddy Chayefsky and Rod Serling materials I found illuminating.

Another dimension of bias which must be prologomenon to any useful discussion of TV drama as an emerging art in the 50s is the metropolitan skew. My first viewing of television with the frequency only a set-owner can achieve began in East Lansing, Michigan, in 1952 when fond relatives decided the austerity of graduate school ought to be leavened with popular entertainment. East Lansing was a one-and-one-half channel town — one commercial VHF channel which picked and chose from three networks (much sports, little culture) and a ludicrously underfinanced UHF channel, whose dial number — 60 — was felt by many on the station itself fo foretell the year when the audience would begin to be measured in two figures. My condition of televisual poverty continued until a Ford Fellowship to study popular culture in New York City in 1955-56 led to a TV critic's job for the rest of the decade. When I compared my pre-New York televiewing experiences with the Museum of Modern Art's nominations, I was reminded sharply of what almost everyone who writes about popular culture in America forgets: how far New York City is from everywhere else — and how even farther is Beverly Hills — with or without synthetic hillbillies. For as a high school teacher of English, who before he went to New York City, hadn't seen five plays of professional quality in his life, I found Paddy Chayefsky paradise. I assigned his "The Catered Affair" (directed by Robert Mulligan for Goodyear Playhouse, May 22, 1955) to two tenth-grade sections. The morning-after was a transcendent experience. They too were inexperienced, Broadway-wise. Yet *they* were exurban sons and daughters of either Michigan State University faculty or General Motors executives. Emotionally they were a long way from the Bronx. But Thelma Ritter as the status happy mother ashamed that her daughter may be pregnant and Pat Henning as the cab driver with almost enough money saved up to buy his own hack made the conflict of values universal in the horrific sense of that term. The touching reconciliation between husband and wife in the bedrom at the final curtain is what *Commentary* reviewers were to sneer at as Paddy's melodrama. I continue to believe what our class concluded: people can transcend their hangups with generosity and love.

Chayefsky was exceedingly gifted at this portrayal of the American vernacular. The rituals of secular American life —

Saturday night prowling as in "Marty," the pre-wedding blast known as "The Bachelor Party," and "The Catered Affair" as a family's social mask — are constitutive of the contemporary American character. No consideration of American television drama in the 50s dares ignore the work (and ultimate defection) of the so-called laureate of the Bronx; indeed it is best to begin with him and his indigenous kitchen-sink drama.

Sidney Chayefsky (the ironic sobriquet Paddy was earned by his frequent attempts to evade Sunday morning K.P. on the pretext of attending Mass while a soldier in England) was born in the Bronx, January 29, 1923 and educated in New York City public schools, City College, and Fordham. He first broke into print at West Clinton High School where he was editor of the literary magazine. While serving in the European theater during World War II, he wrote a GI musical comedy, "No T.O. for Love," which was ultimately produced in London's West End. In late 1950, his television play, "Holiday Song," a fable about the Jewish Holy Days, brought him his first prominence in the fledgling television industry — still for all practical purposes New York City, with a few Eastern Seaboard megalopolitan "network" connections. (It is absolutely essential, in any attempts to make sense of the "golden era" of TV drama to keep firmly in mind how the slow nationalization of the television audience in the early fifties in effect demetropolitanized and parochialized the medium as a communications channel.) Chayefsky preceded his TV career with a stint as a Hollywood screen writer but he had optioned his plays to people who never could raise the money to have them produced: elephantiasis of film budgets thus symbolically drove the ambitious out of sheer frustration to identify with the new TV medium in which unionization and bureaucratization had not yet escalated costs upward on the graph where fiscal timidity joins hands with esthetic emasculation. *Marty* (1953) established him as so important a TV playwright that he began to be besieged by interviewers more anxious than he about his cultural status, much as a stellar academician at a state teachers college is nervously and shyly asked by his best friends, "When is he going to try for the Ivy League (to cite a falling star) or Berkeley?" Hence Chayefsky began parrying ubiquitous questioning about when he was going to leave the vulgar medium of TV for the prestigious one of Broadway or the lucrative one of Hollywood. It is important to observe how he, in effect, succumbed to the status-peddling critics, beginning from what John Kouwenhoven might call a venacular posture of being damn grateful to the new medium for having given him the scope to develop his talents, with no snobbish nonsense about low-brow medium given the least credence to an acceptance of the Big Money from the movies to finance a string of Broadway plays which grow more and more ambitious in an intellectual sense, starting with an adaptation of "Middle of the Night" (original name "December Wedding") and moving through Jewish thematics in "The Tenth Man" (1959) and "Gideon" (1961), and ending with a metaphysical blur on the Russian Revolution. His stature did give him the power to become writer, producer and assistant director on "The Goddess" (1958) which brought him international acclaim at the Brussels World Fair.

Chayefsky forsook the Bronx realism that first established him with "Gideon" (1961), over a decade after his arrival as a TV playwright. He is not a little sensitive about critics praising his phonographic ear. "I'd just like to find," he has said, "a tape recorder half as clever as I am." In a way the comments are a sad index to the slowness with which literary criticism leavens the lumpen judging of other more popular media; questions of literalism vs. artfully contrived simulacra have long since been satisfactorily resolved in discussion, say, of the work of Ernest Hemingway. This, shall we call it, innocence of TV criticism is an important but not a critical factor in the decline of TV drama — and the beginnings of better and more informed criticism could be even more crucial in any efforts to reestablish TV drama as a central genre in the most pervasive medium of American civilization. The isolation of TV criticism in the incipient stages of a national medium may be taken as an emblem of that medium's general isolation from the most sophisticated consciousness available in the American culture, just as the Museum of Modern Art's TV retrospective in 1963 is symbolic of a closing of the cleavage.

When *Marty* appeared as a movie in 1955, the Clinton *News* (May 5, 1955) ran a piece by Leonard B. Stern on Chayefsky, "The Successful Graduate of the Class of 1939," who had been editor-in-chief of *The Magpie* and drama editor of the *News*. The high school reporter asked the returning hero what he considered a most promising field of endeavor for a writer. His reply was that "television is a great medium, an endless medium. There are more opportunities today than at any other time in the past." He also noted with pride that, "I write about people I understand — the $70-$175 a week people."

Marty, as a film, was also a turning point in the history of American popular culture in general, for it presaged all those eruptions of autonomy from underground films and newspapers to Woodstock culture through which the P. T. Barnum syndrome of the film-czar is being replaced by talented ententes such as that formed in 1969 by Harry Belafonte, Barbra Streisand, and Paul Newman. *Marty* as film was a loss to television for it triggered the flight of the unmortgaged (financially or psychologically, no matter, it amounts to the same thing) from the new medium, killing it esthetically while still toddling. Significantly, it was a trumpet of the old film czars who, immensely skillful in adjusting to the shifting sands of fortune in Hollywood, that most miasmic of places, early sensed the shift which would ultimately transform the old style movie capital. Louella Parsons noted in *Cosmopolitan* (May 1955), "Not only is *Marty* a small jewel of a film, but it also marks the end of the great war between the movies and television. Five years ago, I never dreamed Hollywood would make a movie out of a TV drama. [Fifteen years later most of us would never have dreamed that Hollywood would end up making a drive-in of our TVed front room!] But it has finally happened." Miss Parsons noted snippily that although *Marty* had won both the coveted Donaldson and Sylvania Awards as the best TV drama of 1953, it would not win an Academy Award: "The production is too slight and lacks big salaried actors to pull in the audience that helped movies like *From Here to Eternity* and *The High and Mighty* to gross 10 or 15 million dollars." Parsons also observed that the small independent production company was setting the pace in Hollywood "keying itself into the experimental work TV can literally afford to do. (For instance, TV could 'afford' to gamble on Jack Webb a few years ago when his salary was approximately 50 cents a month; at the same time, it was costing the movies 4 million dollars to make a picture like *The Robe*.)" Parsons also pointed out that Burt Lancaster and Harold Hecht could never have produced *Marty* at twice the production budget of $360,000 if high-salaried Lancaster had himself starred in it. (Hecht, parenthetically, had been Paddy's Hollywood agent. In the old days he was the only and very captive audience of Chayefsky who used to make Hecht sit still while he read plays nobody wanted to produce.) And most significantly, Chayefsky had decided to sell *Marty* to the movies "only if he were promised the picture would be filmed with *all the simplicity* [my italics] of the TV production. An unglamorous heroine, realistic actress, no trick camera lighting, no embellishments to detract from the poignant love story of an Italian Bronx butcher and an inhibited school teacher." Hecht was there to see to it that Chayefsky's desires were respected. It was Burt Lancaster's idea, however, to give Ernest Borgnine "his first sympathetic role as the lonely fellow who picks up an even lonelier girl at a cheap dance hall." Parsons concluded her analysis of this quiet revolution by predicting that *Marty* would be able to compete "in its own quiet way" against super films. It was proving that "best sellers" don't necessarily come from between the covers of books, or from the boards of the New York stage. "Only," she concluded pontifically, "because *Marty* is as good as it is has the wall between Hollywood and TV crumbled at last. I'm might glad to see this come to pass."

Another fix on this quiet revolution is a *Variety* headline (June 14, 1955), "WRITERS RIDING CHAYEFSKY MORALE IN PRESTIGE BID." Director-writer Harry Essex contended "Hollywood film makers should learn the important lesson from the already phenomenal success of Hecht-Lancaster's *Marty*. It moved writers from the shabby status of hired hands into the area of top level key figures in the production of motion pictures." Essex pointed out that everyone seemed to be ignoring what he regarded "as the chief reason for the success of this remarkable picture — day-by-day, hour-by-hour, all out participating of writer Paddy Chayefsky in the making of the film." He had taken part in all pre-production conferences with Hecht-Lancaster and Director Delbert Mann — himself, we should not forget, a TV trained director, accustomed to thinking big thoughts in a smallish way. "He was in on all the casting. He was on the set for every moment of the film shooting. At the end of each day the writer met with producer and director, saw and discussed rushes." How different, of course, from the way the average writer has to work in Hollywood, who Essex added bitterly, "finished a script and then when the really significant part of the whole project, bringing it to life, takes place he's off somewhere wondering what they're doing to his baby. More often than not his worries are justified and the father can't recognize his own offspring." Essex concluded his *Marty* induced homily by arguing that the reason there was more creativity in the theatre than in the movies was "precisely the fact that writers are treated with the dignity and respect their contribution calls for."

In a symposium on TV writing published in *Variety* (July 27, 1955); Chayefsky developed for his peers in show business his theory that there were no useful distinctions to be made in his own work between serious and hack writing, between fine and popular art. He noted that from time to time people asked him if he were going to quit TV-writing because of *"Marty's* success as a film," the implication being that he had by then graduated from the esthetic minor leagues and was now a cultural big timer. His defense of the newer medium was straightforward: "There is nothing minor league about television." If that judgment sounds preposterous, one must remember that it was made before Philco Goodyear's Fred Coe abandoned TV drama to producers more willing to meet the advertising agencies' demands for "happy stories about happy people with happy problems." (*Time*, October 10, 1955.) The coterie of writers Coe encouraged (not the least by the high quality of his directors and their casting) and defended against Madison Avenue censors was quite remarkable: Chayefsky, Robert Alan Arthur, Tad Mosel, J. P. Miller, Horton Foote, and Gore Vidal, to name the most productive, and the plays they wrote (and later published) gave the new medium whatever real artistic excitement it had — the Edward R. Murrow tradition of responsible journalism is commendable, indispensable (and also woefully underdeveloped by absolute standards), but it is in the imagined worlds of the dramatist that the medium makes its greatest claim of our serious attention. Most of these creative people would doubtless share the pride in television's tiny flurry of creativity implicit in Chayefsky's autobiographical analysis:

> There was a time [he admitted in the *Variety* symposium on TV writing] when I was annoyed at being called a television writer. I thought of myself as a legitimate playwright, and the term, "television-writer," carried with it a vaguely demeaning connotation. That certainly isn't true any more. I am proud of my work in television and of the company I keep. The television writers I know are the most professional, talented, and responsible young men around. I think they bear their work with dignity, and it is time for the proper respect and attention.

Not that he was a Pollyanna about the medium, for when Simon & Schuster published his first book, *Television Plays* later that same year (1955), he made comments of value to the historian of TV in the 50s; "I enjoy writing television a good deal for personal reasons and because the Philco-Goodyear allows me to write as well as I care to. Most of my friends are not so lucky. They write for shows that demean their talents or twist their good work when they do put effort into it." Chayefsky in fact relished the collaborative creativity that golden era TV drama was at its rarest:

> Rehearsals can be the best part of television, for this is where the real fascination of theater lies — in the quick, nervous, day-to-day maturation of a script, in the sometimes incredible blossoming of actors as they wrench their roles open and expose innumerable hidden subtleties. There is nothing in the professional world to compare to a bunch of responsive theater people engaged in a genuinely co-operative work. On the other hand, nothing is more miserable than those rehearsals in which everyone concerned has contempt for the script, himself, and the entire production.

It was the writer's good fortune as a Ford Fellow studying popular culture in New York City 1955-56 to be allowed to watch, on the bare stages of the Roseland Ballroom, an unfolding *something* like what Chayefsky celebrated. I mention it because the differences were already more evident than the similarities — the play was about the battling around Monte Cassino during World War II, and it was in a new series with a title like the new model Pontiacs it ultimately was the vehicle for, PLAYWRIGHTS '56. First of all there were three non-TV stars, John Forsythe, Kurt Kasznar, and Dina Merrill. The names were insurance; early TV brought along nonentities like Eva Marie Saint and Sal Mineo, who measured up to the challenge. The theme was nostalgic exotica; already World War II was getting far enough away to develop materials that would lead, absurdly, to the fatuities of "Hogan's Heroes." I have no recollection of the theme, even though I spent several days watching director Arthur Penn develop "its meaning." Themes and scenes of perhaps twenty TV plays of substance still stick in my mind, Chayefsky in America sadly overshadowed by British TV playwrights like David Mercer, Troy

Kennedy Martin, Alun Owen, not to mention Harold Pinter. The playwright was there, quietly, and there was a low-keyed intensity of a camaraderie. Coe, a soft-spoken Southerner of great though inobtrusive charisma, helped — not as most TV producers who visualized themselves as ritual lightning rods to keep the lightning of the agencies off the creative talent. But they knew they were making a product more than a program: artifact had displaced art.

Chayefsky also wrote in the preface to his first collection of TV plays that television had been a "kind medium" to him. "I came out of the legitimate theater, and I want to go back again. When I do, I will not be able to calculate the debt I owe to television for the amount of sheer craft I have learned in these past two years. I have never written a script in television of which I was not at least partially proud. I hope to continue writing for the medium as long as I can." In point of fact, Chayefsky — in spite of several well announced feints at return — has boycotted the medium in which some continue to think he did his best work. The reasons he gave in 1957 were both financial and artistic. He got only $1,200 for the script of *Marty*; and never much more than $2,000 at most from Philco-Goodyear Theater. He complained that during his most productive year (9 full-hour and numerous half-hour shows) he earned only $12,000. So he told a *Time* (August 5, 1957) interviewer, he could afford to be demanding, TV paying him so little! "I ask a lot. I insist on veto power when it comes to casting. I ask for veto power on a director. . . . Not many people are willing to make these concessions." In 1957 David Susskind convened on "Open End" (WNTA) Chayefsky and several other Philco-Goodyear expatriates to discuss their abstention from TV. It must be admitted that by then the 34-year-old doyen of TV drama was becoming a trifle stuffy. When the assembled playwrights bemoaned the conformity of the medium and of American culture in general, Susskind reminded them that their absence from TV only added to the mediocrity. Chayefsky then parlayed a gag which he has gotten some little mileage out of since: viz., he had three ideas he was perfectly willing to try on TV's sound stages — one on homosexuality, one on menopause, and the other on the psychopathology of the American Communist. It was clear, this is to say, that the Bronx realist was much more interested in baiting Susskind and Talent Associates' development of classic costume dramas on TV than in enhancing the medium he praised so fulsomely during his own apprenticeship.

Indeed, it is melancholy to observe that the entire crew of ex-TV luminaries holding a televised reunion for "Open End" made their critiques of conformist America from rather unimpregnable redoubts: ranches in Arizona and yachts off the California coast. The high costs of prep schools all figured more prominently in the dialogue than the ethics/esthetics of television.

For a while Chayefsky planned to produce a series of plays on behavioral disorders for the American Psychiatric Association. Dr. Francis J. Braceland, President of the Association was enthusiastic about the project; "It seems to us," he said, "that if anyone can handle psychiatric subject matter, Mr. Chayefsky is the man. He has demonstrated his artistic sensibility in dramatizing behavior patterns for which psychiatrists have many technical names. Everybody exhibits these patterns in varying degrees; but only when carried to extremes do these patterns become a medical concern. If more people learned to recognize them in their own daily behavior, they might have a better chance of modifying them before they got out of hand" (New York *Herald Tribune*, Jan. 4, 1957). But the network demanded control of the scripts, "kookiness" being the *bête noire* of the standardized bureaucrat. "Once they got control," Chayefsky contended "it would be so dehydrated it wouldn't be worth doing. They would try to make the subject matter more palatable, and it can't be done that way." (*Variety*, October 14, 1957). Hence failed what might very well have been an archetype for television entertainment helping orient the mass viewer to the many threatening elements of modern America that are only glossed over now by the "classic" urban folk genres like the western, crime, and situation comedy.

Chayefsky's moral posture and esthetic style eminently qualified him to have become such a pioneer of popular culture, as his *ad hoc* remarks in a piece for the front page of the New York *Times* Drama section (July 15, 1956) suggest, for he rejected the common putdown that his creations were merely little plays about little people:

> I am afraid that what some critics really mean by "little plays" [Chayefsky observed] is that the play had its origins in television. It is a sort of poignant arrogance among some theatre people to suppose that any other dramatic medium is only a stepping stone to Broadway, a sort of minor league, a training school for the nobler demands of the stage. I

could not escape the feeling, after reading some of the reviews of my play, *Middle of the Night* that I was being looked at as a *nouveau riche* who had elbowed his way into an aristocrat's home and while the gentry were by noblesse oblige dutifully courteous, they could not help raising an eyebrow at my choice of necktie.

Chayefsky defended *Middle of the Night* from the charge that it was a little play. He insisted that it dealt with "some of the basic precepts of life: What is love? What is happiness? What is fulfillment?" He wrote about love and happiness and fulfillment in particularly mundane terms because he believed them to be mundane things, "as real as the audience or electric light bulbs, palpable to the touch, recognizable to the senses."

I do not believe [Chayefsky declared] that the richness of life are vague, astral paragraphs of prose available only to esthetes. I believe that all the beauty some poets find in dreams can be found in the involved relationship of a middle-aged man who is concerned about impotence and a highly neurotic girl of twenty-four who devours everyone she knows in her desperate search for warmth.

Chayefsky then defended his lyricism of the commonplace in terms of a scenario he had just written from his TV play *The Bachelor Party*. It is the story of a young accountant who tries to forget the anxieties of prospective fatherhood by taking a fling with a friend who is about to be married.

The hero [Chayefsky wrote] is a man wandering for a night in search of some identity, of some truth and value to his life. His terms of reference are limited by a white-collar job and a two-room apartment in Stuyvesant Town, and he searches for meaning within his family and friends, just as everyone in the audience has to search for his. He speaks in common idiom and the circumstances of his evening are common circumstances. But is he any the less a searcher than Peer Gynt?

He hoped his audience would accept the film as "an amusing, occasionally intense, and even insightful film," but he would be

damned if he thought it a little film because he didn't come out
on a bare stage and announce his intentions in pentameter or "by
abstruse vivification of the language."

Chayefsky's next success was his first original screenplay, *The
Goddess*. It is significant for our purposes that it is the story of a
Hollywood queen of love who has spent a neurotic lifetime
unsuccessfully trying to find love for herself. It is a parable about
the tragedy of the spurious, prefabricated emotions of the mass
media. In *Marty*, for example, the boys hold an impromptu seminar on girlie mags (one fellow clucks his way all *too* slowly
through a gallery of nudes, deploring the existence of such trash
through bathroom squinty eyes). Similarly, they exchange literary
opinions ("Mickey Spillane sure can write") and back their way
into a Saturday-night movie after each lethargically and repeti-
tiously tries to have the other direct the evening's leisure. In *The
Goddess*, also, two succesive generations of unwilling young mothers
attempt to drown out the calls of conscience by turning up the
volume of the jazz on the living room radio. Not the least interesting aspect of Chayefsky is the mirror he holds up to mass man,
revealing to him the inevitable futility of unexamined living
along the midway of mass culture.

Despite the critical success of *The Goddess*. Chayefsky found
that making a career out of writing good films was little less difficult than making a living by writing serious TV drama. He states
his position quite forcefully in his preface to the screenplay of
The Goddess (1958):

> It is a lot harder to make a good movie than you might
> think. I use the word "good" here quite advisedly. What
> I really mean is an "art" film, but I would rather avoid
> any discussion of what is art and what isn't. I don't really
> care what art is as long as it happens. To me, art is simply
> the work that an artist produces, and an artist is a man
> who creates for the single purpose of satisfying himself. An
> "art" film, then, is a picture made by artists because this is
> the kind of movie they themselves would like to see.

Chayefsky then chides "most intelligent people" for forgetting that
this fidelity to personal vision must coexist with an economic
discipline — the film must show a profit. For if the producer of
an art film does not make a profit, he will not have another

chance to create, seriously or otherwise, and "a lot of good his aestheticism will do him then." He goes on to insist that all artists work for what he terms "this inexorable governor of profit": the poet with an eye on publication, the painter aspiring to the walls of a good gallery. The only difference (and trouble) is that it is more difficult to make a profit from a movie.

Even the cheesiest film production will at least have fifty, probably closer to a hundred on its payroll. You have to build sets, rent studio space, purchase thousands of feet of film. Beyond the irreducible crew of thirty-two highly paid technicians, there is the office staff — actors, directors, producers, writer, lawyers and accountant. Even a budget of $500,000 means very few sets, very inexpensive actors and very little location shooting. Working in an art film also means that the creative work for at least half a year at one-fifth their usual incomes, "a sacrifice even dedicated artists are loath to make." And when a film costs $900,000 to make (as did *The Bachelor Party*), "the piquant system of economics that governs moviemaking dictates that it will have to gross about two and a half million dollars before it will return a profit." Even films without "artistic pretensions" have been able to gross the breakeven figure — twice its cost. Hence the art film in such a market is "The wildest gamble you can make."

The producer of an art film cannot afford the "stars" that are the most reliable hedge against box office disaster. Stars who can act are their own independent producers since the rise of television. Thus you must make an art film "quite frankly, in the hurried, slipshod way that any other low-budget Grade B film is made":

> The production of an art film is a shoestring business, demeaned by haggling and skimpiness. The lower the budget, the more chance of profit, so the whole idea is to keep your expenses down. This means slicing days off your shooting schedule, cutting out scenes that would enchance the picture but are not dramatically vital, telescoping three sets into one. . . . You are forced to yield those elegant little colors and gentle shadings that make the difference between the good and the beautiful.

A careful producer can cut corners before an expensive crew comes to them by anticipating bottlenecks; the director can husband shooting time by thoughtful preparation for sequences. Even then the clock is inexorable:

> It means, frankly, racing through difficult and sensitive scenes, settling for half of what you really want, eating your heart out in a frustrated fury of unfulfillment. The idea that a director shoots and reshoots until he has just what he wants is palpable nonsense, especially in an art film. John Cromwell and I let a lot go by in *The Goddess* because we couldn't afford to spend any more time arguing with Kim Stanley over the nuances of her interpretation or with the cameraman to give us a more exquisitively shadowed mood in the lighting. We took what we could get as well as we could get it.

"The point is," Chayefsky admits, "that an art film is never half as good as it should be. An art film must be low-budget, and low-budget means you sacrifice some art."

Talent, "a morale little short of dedication," and luck help to create a film you can be proud of. Distributing it at a profit is the next complication. You must start in art houses, but you cannot stay there; it takes good audiences in 3500 theatres. Because it is two hours and five minutes long it must be the main feature of a twin bill. "How," the problem becomes, "do you get the proprietor of a drive-in theatre outside Joplin, Missouri, to play a long art film starring Kim Stanley as his main feature?"

Although Chayefsky is probably the best-known writer to emerge from the pioneering days of TV drama, the history of his difficulties as TV-and-film-writer are representative of those faced by his colleagues. Until the television industry has the decency to make archival viewing possible, one must take fixes on the ambience for creativity in the medium by examining the failed idealism of talented artists like Chayefsky, who in the more salubrious venues of, say, Toronto or London would have institutionalized sound perceptions about there being no necessary polarity between popular and high culture — a hypothesis brilliantly authenticated in BBC-TV writer Johnny Speight's creation of the Ur-Tory blue-collar Alf Garnett in "Till Death Do Us Part" or the fabulously Rabelaisian generation gap in "Steptoe and Son."

Viewing British television, in fact, makes one question the

limiting of the study of TV drama to one-shot originals, even were they available on archival kinescope and videotape. We should reconsider also such genres as:

—perennial westerns like "Gunsmoke"
—raffish series like "The Honeymooners" with bus-driver Ralph Kramden and sewer-cleaner Ed Norton.
—series like Jack Webb's "Dragnet," treating metropolitan mores shrewdly.
—skit shows with distinctive styles, like Sid Caesar's and Imogene Coca's.
—low-budget poetic drama like those pioneered on Robert Herridge's "Camera 3"
—reality plays like Kraft's on the *Titanic* and the Armstrong-Circle Theatre.
—ritual culture, like the NBC operas, Hallmark Shakespeare.

An adequate critical history of TV drama, beginning in the 50s, ought at least try to show the connections between these forms and one-shot originals, if the latter are indeed the valuable center of theatrical experience on the new medium.

Monday morning quarterbacking aside. I console myself at the perils of looking back through dirty, cracked telescopes because of the amnesiac character of the television industry, by watching a distinguished playwright look into his crystal ball in 1929, as far *before* the start of TV as we are *after*.

Robert Sherwood wrote "After the Talkies-Television" as the lead article for the July 1929 issue of *Scribner's*. *McCall's* had asked him to write it early that spring but he sent the piece to *Scribner's* when he couldn't make the changes *McCall's* asked for. Three years earlier *Scribner's* Robert Bridges had encouraged him by accepting his short story, "Extra! Extra!" "It is, insofar as I know," Sherwood had written Bridges, "the first attempt to indicate (publicly) what Television will be. . . . Most of it will be news to the reader." Sherwood did not share standard egghead prejudices against newer media. He reviewed the "flickers" seriously as an editor and critic for the pre-Luce *Life* in the 1920s. He sensed intuitively and early that sound and color would both revolutionize what he styled the flickers. TV, he was convinced, was not only "inevitable and imminent" but also "one of the most fantastic of all the scientific miracles." Sherwood foresaw that TV would trigger a massive revolution in communications — changes in the home, advertising, political speeches, journalism, radio, cinema, theatre. "It will be posible," Sherwood argued in an early statement of the "You-Are-There" fallacy, "to watch the actual enactment of news events without having to wait for them to appear in the rotogravure sections or in news reels days or weeks later." TV scripts, written for both eye *and* ear, will be different from radio. Humorists and politicians will have to change their styles, too. Sherwood predicted that radio would concentrate on news and music, leaving storytelling to the new medium. Playwright Sherwood also glumly predicted that TV's free entertainment would give that "impractical institution" the theatre a *coup de grace*. Movies would also be decimated. Sherwood also forecast that commercials ("paid propaganda") would become so numerous that they might "cause the public to revolt against the national advertisers and institute a disastrous boycott of nationally advertised goods." Sherwood's boycott has not yet developed, but he was prescient in his common sense explanation of the dynamics of such a sneer-in: "I can state, on the best authority that all Television sets will be equipped, as all radio sets are now equipped, with control switches. Thus, when anyone decides he has been fed to the teeth with visible and audible salesmanship. . . . he has only to turn the little switch and shut the darned thing off." (Cited in John Mason Brown, *The Worlds of Robert E. Sherwood: Mirror to His Times, 1896-1939*, pp. 242-44.)

Sherwood came to see how ineffective that switch was—at least in terms of isolating crude advertising pressures from creative drama — and his own plays were not notably successful on the gradually denatured TV of the 50s and 60s. For however much we become bemused by multiple causation (different demographic audience, McCarthy-era backlash, lure of more money in Hollywood and more prestige on Broadway), Madison Avenue kept indigenous drama from reseeding itself after its first fine flowering because plays about real people contravened its marketing style, for example, as sports telecasts didn't (the finest coverage in the world developed in that precinct of the schedule).

Madison Avenue probably couldn't bring TV drama back to life if it tried, as it has lethargically over the past few years, spending, for example, $100,000 to promote Arthur Miller's *Death of a Salesman*, twenty years after its stage appearance. Both Canada and Britain have done infinitely better for Miller, Williams and Albee than American commercial television has. In 1968 and

1969 National Educational Television has taken the first secure steps to reintroduce indigenous drama on American television — stretching its lean budgets to begin with by importing low-cost British productions, but more and more lately turning to young American playwrights like Ronald Ribman, Paul Foster, and Megan Terry. There is a certain poetic justice in this. For one of the principal NET producers of these plays is the man, Jac Venza, who was still bitter about the difficulties the amnesiac networks gave him in organizing the Museum of Modern Art's Television Retrospective in 1963. Some university would do our understanding of the 1950s and 1960s a service if Venza were asked to organize screenings and symposia — so we can all begin to form our judgments on esthetic fact rather than memory and desire.

Bibliography

GENERAL

As of January 1, 1970, no general history of American literature of the 50s had appeared; but a very useful introduction to the period is provided by *The 1950's: America's "Placid" Decade,* edited by Joseph Satin (1960) for a series providing material for "controlled" research papers.

Allan Angoff's *American Writing Today: Its Independence and Vigor* (1957) reprints the material from a special issue of London's *Times Literary Supplement.* John Fischer and Robert B. Silver's *Writing in America* (1960) is a similar reprinting of material that had appeared in *Harper's* in 1959. Malcolm Cowley's *The Literary Situation* (1954) takes a fashionably dim view of the situation at one of the darkest points during the decade, and Russell Lynes' *The Tastemakers* (1954) touches upon literature, as well as many other aspects of American society, while satirizing the growing conformity in this country. John W. Aldridge developed a similar gloomy thesis in relation to the literature of the period in *In Search of Heresy: American Literature in an Age of Conformity* (1956).

General histories of American literature contain chapters largely devoted to the 50s. The third, revised edition of *Literary History of the United States,* edited by Robert E. Spiller and others (1963) contains two "postscript" chapters on literature since 1945, one by Spiller and Willard Thorp, rounding out the account of the accomplishment of older writers, and the second by Ihab Hassan, introducing the newer writers. Another book edited by Spiller, *A Time of Harvest, American Literature: 1910-1960* (1962) gives the most helpful overview of the decade in its four final chapters— "The Larger Audience" by Henry Popkin, "Theatre Without Walls" by Gerald Weales, "Recent Fiction: *Picaro* and Pilgrim" by R. W. B. Lewis, and "Poetry, Raw or Cooked?" by Willard Thorp. Thorp also deals summarily with the literature of the period in *American Writing in the Twentieth Century* (1960). Two of the final chapters of John M. Bradbury's *Renaissance in the South: A Critical History of the Literature* (1963) are also devoted principally one to the fiction and the other to the poetry and drama of the South during the 50s.

Also very useful to an understanding of the literature of the 50s is a program of interviews with authors first published in the *Paris Review* and later collected in three "series" under the title *Writers at Work* (1958, 1963, and 1967).

An important aspect of American literary activity is discussed in articles collected in David Rosenberg and David M. White's *The Popular Arts in America* (1957), especially a group dealing with detective fiction. Warren French's "The Little Magazines in the Fifties" (*College English*, May, 1961) surveys the efforts to keep alive an avant garde tradition during an uncongenial era. Daniel Wolf and Edwin Francher's *The Village Voice Reader: A Mixed Bag from Greenwich Village* (1962) preserves some of the most important contributions to appear during the first years of the venturesome weekly that was to spearhead the erratic but steadily growing movement away from the tackiness of the 50s.

FICTION

A great deal has been written about the fiction of the 50s, but no one has attempted a comprehensive survey since the appearance of Ihab Hassan's *Radical Innocence: The Contemporary American Novel* (1961). Most recent studies have consisted of a series of loosely connected essays about a limited number of writers. (Hassan helped establish this pattern by devoting more than a third of his book to the study of four "individual talents"—Carson McCullers, Truman Capote, J. D. Salinger, and Saul Bellow.)

Radical Innocence was followed shortly by Irving Malin's *New American Gothic* (1962), which concentrates on Truman Capote, John Hawkes, Carson McCullers, Flannery O'Connor, James

Purdy, and J. D. Salinger, as representatives of a new Gothicism that "is in the main stream of American fiction." The *Four Spiritual Crises in Mid-Century American Fiction* investigated by Robert Detweiler (1963) occur in the works of Philip Roth, J. D. Salinger, William Styron, and John Updike. One of the most highly acclaimed books to treat writers of the 50s, Marcus Klein's *After Alienation: American Novels in Mid-Century* (1964), deals with only James Baldwin, Saul Bellow, Ralph Ellision, Bernard Malamud, and Wright Morris. Jonathan Baumbach's *The Landscape of Nightmare: Studies in the Contemporary American Novel* (1965) more ambitiously takes on nine writers (Bellow, Ellison, Malamud, Morris, O'Connor, Salinger, Styron, Edward Lewis Wallant, and Robert Penn Warren), and John W. Aldridge's *Time to Murder and Create* (1966) collects unrelated essays on Styron, Mary McCarthy, Bellow, Mailer, Updike, and John Cheever, as well as earlier writers, some British. David D. Galloway's *The Absurd Hero in American Fiction* (1966, Revised 1969) is in the more usual pattern, dealing at great length with only four writers— Bellow, Salinger, Styron, and Updike. Howard M. Harper, Jr.'s *Desperate Faith* (1967) focuses on a similar grouping (Baldwin, Bellow, Mailer, Salinger, Updike), and Helen A. Weinberg's *The New Novel in America: The Kafkan Mode in Contemporary Fiction* (1969) is limited to consideration of Bellow, Herbert Gold, Malamud, Roth, and Salinger. Jack Ludwig's *Recent American Novelists* (UMPAW No. 22, 1962) and Irving Malin's *Jews and Americans* (1965) drop more names than the other books, but the former is a hurried 38-page survey and the latter deals with fiction from an ethnic rather than a period viewpoint.

Maxwell Geismar's *American Moderns: From Rebellion to Conformity* (1958) is a collection of unconnected reviews and essays that disappointed those who expected this book to carry forward the multi-volumed history of American fiction from 1900 to 1940 that he had produced earlier. Edmund Fuller's *Man in Modern Fiction: Some Minority Opinions on Contemporary American Writing* (1958) is useful as a revelation of conservative academic critics' distaste for recent developments in American writing. The final chapter of Walter Allen's *The Modern Novel in Britain and the United States* (1964) is a more sympathetic survey of American novels of the World War II and post-war periods. The important short story writers of the 50s are also placed judiciously into a larger context in William Peden's *The American*

Short Story: Frontier in the National Defense of Literature (1964).
One of the most provocative books to touch upon the period,
Leslie Fiedler's *Love and Death in the American Novel* (1960) surveys the whole range of American fiction in developing an elaborate thesis about the preoccupations of our native writers.

Two books that deal specifically with Southern fiction are principally devoted to the writings of the 50s: Louise Y. Gossett's *Violence in Recent Southern Fiction* (1965) and Frederick J. Hoffman's *The Art of Southern Fiction* (1967), one of the last works
completed by this outstanding critic of twentieth-century fiction.

Several collections of essays — some original and some reprinted
— by various critics deal largely with writings of the 50s — Joseph
J. Waldmeir's *Recent American Fiction: Some Critical Views*
(1963), Harry T. Moore's *Contemporary American Novelists*
(1964), Richard Kostalanetz's *On Contemporary Literature* (1965),
and Marcus Klein's *The American Novel Since World War II*
(1969). Pierre Brodin's *Présences contemporaines: Écrivains
américains d'aujourd'hui* (Paris, 1964) provides valuable insights
into foreign attitudes toward post-World-War II American writing.
Of special interest are essays about several writers generally ignored
in domestic studies — James Jones, Anais Nin, J. F. Powers, and
Harvey Swados. A valuable theoretical article is Eugene Mc-
Namara's "The Post-Modern American Novel" (*Queen's Quarterly,*
1962). Examples of the writing of many of the novelists of the
period are included in Herbert Gold's collection *Fiction of the
Fifties* (1959).

The treatment of individual novelists so far has been uneven.
Many of the most useful accounts are found in three series that
were launched during the 60s: the book-length Twayne United
States Authors Series (hereafter abbreviated TUSAS), and the
short pamphlets comprising the University of Minnesota Pamphlets
on American Writers (hereafter UMPAW) and the Eerdmans'
series on Contemporary Writers in Christian Perspective (CWCP).
A semi-annual "round-up" of books and articles about modern
American novelists appears in *Modern Fiction Studies.*

JAMES AGEE (1909-1955) — The first book-length study of this versa-
tile author is Peter Ohlin's *Agee* (1965), which was followed
by Kenneth Seib's less useful, but more fully documented
James Agee: Promise and Fulfillment (1968). Michael Mor-
risroe, Jr.'s "A Point of Focus in James Agee's *A Death in*

the Family" (*Twentieth Century Literature,* October, 1966)
is probably the best reading of the novel based on the
assumption that the italicized portions are essential to its
structure. Of great value to an understanding of Agee's
work is *Letters of James Agee to Father Flye* (1962).

JAMES BALDWIN (1922-   ) — The first book about Baldwin, Fern
Marja Eckman's *The Furious Passage of James Baldwin*
(1966) is principally biographical. Baldwin has also written
extensively about himself in *Notes of a Native Son* (1955)
and *The Fire Next Time* (1963). An important episode in
Baldwin's career is examined in Maurice Charney's "James
Baldwin's Quarrel with Richard Wright" (*American Quarterly,* 1963). C. W. E. Bigsby's collection *The Black American Writer* (1969) contains three essays on Baldwin: the
novelist's own "Disturber of the Peace: James Baldwin,"
Brian Lee's "James Baldwin: From Caliban to Prospero,"
and Mike Thelwell's "*Another Country*: Baldwin's New
York Novel."

SAUL BELLOW (1915-   ) — The first full-length study of Bellow
is Tony Tanner's *Saul Bellow* (1965). More recent are
Keith M. Opdahl's *The Novels of Saul Bellow: An Introduction* (1967), John J. Clayton's *Saul Bellow: In Defense of
Man* (1968) and Irving Malin's *Saul Bellow's Fiction* (1969).
Briefer surveys are Earl Rovit's *Saul Bellow* (UMPAW No.
65) and Robert Detweiler's *Saul Bellow: A Critical Essay*
(CWCP), both published in 1967. *Critique: Studies in Modern Fiction* devoted a special issue in 1965 to Bellow, containing articles by Robert D. Crozier, Allen Guttmann,
James C. Mathis, and James Dean Young, as well as a checklist. Irving Malin has collected another group of essays
about the novelist in *Saul Bellow and the Critics* (1967).
Bellow's statements on the composition of *The Adventures
of Augie March,* used in Mr. Jones' essay, appear in "How
I Wrote Augie March's Story" (*New York Times Book
Review,* January 31, 1954), a statement by Bellow quoted
in the *New York Herald Tribune Book Review* (October
11, 1953), and two notes in the *Saturday Review of Literature* — Bernard Kalb's "The Author" (September 19, 1953)
and Laura Hobson's "Trade Winds" (August 22, 1953).

RALPH ELLISON (1914-   ) — Ellison has written about himself in
The Writer's Experience (1964, with Karl Shapiro as co-

author) and "On Becoming a Writer" (*Commentary*, 1964). Robert Bone discusses Ellison's work in both *The Negro Novel in America* (Revised Edition, 1965) and *Anger and Beyond: The Negro Writer in the United States* (edited by Herbert Hill, 1966). C. W. E. Bigsby's *The Black American Writer* (1969) contains an interview with Ellison by Allen Geller and Michael Allen's "Some Examples of Faulknerian Rhetoric in Ellison's *Invisible Man*."

WILLIAM FAULKNER (1897-1962) — Relatively few of the many books and articles about Faulkner are principally concerned with his writings during the 50s. Warren Beck's *Man in Motion: Faulkner's Trilogy* (1961) is an intensive study of the Snopes family saga, and Joseph Gold's *William Faulkner: A Study in Humanism, From Metaphor to Discourse* (1966) is largely devoted to *Requiem for a Nun, A Fable, The Town,* and *The Mansion.* Important studies of Faulkner's Yoknapatawpha epic are Cleanth Brooks' *William Faulkner: The Yoknapatawpha Country* (1963) and Elizabeth Kerr's *Faulkner's "Little Postage Stamp of Native Soil"* (1969). Martin J. Dain's *Faulkner's County: Yoknapatawpha* (1964) is a collection of photographs of scenes Faulkner wrote about. James B. Meriwether has provided a detailed discussion of other writings about Faulkner for *Fifteen Modern American Authors,* edited by Jackson R. Bryer (1969).

ERNEST HEMINGWAY (1899-1961) — None of the many books about Hemingway focus on the 50s. The standard account of the novelist's life and work is Carlos Baker's *Ernest Hemingway: A Life Story* (1969). Philip Young revised his valuable *Ernest Hemingway: A Reconsideration* in 1966 and wrote a short introduction to the author, *Ernest Hemingway* (UMPAW No. 1, 1959) to launch a widely distributed pamphlet series. Audre Hanneman's *Ernest Hemingway: A Comprehensive Bibliography* (1967) is a detailed listing of writings by and about the novelist. Its utility is explained and other writings about Hemingway are commented upon in the late Frederick J. Hoffman's contribution to *Fifteen Modern American Authors,* edited by Jackson R. Bryer (1969).

JACK KEROUAC (1922-1969) — Kerouac's essay "The Origins of the Beat Generation" is reprinted from *Playboy* (June, 1959) in Thomas Parkinson's *A Casebook on the Beat* (1960), which also contains specimens of Kerouac's prose. No book has yet been devoted to Kerouac, but he is discussed in Frederick Feied's *No Pie in the Sky* (1964). Ann Charters has compiled *A Bibliography of Works by Jack Kerouac* (1967).

NORMAN MAILER (1923-   ) — The major source of information about Mailer's literary career is his own *Advertisements for Myself* (1959). Valuable interviews also appear in *Writers at Work* (Third Series, 1967) and *Playboy* (January, 1968). The first book-length critical study of this controversial author is Donald L. Kauffmann's *Norman Mailer: The Countdown* (1969). It was preceded by a short survey of his career, Richard Foster's *Norman Mailer* (UMPAW No. 73, 1968), and it has been followed by Barry Leeds' *The Structured Vision of Norman Mailer* (1969).

BERNARD MALAMUD (1914-   ) — The first book-length study is Sidney Richman's *Bernard Malamud* (TUSAS No. 109, 1966). Malamud and Philip Roth are also discussed in a pamphlet by Glenn Meeter (CWCP, 1968). A collection of the novelist's works entitled *The Malamud Reader* (1967) has been edited by Philip Rahv, and Rita Nathalie Kosofsky has prepared *Bernard Malamud: An Annotated Checklist* (1969).

MARY MCCARTHY (1912-   ) — Two book-length studies of Miss McCarthy's exciting life have appeared: Barbara McKenzie's *Mary McCarthy* (TUSAS No. 108, 1966) beat out Doris Grumbach's *The Company She Kept* (1967). Briefer male appraisals are Irvin Stuck's *Mary McCarthy* (UMPAW No. 72, 1968) and John Chamberlain's "The Novels of Mary McCarthy" in *The Creative Present: Notes on Contemporary American Fiction* (edited by Nona Balakian and Charles Simmons, 1963). Sheril E. Goldman has compiled *Mary McCarthy: A Bibliography* (1968).

WRIGHT MORRIS (1910-   ) — The pioneering book-length study of this Midwestern author is David Madden's *Wright Morris* (TUSAS No. 71, 1964). A shorter account of his work is Leon Howard's *Wright Morris* (UMPAW No. 69, 1968). Morris discusses his views on literature in *The Territory Ahead* (1958).

VLADIMIR NABOKOV (1899-   ) — Nabokov has written about himself in *Speak, Memory: A Memoir Revisited* (1966, a revision of *Conclusive Evidence,* published in 1951). The first book-length studies of his work appeared in 1967: Andrew Field's *Nabokov: His Life in Art* and S. Page Stegner's *Escape into Aesthetics: The Art of Vladimir Nabokov.* A special issue of *Wisconsin Studies in Contemporary Literature* (Spring, 1967) has been enlarged into *Nabokov: The Man and His Work,* edited by L. S. Dembo (1967, with a bibliography by Jackson R. Bryer and Thomas Bergin.) Another collection of criticisms and reminiscences is *Nabokov!,* edited by Alfred Appel, Jr., and Charles Newman (1970). One of the few books to be devoted to a single novel published during the 50s is Carl R. Proffer's *Keys to "Lolita"* (1968). An annotated *Lolita* appeared in 1970.

ANAIS NIN (1903-   )—Miss Nin's hermetic fiction (largely published between 1947 and 1961) has not yet attracted many readers; but with the publication of her diaries, beginning in 1966, she has been increasingly recognized as a key figure in understanding the International *avantgarde* movement since the 1930s. The first book-length study of her work, Oliver Evans's *Anais Nin* (1968) is disappointing, because as Evans recognizes, rationalistic criticism does not help much in approaching her work. Better understanding of her life and work is being fostered, however, by *Under the Sign of Pisces; Anais Nin and Her Circle,* a quarterly journal, published beginning in 1970, by Richard Centing.

FLANNERY O'CONNOR (1925-1964) — The first full-length study is Carter W. Martin's *The True Country:Themes in the Fiction of Flannery O'Connor* (1969). She was earlier discussed in Stanley Edgar Hyman's *Flannery O'Connor* (UMPAW No. 54) and Robert Drake's *Flannery O'Connor* (CWCP), both published in 1966. That same year saw the publication of Melvin J. Friedman and Lewis A. Lawson's *The Added Dimension: The Art and Mind of Flannery O'Connor,* a memorial collection of essays by various critics, with an extensive bibliography. Robert E. Retler's *Flannery O'Connor* (1968) is a collection of reprinted essays by several critics.

JAMES PURDY (1923-   ) — The first separate publication devoted to Purdy is Bettina Schwarzschild's *The Not-Right House: Essays on James Purdy* (University of Missouri Literary Frontiers Series No. 5, 1968). Purdy has launched an

unusual program of recording his writings, beginning with
63: Dream Palace and *Color of Darkness* (Spoken Arts
Records).

J. D. SALINGER (1919-   ) — The only book-length study of Salinger to appear before 1970 is Warren French's *J. D. Salinger*
(TUSAS No. 40, 1963), although many books have been
announced and many essays published about this popular
writer. An earlier brief account is Frederick L. Gwynn and
Joseph L. Blotner's *The Fiction of J. D. Salinger* (1958),
and two later appreciations are James E. Miller, Jr.'s *J. D.
Salinger* (UMPAW No. 51, 1965) and Kenneth Hamilton's
J. D. Salinger (CYCP, 1967). The earliest collection of
essays by various writers about Salinger is Henry Anatole
Grunwald's *Salinger: A Critical and Personal Portrait*
(1962). There are also four "casebooks," generally focused
on *The Catcher in the Rye*: William F. Belcher and James
W. Lee's *J. D. Salinger and the Critics* (1962), Marvin
Laser and Norman Fruman's *Studies in J. D. Salinger*,
Malcolm M. Marsden's *If You Really Want to Know: A
Catcher Casebook,* and Harold P. Simonson and E. P.
Hager's *Salinger's "Catcher in the Rye": Clamor vs. Criticism*
(all 1963). Two special issues of magazines are devoted
to Salinger: the Winter, 1963 issue of *Wisconsin Studies in
Contemporary Literature,* which contains nine articles and
Donald M. Fiene's extensive bibliography of writings by and
about Salinger, including many in foreign languages; and
the autumn, 1966 issue of *Modern Fiction Studies,* which
contains seven articles and a selected checklist of criticism
by Maurice Beebe and Jennifer Sperry.

ELIZABETH SPENCER (1921-   ) — The first separate study of Miss
Spencer's work is Nash K. Burger's "Elizabeth Spencer's
Three Mississippi Novels" (*South Atlantic Quarterly*, 1964).

JOHN STEINBECK (1902-1968) — None of the books published before
1970 devotes much space to Steinbeck's writings after 1945.
Journal of a Novel: The "East of Eden" Letters (1969) prints
the letters that the novelist wrote to his editor, Pascal Covici,
while the novel was in progress. Lawrence William Jones
has also completed a book-length study of Steinbeck's later
novels as fables. A special Steinbeck issue of *Modern
Fiction Studies* (Spring, 1965) contains no articles on
the novels of the 50s, but does contain a bibliography

of writings about them compiled by Maurice Beebe and Jackson R. Bryer. Warren French has surveyed Steinbeck scholarship for Jackson R. Bryer's *Fifteen Modern American Authors* (1969). This survey is being constantly updated by the contributors to the *Steinbeck Journal*, edited since 1968 by Tetsumaro Hayashi.

WILLIAM STYRON (1925-   ) — The first short accounts of Styron's career are Robert H. Fossum's *William Styron: A Critical Essay* (CWCP, 1968) and Cooper R. Mackin's *William Styron* in a new pamphlet series devoted to Southern Writers (1969). Styron's work during the 50s has been overshadowed lately by the furore over his *The Confessions of Nat Turner,* but his work was earlier the subject of a special issue of *Critique: Studies in Modern Fiction* (1966).

POETRY

No comprehensive study of American poetry during the 50s had appeared by 1970. The most useful guide to the period is the *Proceedings* of the *National Poetry Festival,* held in the Library of Congress, October 22-24, 1962. Many leading figures of the 50s read from their work during this gathering. The book includes general statements by Louise Bogan, Stanley Kunitz, Sir Herbert Read and Morton D. Zabel, as well as transcriptions of remarks and readings by John Berryman, Gwendolyn Brooks, Richard Eberhart, Kenneth Rexroth, Richard Wilbur and many others. Allen Ginsberg and the other Beat poets did not participate.

Other books that deal with some of the poets who were particularly active during the 50s are David Ossman's *The Sullen Art: Interviews with Modern American Poets* (1963), Stephen Stepanchev's *American Poetry since 1945* (1965), Ralph J. Mills, Jr.'s, *Contemporary American Poetry* (1966), which brings together many of Mills' excellent essays for *Northwestern University Tri-Quarterly,* and M. L. Rosenthal's *The New Poets: American and British Poetry since World War II* (1967). A brief introduction to the work of the period is Glauco Cambon's *Recent American Poetry* (UMPAW No. 16, 1962)

The most comprehensive and useful survey of the Beat Generation is Thomas Parkinson's *A Casebook on the Beat* (1961), which contains excerpts from the work of Ginsberg, Kerouac, Ferlinghetti and six others, as well as the most impotrant critical statements made for and against the movement at its height by Kenneth Rexroth, Norman Podhoretz, Henry Miller, John Ciardi, and others.

Other collections that preserve something of the distinctive flavor of the Beat movement are Gene Feldman and Max Gartenberg's *The Beat Generation and The Angry Young Men* (1958), linking rebel movements in the United States and England; the second issue of *Evergreen Review,* "San Francisco Scene" (1957); Seymour Krim's *The Beats,* Stanley Fisher's *Beat Coast East: An Anthology of Rebellion,* Lawrence Ferlinghetti's *Beatitude Anthology,* and Donald Allen's *The New American Poetry* (all published in 1960). The fullest records of the movement are in its short-lived journals — *Beatitude, Underhound,* and *Journal for the Protection for All Beings* (all published in San Francisco, circa 1960). A rambling history and defense of the movement is Lawrence Lipton's *The Holy Barbarians* (1959). The Beat movement is discussed in relation to traditional Bohemianism in America in the late Frederick J. Hoffman's *Marginal Manners: The Variants of Bohemia* (1962) and Kingsley Widmer's *The Literary Rebel* (1965). The movement faded as suddenly and surprisingly as it surfaced, and the only retrospective study appears to be David Kherdian's *Six Poets of the San Francisco Renaissance: Portraits and Checklists* (1967).

GWENDOLYN BROOKS (1917-   ) — No full-length study has been made of Miss Brooks' Pulitzer-prize winning work, but she is celebrated in C. W. E. Bigsby's *The Black American Writer* (1969) by Dan Jaffe's "Gwendolyn Brooks: An Appreciation from the White Suburbs."

RICHARD EBERHART (1904-   ) — Bernard F. Engel has edited and introduced a collection of essays, *The Achievement of Richard Eberhart* (1968), and Ralph J. Mills, Jr., summarizes the poet's career in *Richard Eberhart* (UMPAW No. 55, 1966).

ALLEN GINSBERG (1926-   ) — The first book about this leading Beat is Jane Kramer's *Allen Ginsberg in America* (1969). Thomas F. Merrill has also prepared a book-length critical study, *Allen Ginsberg* (TUSAS No. 161, 1969). J. W. Ehrlich's *Howl of the Censor* (1962) provides a transcript of the much-publicized trial in San Francisco at which *Howl and Other Poems* was found not obscene. Edward Z. Menkin has contributed "Allen Ginsberg: A Bibliography and

Biographical Sketch" to *Thoth,* a graduate student magazine at Syracuse University (1967).

THEODORE ROETHKE (1908-1963) — The first separately published study of the poet was Ralph J. Mills, Jr.'s *Theodore Roethke* (UMPAW No. 30, 1963). Arnold Stein's *Theodore Roethke: Essays on the Poetry* (1965) contains a group of nine analyses and appreciations by leading critics and poets. The first book-length study of the poet was Karl Malkoff's *Theodore Roethke: An Introduction to His Poetry* (1966), but by far the most important book so far about Roethke — and one of the most distinguished works about any writers of the 50s — is the late Allen Seager's monumental biography, *The Glass House: The Life of Theodore Roethke* (1968). William J. Martz's *The Achievement of Theodore Roethke* (1966) is a valuable collection of poems with introductory editorial commentary.

WALLACE STEVENS (1879-1955) — The appearance of the *Collected Poems* (1954) has inspired a great number of books about Stevens, of which John Enck's *Wallace Stevens: Images and Judgments* (1964), Joseph Riddel's *The Clairvoyant Eye: The Poetry and Poetics of Wallace Stevens* (1965), Frank Doggett's *Stevens' Poetry of Thought* (1966), and Robert W. Buttel's *The Making of "Harmonium"* (1967) especially deserve attention. Several books collect distinguished essays about Stevens' work: Ashley Brown and Robert S. Haller's *The Achievement of Wallace Stevens* (1962), Marie Borroff's *Wallace Stevens: A Collection of Critical Essays* (1963), and Roy Harvey Pearce and J. Hillis Miller's *The Art of the Mind: Essays on the Poetry of Wallace Stevens* (1965). Joseph Riddel surveys criticism of Stevens for Jackson R. Bryer's *Fifteen Modern American Authors* (1969). Riddel and Bryer have also published with Samuel French Morse *A Wallace Stevens Checklist and Bibliography of Criticism* (1963). Morse's *Wallace Stevens: Life as Poetry* was added to the Pegasus American Authors Series in 1970.

RICHARD WILBUR (1921-   ) — The first book-length study of the poet is Donald Hill's *Richard Wilbur* (TUSAS No. 117, 1967). Kent State University Press has announced a bibliography of writings by and about Wilbur as part of its series on American writers.

WILLIAM CARLOS WILLIAMS (1883-1963) — A number of books

about Williams have appeared since his death. Principal among them are Linda W. Wagner's *The Poems of William Carlos Williams: A Critical Study* (1964), Alan Ostrom's *The Poetic World of William Carlos Williams* (1966), and Sherman Paul's *Music of Survival: A Biography of a Poem by William Carlos Williams* (1968). J Hillis Miller's *William Carlos Williams: A Collection of Critical Essays* (1966) brings together varied appraisals.

DRAMA

The major history of the American play during the 50s is Gerald Weales' *American Drama since World War II* (1962). A shorter account is the late Alan Downer's *Recent American Drama* (UMPAW No. 7, 1961) ._ Later studies are Jean Gould's *Modern American Playwrights* (1967), Alvin B. Kernan's *The Modern American Theatre: A Collection of Critical Essays* (also 1967) and Martin Gottfried's *A Theatre Divided: The Postwar American Stage* (1968). Many plays of the period are commented upon in Winifred Dusenbery's *The Theme of Loneliness in the Modern American Drama* (1960). Norma Miller explains one of the most important movements during this period in "America's Endeavor to Establish a National Theatre: The American National Theatre and Academy" in *Salon* (1961). One of the most useful guides to the history of the American theatre remains the annual volumes of the *Ten Best Plays* series, edited by Burns Mantle until 1940 and thereafter by John Chapman (until 1952) and Louis Kronenberger.

ARCHIBALD MACLEISH — Signi Falk's *Archibald MacLeish* (TUSAS No. 93, 1965) discusses the entire career of the poet/playwright. Essays prompted by the production of *J.B.* have not been collected, but William E. Taylor's *Modern American Drama: Essays in Criticism* (1968) contains Donna Gerstenberger's "Three Verse Plays and the American 50s," which deals with MacLeish, Richard Eberhart, and Djuna Barnes.

ARTHUR MILLER (1915-   ) — Dennis Welland's *Arthur Miller* (1961), Sheila Huttel's *Arthur Miller: The Burning Glass* (1965), Edward Murray's *Arthur Miller: Dramatist* (1967) and Leonard Moss's *Arthur Miller* (TUSAS No. 115, 1968) are all full-length studies of the dramatist. Robert W. Corrigan has also edited *Arthur Miller: A Collection of Critical Essays* (1969), and Tetsumaro Hayashi has compiled a bibliography, *Arthur Miller Criticism (1930-1967)* (1969).

EUGENE O'NEILL (1888-1953) — Many books have been written about O'Neill's life and works; but despite the excitement attendant upon the production of *Long Day's Journey into Night* and the excellent film made from it, it has not been the subject of a separate book-length study. The best essay about O'Neill's later works is in Robert Brustein's *The Theatre of Revolt* (1964). The standard biography of the playwright is Barbara and Arthur Gelb's *O'Neill* (1962). John Henry Raleigh prepared a survey of the criticism of O'Neill's work for Jackson R. Bryer's *Fifteen Modern American Authors* (1969).

TENNESSEE WILLIAMS (1914-   ) — Books about this fascinating playwright abound, beginning with three published in 1961: Signi Falk's *Tennessee Williams* (TUSAS No. 10), Benjamin Nelson's *Tennessee Williams: The Man and His Work,* and Nancy M. Tischler's *Tennessee Williams: Rebellious Puritan.* Since then there have been Francis Donahue's *The Dramatic World of Tennessee Williams,* (1964), Esther M. Jackson's *The Broken World of Tennessee Williams* (1965) and many more, mostly reminiscences of friends and relatives. A good introduction to the playwright and his work is Gerald Weale's *Tennessee Williams* (UMPAW No. 58, 1965).

TELEVISION AND FILM

No history of the visual media in the 50s had appeared by 1970, although the decade was crucial in the development of both arts. A useful article is "Special Report: Television Drama, Unkept Promise" (*Action, The Magazine of the Directors Guild of America,* March-April, 1969) A convenient list of important American directors and their films is Andrew Sarris' *The American Cinema: Directors and Directions,* 1929-1968 (1969).

ABOUT THE CONTRIBUTORS

C. W. E. BIGSBY (Black Literature) received his Ph.D. in American Studies at The University of Nottingham. Earlier he had studied in England at Sheffield and in the United States at Kansas State University. He has twice participated in the Salzburg American Studies seminar in Austria, and he has been a visiting professor at the University of Missouri — Kansas City. Besides many articles, he has published *Confrontation and Commitment: A Study of Contemporary American Drama, 1959-1966* (1967) in both British and American editions, and *Edward Albee* (Edinburgh, 1969). He has recently edited a two-volume collection of essays, *The Black American Writer* (1970). He is a lecturer in the Department of British and American Studies at the University of East Anglia at Norwich, England.

JACKSON R. BRYER (Eugene O'Neill) is one of the most active young scholars in this country. He was managing editor of *Wisconsin Studies in Contemporary Literature,* and he is now editor of the American Literature section of the annual *PMLA* bibliography. He has compiled many bibliographies of American writers, as well as *The Critical Reputation of F. Scott Fitzgerald* (1967) and *Fifteen Modern American Authors* (1969). *F. Scott Fitzgerald in His Own Time: A Miscellany* is now in press. He has collaborated on the bibliographies for all the books in this series and wrote about Rodgers and Hammerstein's musical drama for *The*

Forties. He is an Associate Professor of English at the University of Maryland.

PASCAL COVICI, JR. (John Steinbeck) is the son of Steinbeck's long-time friend and editor and a member of the faculty of Southern Methodist University. He is the author of *Mark Twain's Humor: The Image of a World* (1962), and he is preparing a revised edition of *The Portable Steinbeck.* He also contributed an essay on Steinbeck to *The Thirties.*

WILLIAM FREEDMAN (Bernard Malamud), after receiving his Ph.D. from the University of Chicago and teaching at Brooklyn College, has joined the English faculty of the University of Haifa, Israel. Although trained in 18th century literature, he has written extensively about 19th and 20th century American authors, and he has contributed essays on Henry Roth and Lionel Trilling to *The Thirties* and *The Forties,* respectively.

KENNETH FRIELING (Flannery O'Connor) will edit the projected volume on *The Sixties,* which will contain essays on contemporary trends chosen from entries in a nation-wide contest for young critics. Frieling, who has interrupted his graduate studies at Ohio University to teach at the University of Missouri — Kansas City, is also a painter and designer.

LOIS GORDON (Richard Eberhart) is the author of *Strategems to Uncover Nakedness* (1968), a study of Harold Pinter's plays, as well as essays on Samuel Beckett and Pinter. She is preparing a full-length psychoanalytically-oriented study of Beckett's plays in collaboration with her husband. After receiving her doctorate at Wisconsin, she taught at CCNY and UM-KC before moving to Fairleigh-Dickinson University.

SHELDON GREBSTEIN (Ernest Hemingway) has contributed *Sinclair Lewis* (1962) and *John O'Hara* (1968) to the Twayne United States Authors Series. He has also edited *Perspectives in Contemporary Criticism* (1968) and published many articles and book reviews. He wrote on Hemingway earlier for *The Thirties* and shifted to Nelson Algred in *The Forties.* He is Professor of English and Director of Graduate English Studies at the State University of New York at Binghamton.

PATRICK D. HAZARD (Television Drama) is one of the busiest men in the profession, constantly flying to literary and mass-media conferences in England, Africa, and Australia. Still he has found time to prepare a guide to Hawaii and to write books like *TV As Art* and *Language and Literacy Today*. His major project is a comprehensive history of radio and television. He is Professor of English at Beaver College, Glenside, Pennsylvania.

WILLIAM HOFFA (Norman Mailer) is a student of Henry James, who has been working frequently in London recently. A graduate of Wisconsin, he teaches at Vanderbilt University.

DAN JAFFE (Theodore Roethke) has published poems in many nationally circulated magazines and is the author of *Dan Freeman* (1967), a poetic account of the man recognized as the first to file under the Homestead Act. He has written about Archibald MacLeish for *The Thirties* and the poetry of World War II for *The Forties,* and he organized the American Poets Series at the Jewish Community Center in Kansas City. He is Associate Professor of English at the University of Missouri — Kansas City, and gives frequent readings from his works (including a "jazz opera," *Without Memorial Banners)* throughout the Midwest.

KENNETH JOHNSON (Richard Wilbur) is a widely published poet, who is preparing a selection of his works for publication. He has also written on Robert Lowell for *The Forties.* He is a member of the faculty at Suffolk University, Boston.

DAVID R. JONES (Saul Bellow) is one of the dynamic young assistant professors who have helped keep the English program vigorous at the University of Chicago. He received his doctorate from Princeton and spent a year in Ireland on research for a forthcoming book on Yeats and the Irish Theatre.

SY KAHN (Archibald MacLeish), after teaching in Wisconsin and Florida, has become Chairman of the new Department of Drama and director of theatrical activities at the University of the Pacific, Stockton, California. Despite the demands made upon his time by his theatrical directing, he has produced a number of books of poems: *Our Separate Darkness, Triptych* (with Paul Ramsey and Jane Taylor), *The Fight is with Phantoms, A Later Sun* (with Don Gray) and *Another Time* (with Roger Mitchell). During 1970-71 he will be at the University of Vienna on his third Fulbright grant. Previously he has visited the University of Salonika (Greece) and the University of Warsaw. He has also contributed to *The Thirties* (Kenneth Fearing) and The *Forties* (Eugene O'Neill).

MARK LEAF (William Faulkner) is in charge of the American Studies program at the University of Durham (England), one of the five distinguished participants in a program to bring American students to Europe. In the spring of 1969, he was also a visiting professor at the University of Missouri — Kansas City.

JORDAN Y. MILLER (Tennessee Williams) is one of the most prolific students of American drama. His publications include *American Dramatic Literature* (an anthology, 1961), *Eugene O'Neill and the American Critic* (1962), and *Playwright's Progress: O'Neill and the Critics* (1965). He also wrote the article about O'Neill for *American Winners of the Nobel Literary Prize* (1968), and he has contributed articles on Maxwell Anderson to *The Thirties,* American Drama of World War II to *The Forties,* and Lorraine Hansberry to *The Black American Writer.* After a distinguished career at Kansas State University, he recently became Chairman of the Department of English at the University of Rhode Island.

DONALD PEASE (James Purdy) is attending the University of Chicago Graduate School on a humanities fellowship. Although this book contains his first published critical essay, he has had an experimental ritualistic drama, *The Confession,* produced while teaching at the University of Missouri — Kansas City.

DAVID G. PUGH (Elizabeth Spencer) is one of the veterans of the "decades" series. A student of popular literature, he wrote about the proletarian novelists for *The Thirties* and Frederick Wakeman's *The Hucksters* for *The Forties.* He and Elizabeth Spencer were also colleagues for two years at the University of Mississippi. He now teaches at Western Michigan University, Kalamazoo.

GENE RUOFF (James Agee) has also contributed to both *The Thirties* (The New Criticism) and *The Forties* (Truman Capote). He is also interested in American popular literature, although his graduate studies at Wisconsin have centered on Wordsworth. Both he and his wife (also a nineteenth-century scholar) teach at the University of Illinois— Chicago Circle.

DONALD SHEEHAN (Wallace Stevens) is the only contributor to prepare a series of essays on the same writer for *The Thirties, The Forties,* and *The Fifties.* He teaches humanities and modern poetry at the University of Chicago, and he has also published articles on Stevens — as well as poetry of his own — elsewhere. Earlier he was managing editor of *Wisconsin Studies in Contemporary Literature.*

ELEANOR WIDMER (Mary McCarthy) teaches in the Department of Literature at the University of California, San Diego. She is the author of *Mister Jack,* a novella, and *Is it an Owl?,* a children's story, as well as essays on twentieth-century fiction (including analyses of John Dos Passos in *The Thirties* and Malcolm Lowry in *The Forties*). She has also edited two anthologies, *Literary Censorship* and *Freedom and Culture.* She took her graduate degrees at Columbia and the University of Washington.

KINGSLEY WIDMER (The Beats) was raised in Midwestern small towns and educated at diverse labors. His teaching positions have included the Universities of Minnesota, Washington, California (Berkeley), Tel Aviv (Israel), Simon Fraser (Canada) and Nice (France). His many literary studies range from Milton to Mailer and include *The Art of Perversity: D. H. Lawrence, Henry Miller, The Literary Rebel* and *The Ways of Nihilism: Melville's Short Novels.* A social as well as literary critic, he has also frequently written on contemporary education, censorship, and radicalism. (His far-flung interests are brought into focus in his essay on the effects of the Atomic Bomb in *The Forties,* as well as in his analysis for this book of the Beat phenomenon.) Currently, he is Professor of Comparative Literature at San Diego State College.

Index